# Economic Liberalization and Integration in East Asia

# Economic Liberalization and Integration in East Asia

## A Post-Crisis Paradigm

Yung Chul Park

OXFORD
UNIVERSITY PRESS

# OXFORD

UNIVERSITY PRESS

Great Clarendon Street, Oxford OX2 6DP

Oxford University Press is a department of the University of Oxford.
It furthers the University's objective of excellence in research, scholarship,
and education by publishing worldwide in

Oxford New York

Auckland Cape Town Dar es Salaam Hong Kong Karachi
Kuala Lumpur Madrid Melbourne Mexico City Nairobi
New Delhi Shanghai Taipei Toronto

With offices in

Argentina Austria Brazil Chile Czech Republic France Greece
Guatemala Hungary Italy Japan Poland Portugal Singapore
South Korea Switzerland Thailand Turkey Ukraine Vietnam

Oxford is a registered trade mark of Oxford University Press
in the UK and in certain other countries

Published in the United States
by Oxford University Press Inc., New York

British Library Cataloguing in Publication Data

Data available

Library of Congress Cataloging in Publication Data

Data available

Typeset by Newgen Imaging Systems (P) Ltd., Chennai, India
Printed in Great Britain
on acid-free paper by
Biddles Ltd., Kings Lynn, Norfolk

ISBN 0–19–927677–3 (Hbk.)  978–0–19–927677–6

10 9 8 7 6 5 4 3 2 1

To the memory of my Mother

# Preface

East Asia covers a land mass of 15,850 thousand square km, accounts for roughly 20 percent of world GDP, and is home to more than 2 billion people from 15 countries plus Taiwan and Hong Kong.

They are ASEAN 10, China, Japan, South and North Korea, and Mongolia. East Asia is a region where economic development miracles abound, beginning with Japan during the post-war period to the region's newly industrializing economies of Hong Kong, Singapore, South Korea and Taiwan. Finally, there is China. According to Stiglitz, East Asia, even after the Asian crisis of 1997–98, remains the best model of development the world has seen today.

The Asian financial crisis altered what appeared to be an invincible image of East Asia as an economic powerhouse challenging the West's dominance in the global economy. A region that was proud of its miraculous economic achievements was suddenly reduced to a region of corruption, non-transparency, inept governments, mismanaged financial systems, and industrial conglomerates bent on excessive investment and expansion with borrowed money. It was not clear whether there was anything right in East Asia. The Asian crisis understandably provoked a re-examination of the East Asian development paradigm. Many observers claim that capitalism proved its superiority in the latter half of the 1990s.

Seven years after the crisis, East Asia is at a crossroads. If they subscribe to the Washington Consensus view of the world economy, East Asian countries should not hesitate to replace the pre-crisis model of development entirely with an Anglo-American system of capitalism. On the other hand, if the problems associated with the imperfections of international financial markets are more to blame as the causes of the crisis, East Asia would be better off by staying with a traditional East Asian model and at most, reforming it to be compatible with changes in the domestic and global economic environment. This book searches for a new development paradigm that could help East Asian countries adapt to societal and political changes taking place in the region while retaining their pre-crisis vitality and competitiveness for durable growth in integrating into the global economy.

This book grew out of a study in which I participated on a new development paradigm for Asia organized by the Asian Development Bank Institute (ADBI) under the leadership of Masaru Yoshitomi, who served as dean of the institute at the time. I am grateful to Mr. Yoshitomi for his generous financial support and his numerous suggestions for improvement. I have since added several chapters on economic integration in East Asia to a paper I wrote for the institute to complement the analysis of economic liberalization in the region.

In writing this book, I have benefited a great deal from comments and discussions with many colleagues and friends who read all or parts of earlier drafts. Hugh Patrick and Stephan Haggard read the first draft. Their helpful comments assisted me a great deal in restructuring the book's contents. Hugh, gracious in his support, read a third draft and provided detailed input. In many places, I literally copied his suggested changes with his permission. I owe him a lot for what this book is now.

I have been working on financial developments, integration, and macroeconomic policy issues in East Asia with Barry Eichengreen, Charles Wyplosz, and Robert McCaulley. They have been instrumental in advancing many of my arguments in this book. Charles guided me in understanding the process of economic integration in Europe, which gave me new perspectives on possible processes applicable to East Asia. Bob was always available whenever I had questions on global and regional market development. Barry suggested a number of important clarifications on East Asian economies that I referred to in analyzing economic, social, and political developments in addition to future development paradigms in East Asia. Whenever my thinking went astray, he brought me back on course. This book would be much less focused without his incisive criticism.

Several chapters of this book were presented to conferences at NBER and the Brookings Institution. At these conferences and elsewhere Dani Rodrik was patient enough to discuss many issues on globalization. Jong Wha Lee and So Young Kim, my colleagues at Korea University, offered many suggestions for clarification on exchange rate policy and capital market deregulation in East Asia in Chapters 16 and 17.

When I began working on this book, the late Rudi Dornbusch was gravely ill. Yet he was willing to listen to all sorts of problems I had in writing the book. He taught me practically all I know about exchange rate economics. With Rudi around I would be a better economist and have written a better book. It is difficult to put into words how much I miss him.

Carol Bestley and Jennifer Wilkinson at Oxford University Press expedited the publication of this book. Without their support, the book's release would have been further delayed. Special thanks go to Edwin Pritchard. Finally, Daniel Yang at the Korea Development Institute (KDI) and Maggie Shade did meticulous work in checking many numerical and typographical errors which escaped my attention.

*Seoul*
*August 2005*

# Contents

# Contents

## Contents

# List of Figures

# List of Tables

# List of Abbreviations

| | |
|---|---|
| ABF | Asian Bond Fund |
| ABMI | Asian Bond Market Initiative |
| ADB | Asian Development Bank |
| AMC | asset management company |
| AMF | Asian Monetary Fund |
| APEC | Asia Pacific Economic Cooperation |
| AFTA | ASEAN Free Trade Area |
| AREAR | Annual Report on Exchange Agreements and Restrictions |
| ASA | ASEAN swap arrangement |
| ASEAN | Association of South East Asian Nations |
| BBC | basket, band, and crawl |
| BIS | Bank for International Settlements |
| BSA | bilateral swap arrangement |
| CER | Closer Economic Relations trade agreement |
| CMI | Chiang Mai Initiative |
| CPF | Central Provident Fund |
| CPI | Consumer Price Index |
| EME | emerging market economy |
| EMEAP | Executive Meetings of East Asia and Pacific |
| EMS | European Monetary System |
| EU | European Union |
| FDI | foreign direct investment |
| FTA | free trade agreement |
| GATT | General Agreement on Tariffs and Trade |
| GDP | gross domestic product |
| GLB | Gramm-Leach-Biley |
| ICT | information and communication technology |

## List of Abbreviations

| | |
|---|---|
| IFI | international financial institution |
| IFS | International Financial Statistics |
| IMF | International Monetary Fund |
| IT | information technology |
| KKZ | Kaufmann, Kraay, and Zoido-Lobaton |
| NIE | newly industrializing economy |
| NPL | nonperforming loan |
| ODA | official development assistance |
| RTA | regional trade agreement |
| SEC | Securities and Exchange Commission |
| SME | small and medium sized enterprises |
| TFP | total factor productivity |
| WTO | World Trade Organization |

Part I

# Successes and Failures of the East Asian Development Paradigm

# 1

# Introduction

The decade since the mid-1990s has been a tumultuous time of economic and political changes that have altered the course of development in East Asia. Several countries, which once built the East Asian miracle, fell victim to a devastating financial crisis in 1997–98, plunging the entire region into economic turmoil. Against all the odds and earlier expectations these countries were able to bounce back quickly from the near financial melt-down a year after they succumbed to it.

In the wake of the crisis, most East Asian economies, including the crisis-hit ones, embraced liberal economic reforms that would deregulate and open their financial and trade regimes and in doing so, usher in the economic system of Anglo-American societies—the US, UK, Canada, and Australia—that is characterized by unfettered competition, free enterprise, property rights, and political democracy with a government of limited powers, the system which for the sake of comparison with the East Asian one will be referred to throughout this study as the Anglo-American model of free capitalism. This system was expected to replace the development paradigm that had been instrumental in East Asia's economic ascendancy before the crisis. Seven years into the liberal reforms, East Asia is not yet halfway there as far as Anglo-Americanization is concerned.

While much of East Asia has been struggling to regain its pre-crisis dynamism, with Japan languishing in a decade-long recession, China has been racing ahead with a dizzying speed of growth. China is no longer a regional economic power; it has become a global power to be reckoned with.

The financial crisis of 1997–98 has set in motion two interrelated initiatives for financial cooperation and integration in the region promoted by the group of East Asian economies known as ASEAN+3, the three being China, Japan, and South Korea. One has been the Chiang Mai Initiative and the other, the Asian Bond Market Initiative. These two initiatives were followed by a proliferation of bilateral free trade agreements (FTAs), sidetracking East Asia from the region-wide free trade movement that has been carried out under the auspices of the GATT/WTO and APEC.

ASEAN+3, which for all practical purposes is synonymous with East Asia, has made considerable progress in institutionalizing financial and policy cooperation and has been engaged in negotiating or discussing some seventeen bilateral FTAs within the organization and with partners from outside of the region. China has been at the center of East Asia's integration. With the advantage of its large market and potential for growth, China has been able to take a more assertive stance in managing regional affairs and has assumed a greater leadership role in regional economic integration few foresaw a decade before.

The ASEAN+3 states are committed to open regionalism and are expected to continue liberalizing and opening their markets for goods and services and also deregulating their capital accounts over time. However, the bifurcation of their strategy of regional integration between bilateral FTAs for trade and a multilateral approach for regional financial integration may run into disunity of and conflicts of interest among the ASEAN+3 states. This dissonance may in the end not advance either economic integration in the region or their integration into the global economic system.

Since the crisis, many East Asian economies have recorded persistent surpluses on their current accounts vis-à-vis the US, which have been sterilized to add to their foreign exchange reserves. No doubt, the export-led development strategy that is in part supported by an exchange rate policy that has kept many East Asian currencies undervalued has contributed to the imbalance. However, the major culprit of the region's surplus has been the sharp decrease in investment demand, caused by the crisis and subsequent structural reform, while savings as a share of GDP have remained stable. The growing imbalance in trade has become the point of contention, posing the risk of destabilizing the global financial system and provoking trade frictions and straining transpacific economic relations between the US and East Asia. Unfortunately, neither side of the Pacific has been able to agree on how to go about resolving it.

East Asia is known for and used to many miracles—the Japanese miracle of the post-war economic recovery, the East Asian miracle, and of late the Chinese miracle of near double-digit growth for more than two decades (Lin, Cai, and Li 2003). And now there is East Asia's political miracle. Excluding China, 'there is a great swath of democracy in Asia's East from Japan in the North down to Indonesia in the South' (*The Economist* 2004: 11).

Indisputably, democratization has brought about fundamental changes in governance at every level of society, the social welfare system, and industrial relations.

What do these economic, social, and political changes collectively portend for the future of East Asia in its quest to catch up with the living standards of advanced countries in Europe and North America and integrate into the global economic system? The purpose of this study is to analyze the implications of the major developments described above for East Asia's economic liberalization and integration into the global economy and prospects for its economic relations with the US and Europe. To this end, this study begins with an examination of the achievements and failures of the pre-crisis East Asian development paradigm, which was a highly regulated mixed economy model, and then moves on to a critical review of the Anglo-American reform upon which East Asian economies embarked early in the 1990s.

Is the East Asian development model, as described by the World Bank study of the East Asian miracle (World Bank 1993), so outdated and out of touch with the realities of a new global economy that it should be repudiated in favor of an alternative system, such as Anglo-American capitalism? The Anglo-Americanization of East Asia, whether it was what the IMF and World Bank intended in imposing policy conditionality for their rescue financing, has been hampered by the region's limited institutional capacity for liberal reform and in some cases has been stalled by local opposition to it. On the basis of this and other experiences of economic liberalization, this study concludes that neither Anglo-Americanization nor staying with the old regime is a realistic alternative and goes on to propose that the old system be reformed in a way that could help East Asian economies adapt to societal and political changes taking place in the region while regaining their pre-crisis vitality and competitiveness for durable growth.

What would be the critical components of reform they might undertake in developing a new paradigm of development? Although East Asian economies will not fully accept the Anglo-American market-oriented reform, neither will they retreat from opening their markets and hence from economic globalization as long as they pursue an export-led development strategy. This study concludes that they are most likely to settle on a mixed economy model that melds the state and market, and is more open and much less regulated than the old model. This study then proposes an agenda for reform of the financial, corporate, and public sector that would be critical to developing such an economic system.

• *Plan of the Book*

East Asia covers a huge territory, is home to almost 2 billion people, and in 2003 accounted for 23 percent of total world gross domestic product. It would indeed be presumptuous to talk about a new paradigm for all of East Asia, just as it would be to define the pre-crisis East Asian development model as if it applied to all East Asian economies.

This book consists of six parts. Part I examines the successes and failures of the East Asian development model. In Chapter 2, this study defines and illustrates the conceptual framework of the East Asian development model and delineates some of its unique features and basic strengths that have been highlighted by many studies on East Asia's economic rise. This is followed in Chapter 3 by the development policies of East Asia's emerging economies. Chapters 4, 5, and 6 are devoted to an in-depth evaluation of the failures of the East Asian economic system, focusing on the governance system and the financial and corporate sector to determine the extent to which they exposed East Asian economies to speculative attacks.

The four chapters from 7 to 10 constitute Part II, devoted to analyzing the causes and consequences of the 1997–98 Asian crisis. Chapter 8 reviews alleged or actual causes of the crisis to set the stage for reform of the East Asian model. And a good starting place would be the IMF reform programs drawn up for the management of the crisis in Indonesia, South Korea, and Thailand. This is because the IMF programs in general espoused policies advanced by the Washington Consensus on market deregulation and opening. The Fund saw as critical the need to identify the causes of the crisis, what it thought should be done to prevent a financial collapse and speed up the recovery in these countries. A critical review of the IMF programs in Chapters 9 and 10 shows that they were plagued by an incorrect diagnosis of the causes of the crisis and hence a wrong prescription. Chapter 9 argues that none of the alleged causes of the crisis were serious enough to bring Indonesia, South Korea, Malaysia, and Thailand to the brink of a financial meltdown, though they increased the probability of a crisis.

Having suffered such a traumatic crisis, it is necessary to re-examine whether the old East Asian development model would be viable for the post-crisis development of the region and for replication elsewhere in the 21st century. The consensus view is that this should not be the case: East Asia needs a new paradigm of economic development. Although the economic profession is divided on whether the causes of the crisis were primarily the loss of foreign exchange reserves and associated panic or rooted in the structural and insolvency problems, there is little doubt that the old East Asian model will not survive political, economic, and techno-logical changes taking place in and around East Asia.

In view of this need for overall reform, this study presents in Part III from chapters 11 through 14 an agenda for structural and institutional changes in the public, corporate, and financial sectors that are vital for construct-ing a new post-crisis paradigm of development. Chapter 11 discusses the pros and cons of East Asia's large family-owned corporations and groups. Although there is an urgent need for improving the governance of these groups, this study argues that democratization and market opening will eventually bring about their transformation into modern corporations built on global standards of governance and transparency. In other chap-ters of Part III, it will be shown that the new paradigm demands institution building for a new governance system, new social welfare policies and industrial relations built on a set of democratic institutions, rules, and norms. In the new paradigm, the role of government will be leading social rather than economic development. This does not, however, mean that there is no room for industrial policy in the new paradigm.

Part IV turns to deregulation and opening of financial markets in Chapters 15 through 17. One important conclusion of Chapter 15 is that although East Asian economies are not likely to deviate from the general trend toward economic liberalization, they will retain many features of their financial sectors specific to East Asia, including bank-oriented financial systems.

Following the IMF structural reform, East Asia's emerging economies moved to free floating currencies, instituted an inflation targeting system, and laid out a plan for gradual deregulation of capital account transac-tions. Seven years after the initiation of the reform, it is common know-ledge that East Asian floaters in reality intervene extensively in the foreign exchange market and have retained many of the capital controls of the pre-crisis regime. Chapters 16 and 17 explain why the East Asian economies have been reluctant to liberalize their capital accounts and have chosen to move to the middle of the spectrum of the exchange rate system. The export-led development strategy, which the East Asian economies have never given up, has made it necessary to intervene in the foreign exchange market.

Part V deals with issues concerning economic cooperation and integra-tion in East Asia. Chapter 18 discusses trade liberalization and integration in East Asia, focusing on the new wave of bilateral free trade agreements (FTAs). This discussion is followed in Chapter 19 by a review of recent develop-ments concerning the Chiang Mai Initiative (CMI) and the Asian Bond

Market Initiative (ABMI) to trace the evolution of regional financial cooperation and integration in the region. Trade and financial market integration have encountered many constraints and suffered from the absence of leadership that could reconcile the varying interests of different economies to obtain consensus on a regional integration agenda. In Chapter 20 this study speculates on the prospects for regional economic integration: it will be sustained, but at best move at a snail's pace. Part VI, comprising Chapters 22 through 25, summarizes the findings and arguments of the preceding five parts to present the main features of a new development model for East Asia and the main messages of the study.

# 2

# Characteristics and Accomplishments of the East Asian Development Paradigm[1]

## 2.1. East Asian Development Models of Four Different Generations

East Asia is often referred to as a sub-region of Asia that includes the ASEAN states, China, Japan, South Korea, Taiwan, and Hong Kong. Development experiences of these economies have been extensively analyzed by many studies, the most notable being the East Asian miracle by the World Bank in 1993. The ten ASEAN members and the three Northeast Asian economies—China, Japan, and South Korea—known as ASEAN+3 have worked together to create regional arrangements for financial cooperation and policy coordination for deeper economic integration in the region. East Asia is where there has been a new wave of bilateral free trade agreements. The Asian crisis in 1997–98 and the integrationist movement that has followed, have therefore again attracted a great deal of interest in analyzing the past and future prospects of East Asia's economic development among economists and economic policymakers of both developed and developing countries.

This study analyzes the development experiences of East Asia's emerging economies that include the original ASEAN five, Hong Kong, South Korea, and Taiwan. China is also an emerging economy, but because of its size and different pattern of development, it is only proper to treat it as a separate entity. Cambodia, Laos, Myanmar, and Vietnam are East Asia's developing economies. Japan is not covered in this study except for brief description of

---

[1] This chapter draws on the World Bank (1993) as a primary source of reference. For recent studies on a re-examination of the East Asian miracle, see Yoshitomi (2003), Stiglitz and Yusuf (2001), Quibria (2002), and the ADB (1997).

the Japanese model of development during the post-war period until the mid-1970s to set the stage for comparative analyses of models of different countries belonging to different generations in East Asia.

China's remarkable growth and structural transformation are beyond the scope of this study; they are presented in a rather cursory manner for comparison with the experiences of the region's other emerging economies. Throughout this study, East Asia's emerging economies and emerging East Asia will be used interchangeably, as will East Asia's developing economies and developing East Asia. For analytic purposes, Hong Kong, Singapore, South Korea, and Taiwan are separated out as a group of so called newly industrializing economies (NIEs), a term which was in common usage in the 1990s, or the region's more advanced economies in this study. East Asian economies in this study include ASEAN, China, Hong Kong, Taiwan, and South Korea.

At the outset, it should be noted that 'East Asian development model' is a term used to explain the workings of the economic systems of emerging economies of the region with a view to identifying the distinctive features responsible for rapid growth with equity in the region. In terms of this broad definition, there may be as many East Asian models as there are East Asian economies, each with different cultural and historical backgrounds and each at different stages of development.

However, the East Asian economies covered in this study share a number of structural characteristics that separate them from many other developing economies. It is the combination of these characteristics that make them unique as compared with other countries in different regions. Throughout this study 'the East Asian model' will be referred to as a development paradigm that captures most of the common characteristics found in a variety of models of different generations and countries in the region. In subsequent chapters, the East Asian development model, development paradigm, economic system, and development strategy will be used interchangeably to explain the development process of East Asia.

## • Product Cycle Development

For analytic purposes, it is convenient to divide East Asia into five groups of economies along the ladder of comparative advantage, layered by differences in their factor endowments. As an economic superpower, Japan is the most advanced country with comparative advantage in high technology industries. Following Japan there is a second tier of countries—East

Asia's NIEs. The third tier consists of the five middle-income countries of ASEAN—Indonesia, Malaysia, the Philippines, Thailand and Malaysia.

The fourth group comprises developing economies of East Asia. The region's less developed economies are gearing up for an economic take-off after a long period of dormancy and are likely to follow a variant of the export-led development strategy of other East Asian economies. Although they have shown potential for rapid growth and industrialization, their development experience is not long enough to warrant an in-depth analysis. By virtue of its size and industrial diversity, which includes a space industry, China does not belong to any particular group described above: it constitutes a group unto itself. Depending on the industry, it maintains either competitive or complementary relations with its neighbors.

Excluding the group of less developed countries and China, the other three groups then roughly correspond to three similar but differentiable development models of different generations since the Second World War. The Japanese model of a developmental state that created the Japanese economic miracle after the war and subsequently paved the way for Japan's rise as a global economic power can be identified as the first generation East Asian development model.

A developmental state or a state with a strong government is one that has the ability to credibly commit itself to long-term development goals and choose appropriate policies that would enable them to attain those goals. Many East Asian economies, some of which were authoritarian, fit into this category of 'strong' states. The ability to make long-term policy commitments drew in part on the political independence from private actors that strong governments enjoyed and which, in turn, allowed control of the policy agenda. The governments in Japan, South Korea, and Taiwan were perceived to possess these abilities, although it is not clear why and how these countries came to support strong governments. In general, history, culture, tradition, such as the Chinese mandarin system, and path dependence are all likely factors that have contributed to the emergence of strong and efficient governments in East Asia.[2]

---

[2] Since so many factors are involved in establishing an efficient, relatively independent, and corruption-free bureaucracy, it is not clear how developing countries should go about building one. Following Bardhan (1996), it appears that redistributive reforms may help lay a social foundation conducive to the emergence of a strong government. However, the effective implementation of the reforms he suggests often requires the existence of a strong government, taking us back to square one. According to Bardhan, distributive equality and the homogeneity of societies in East Asia helped create and sustain communal institutions, which in turn were able to provide local public goods and to enforce social rules and regulations and property rights. Effective communal institutions are then able to help maintain a high quality bureaucracy since these institutions do not allow interest groups to easily control local politics. In addition, see

The Japanese model of the post-war period up to the late 1970s is characterized by industrial policy, export orientation, a bank-based financial system, and state support for big business groups. In conducting industrial policy, the Japanese economic bureaucracy, largely insulated from political intervention, was picking and supporting winner industries through credit and tax breaks and helping the adjustment process of loser industries such as shipping, coal, and mining. During this period, Japanese industrial policy was effective in part because it placed a strong emphasis on savings, education, training, and import of foreign technology. As in other contemporary East Asian economies, large business groups dominated many of Japan's industries.[3] Business relations among these groups and large firms were characterized by long-term, repeat business, and less than arms-length relations, which relied more on trust than legal contracts.

The financial system was bank rather than capital market based to deal with the lack of public information on firms and their asymmetry. Industrial groups and large corporations heavily depended on their main banks as major creditors, monitors, and organizers of implicit loan syndications. In the absence of efficient capital markets, Japanese banks supplied long-term financing as well by rolling over short-term loans.[4]

By and large the Japanese model was successfully emulated by several East Asian economies, namely Hong Kong, Singapore, Taiwan, and South Korea beginning in the 1960s, eventually earning accolades for creating an East Asian miracle. Some of the features of the development strategies pursued by these countries, which are analyzed in the next chapter, may constitute the second generation East Asian development paradigm.

About a decade later, several Southeast Asian economies went on to replicate the second generation model with considerable success. Their development experience constitutes the third generation model. Compared with the second generation model, it is distinctive in that the Southeast Asian economies depended much more on foreign direct investment as sources of capital and technology, were more specialized in resource-based exports, did not acquire many features of a developmental state, and managed a relatively loose industrial policy framework.

---

Haggard (2000: 20) on the contribution of the developmental state and strong government to economic development.

[3] After the Second World War, the pre-war Zaibatsu families in Japan were broken up by the occupation authorities, and control over large companies was vested in management. Unlike in other East Asian economies, the dominant mode of big business organization has been management, rather than family-controlled companies in Japan.

[4] On the Japanese model, see Patrick and Park (1994) and Aoki and Patrick (1994).

The evolution of three generations of models in East Asia follows the pattern of development predicted by the product cycle hypothesis (Vernon 1966), when it is extended to industrialization in different countries at different stages of development in a region.[5] In this framework, Japan is the leading innovative country, which creates a new product and then begins to export when its supply exceeds the domestic demand. With the diffusion of innovations and migration of the production process over time, the follower countries, which used to import the product, learn to produce it for their domestic markets. In the East Asian context, the East Asian NIEs are the followers right behind Japan.

Over time these East Asian NIEs become more competitive in producing and saturate their domestic markets for the product. They then start exporting it by first making inroads into Japan's export markets—for example ASEAN—and eventually by penetrating Japan's (the innovator's) domestic market. In the end, Japan (the innovator) becomes a net importer of the product it first invented.

While the second tier countries—the East Asian NIEs—are catching up with the leading innovator (Japan) they are also pursued by other economies in the third tier on the ladder of competitive advantage (Malaysia and Thailand, for example). When the third tier countries complete import substitution of the product in question, they begin to penetrate the home markets of the second tier countries (NIEs). By then the second tier countries have probably become innovators themselves or begun import substitution of a new product invented by the leading innovator country (Japan). Thus, a development cycle for the second tier countries moves from rising imports of the product from the innovator to rising imports from the third tier countries and then to a new product.

- *The China Miracle: The Fourth Generation Model*

While some of the Southeast Asian economies were following in the footsteps of the East Asian NIE's development experience, China embarked on economic reforms of its own. This resulted in market liberalization and opening towards the end of the 1970s after the failure of the leap forward development strategy in the 1960s and the 1970s. The remarkable success of China in industrialization and improving living standards, which is often referred to as the Chinese miracle, may be classified as the fourth generation East Asian development model.

---

[5] According to the Japanese metaphor, this process is known as the flying geese pattern of development: see Akamatsu (1961) and Ito (2000).

Just like other East Asian economies, it has relentlessly and successfully pursued an export-led development strategy, relying largely on foreign invested firms, which have accounted for 40 percent of China's total exports in recent years. As a result of this success, China has replaced the US as the most important destination of exports for all East Asian economies. Unlike other large countries, China exports a large share of its output: its exports as a share of GDP rose to almost 30 percent of GDP in 2003, twice the average share of other large countries. Unlike other East Asian economies, however, its demand for imported raw materials and other intermediate and final goods is expected to grow as fast as its exports. Assuming China will be able to sustain its current rate of growth, it will remain the growth engine in the region and will reduce East Asia's dependence on the US market.

China imports raw materials, capital goods, and parts and components from Japan, South Korea, and other Asian countries to produce a large variety of manufactured products that are exported to the US and Europe. China, the US and other East Asian economies have in the process developed a triangular trade relationship in which China has become a large assembly plant for East Asia's exports, the US the final market, and Japan and other East Asian economies suppliers of capital, technology, and raw materials. If China maintains the current level of growth for some time in the future, the triangular trade relationship will deepen. China is also distinctive in that it is a communist regime and as such would continue through path dependency of its socialist heritage, even if it tried to move away.

## 2.2. Accomplishments of the East Asian Development Model

Among the many economic achievements of East Asia before the crisis, the most notable was rapid growth, as shown in Table 2.1. From 1960 to the early 1990s, East Asia grew on average three times as fast as Latin America and South Asia. Between 1960 and 1985, real income per capita more than quadrupled in Japan, Taiwan, Hong Kong, Singapore, and South Korea. A second significant accomplishment was declining inequality as the rewards of rapid growth were evenly spread throughout the populations.[6] A third was the quick reduction of the technology gap vis-à-vis

---

[6] During this high growth period, it is not clear to what degree inequality declined. Japan, Korea, and Taiwan had relatively low inequality before the onset of rapid growth. But it should also be noted that inequality has worsened in the Philippines, Malaysia, and Thailand. See Quibria (2002) on income distribution in East Asia (section 2).

advanced countries via massive investment in human capital, importation of foreign technology, export orientation, and deregulation of foreign direct investment as a channel of acquiring new and advanced technology.

There is voluminous literature on the economic and social factors that contributed to East Asia's rapid growth and reduction in poverty rates. Even before the publication of the World Bank miracle study, characteristics of the East Asian economies, especially regarding the phenomenal increases in savings, investment, and exports, had been extensively documented with different analysts emphasizing different aspects of East Asia.[7] Of these contributions, the World Bank miracle study (1993) was the most rigorous and comprehensive analysis of East Asia's meteoric economic rise. It defines the East Asian model as a functional framework of growth in which macroeconomic stability, superior accumulation of physical and human capital, efficient allocation, and catching up with advanced foreign technology were important elements that supported rapid growth with equity.

How then were East Asian economies able to acquire all these prerequisites for rapid growth? In large measure they did so by successfully pursuing a set of policies that combined fundamentals and interventions. This policy regime was complemented by a governance mechanism that made the policies credible to the polity. That is, East Asia's economic rise was built on its success in constructing governance and market supporting institutions that secured foundations for rapid growth and in developing policies that these institutions supported.

A similar assessment can be found in an ADB study published in 1997 (ADB: 18) that argues that the East Asian development process 'was the outcome of a fortunate combination of initial potential that capable governments harnessed through export promotion and increasingly effective market supporting institutions.' Although the list of factors the study claims to have contributed to East Asia's economic ascendancy was long and formidable, it was more hopeful than others in recommending other developing countries to follow in East Asia's wake. This optimistic view had not been supported by evidence even before the onset of the Asian crisis; a large number of developing countries had emulated the East Asian development strategy only to fail to replicate it. Since the Asian crisis, few international financial institutions and development experts have been willing to extol the virtues of the East Asian development model to contemporary developing countries, at least not in its old paradigm.

---

[7] See Yusuf (2001), Quibria (2002), and Yoshitomi (2003).

**Table 2.1.** GDP Growth, Saving, Investment, and Exports in GDP in East Asia

| Countries | 1960–9 | 1970–9 | 1980–9 | 1990–6 | 1997 | 1998 | 1999–2003 |
|---|---|---|---|---|---|---|---|
| **China** | | | | | | | |
| GDP growth rate (I) | 3.02 | 7.44 | 9.75 | 10.49 | 8.80 | 7.80 | 8.00 |
| Saving (% of GDP) (II) | — | 30.50 | 34.90 | 40.86 | 41.47 | 40.77 | 40.24 |
| Investment (% of GDP) (III) | 9.64 | 14.75 | 35.43 | 38.94 | 38.00 | 37.40 | 38.60 |
| Export (% of GDP) (IV) | — | 3.79 | 9.21 | 15.78 | 20.34 | 19.39 | 24.40 |
| **Hong Kong** | | | | | | | |
| (I) | 9.91 | 9.29 | 7.33 | 5.13 | 5.10 | −5.00 | 3.84 |
| (II) | 22.42 | 30.80 | 34.10 | 32.23 | 30.25 | 29.40 | 30.75 |
| (III) | 28.76 | 25.31 | 28.12 | 29.91 | 34.50 | 29.14 | 25.06 |
| (IV) | 78.65 | 88.25 | 108.35 | 141.09 | 110.66 | 106.41 | 123.45 |
| **Indonesia** | | | | | | | |
| (I) | 3.74 | 7.82 | 5.66 | 7.39 | 4.50 | −13.10 | 3.40 |
| (II) | 7.97 | 24.97 | 31.47 | 32.34 | 31.48 | 26.53 | 22.95 |
| (III) | 4.82 | 9.86 | 27.72 | 31.19 | 31.80 | 16.80 | 15.38 |
| (IV) | 10.44 | 22.37 | 24.91 | 23.19 | 26.09 | 52.78 | 36.93 |
| **Japan** | | | | | | | |
| (I) | 10.44 | 5.28 | 3.85 | 2.26 | 1.80 | −1.10 | 1.09 |
| (II) | 35.15 | 35.47 | 31.67 | 31.62 | 29.80 | 28.72 | 26.77 |
| (III) | 34.63 | 34.45 | 29.79 | 30.03 | 28.55 | 26.76 | 25.88 |
| (IV) | 9.78 | 11.71 | 12.64 | 9.57 | 10.745 | 10.672 | 10.84 |
| **Korea, South** | | | | | | | |
| (I) | 8.25 | 8.53 | 7.56 | 7.61 | 4.70 | −6.90 | 6.38 |
| (II) | 8.67 | 22.25 | 31.37 | 36.35 | 35.78 | 37.87 | 33.15 |
| (III) | 15.57 | 25.02 | 29.63 | 37.64 | 36.00 | 25.00 | 29.58 |
| (IV) | 7.91 | 24.95 | 32.99 | 24.02 | 26.87 | 38.29 | 32.21 |

| | | | | | | | |
|---|---|---|---|---|---|---|---|
| **Malaysia** | | | | | | | |
| (I) | 6.55 | 7.73 | 5.90 | 9.47 | 7.30 | −7.40 | 4.94 |
| (II) | 21.85 | 27.10 | 32.95 | 38.07 | 43.89 | 48.67 | 44.36 |
| (III) | 13.53 | 17.73 | 29.81 | 38.73 | 43.00 | 26.70 | 23.80 |
| (IV) | 42.60 | 44.13 | 54.30 | 71.76 | 77.26 | 99.44 | 103.32 |
| **Philippines** | | | | | | | |
| (I) | 5.06 | 5.79 | 2.01 | 2.81 | 5.20 | −0.60 | 3.72 |
| (II) | 18.53 | 24.89 | 22.76 | 15.43 | 14.21 | 12.40 | 17.85 |
| (III) | 13.13 | 15.58 | 21.04 | 22.90 | 24.80 | 20.30 | 19.72 |
| (IV) | 14.95 | 21.51 | 20.80 | 20.97 | 30.64 | 45.26 | 44.97 |
| **Singapore** | | | | | | | |
| (I) | 9.58 | 9.41 | 7.43 | 9.00 | 8.60 | −0.90 | 3.60 |
| (II) | −3.99 | 28.61 | 41.29 | 46.90 | 51.99 | 53.35 | 46.44 |
| (III) | 29.99 | 47.41 | 42.58 | 35.31 | 39.20 | 32.30 | 24.70 |
| (IV) | — | — | 58.07 | 139.08 | 131.75 | 134.61 | 265.33 |
| **Thailand** | | | | | | | |
| (I) | 7.82 | 7.51 | 7.30 | 8.60 | −1.40 | −10.50 | 4.70 |
| (II) | 18.66 | 22.26 | 26.53 | 36.19 | 35.66 | 35.23 | 32.83 |
| (III) | 24.92 | 30.04 | 29.39 | 41.20 | 33.70 | 20.40 | 23.30 |
| (IV) | 16.31 | 19.03 | 23.29 | 29.71 | 37.59 | 47.27 | 52.61 |
| **Taiwan** | | | | | | | |
| (I) | 13.62 | 19.98 | 9.88 | 6.73 | 6.70 | 4.60 | 3.20 |
| (II) | 20.57 | 31.18 | 32.94 | 26.87 | 25.60 | 25.44 | 24.05 |
| (III) | 21.64 | 29.65 | 23.88 | 24.47 | 23.96 | 24.72 | 19.88 |
| (IV) | 22.41 | 44.10 | 51.67 | 40.22 | 41.89 | 41.22 | 44.38 |

*Sources:* World Bank indicators 2003 and 2004, Penn World Table 6.1, and Asian Development Bank key indicators (various issues).

In the following section, this chapter identifies (i) initial conditions, (ii) cultural factors, and (iii) institutions unique to East Asia. Policies that were conducive to an economic take-off and to sustaining rapid growth are reviewed in Chapter 3.

## 2.3. Initial conditions, Asian values, and Institutions

Many studies on the East Asian economic miracle identify a number of initial conditions that buttressed the economic take-off in South Korea, Taiwan, Hong Kong, and Singapore in the early 1960s.[8] One such factor was poor resource endowments, which provided incentives to follow an outward looking development strategy instead of the import substitution favored by Latin American countries. Another was the availability of a relatively well-educated labor force. A third was a low degree of inequality of income and wealth distribution, which made it possible to mobilize public support for industrialization as the relative equality helped reduce pressure on distributive policies. A fourth factor was labor market flexibility, which facilitated labor migration from rural agriculture to urban manufacturing sectors. Finally, these countries had the advantage of having a high quality bureaucracy, which was able to create and manage a relatively efficient developmental state that played a pivotal role in the allocation of resources.

As for the so-called Asian values that contributed to the East Asian miracle, those values of Confucianism that include a work ethic, thrift, emphasis on education, a meritocratic system, and the maintenance of order and respect for hierarchy, are claimed to be conducive to developing a modern technological economy.[9] Asian values are also believed to have supported a number of key institutions unique to East Asian societies, which had an important role in sustaining rapid growth. They were: the paternalistic brand of authoritarian governments that made possible the emergence of developmental or hard states; the Japanese lifetime employment system and Keiretsu networks; Chaebol and large family-owned business groups, and family-based networks of overseas Chinese businesses in Southeast Asia.

How significant were these values as factors responsible for such rapid growth? There is of course, no easy way to quantify the contribution of

---

[8]  A representative of these studies is Yoshitomi (2003).
[9]  For a discussion on the Asian values, see Zakaria's interview with Lee Kuan Yew (1994).

East Asia's cultural values to its economic success. Even in a conceptual framework, it is difficult to identify a causal relationship between cultural values and economic development. As Fukuyama (2004) notes, culture may not have a direct effect on either economic or social behavior. Instead, as he argues, although many of these Asian institutions were not as harmful as often asserted, the basic explanation for East Asia's economic success lies in conventional factors such as factors of production, technology, and political stability. Analyzing the causes of the Asian crisis six years earlier, however, Fukuyama (1998) was more critical about Asian institutions: they became obstacles to growth as demonstrated by the crisis. In Fukuyama's view, the crisis undermined the argument that there was a distinct set of Asian values on an economic and a political level. He even predicted that the crisis would lead to a convergence of institutions between East and West.

About four years before Fukuyama (1998), Zakaria (1994: 126) concluded after an interview with Lee Kuan Yew that most of the attributes of Asian culture were once part of the West. Modernization and economic growth would lead to a convergence of East Asian to Western institutions because 'to be modern without becoming more Western is difficult: the two are not wholly separable'. Disputing the convergence argument, however, Johnson (2001) claims that underregulation and the loss of autonomy by the economic bureaucracy to cultivate growth industries in the face of the vested interests represented by the Liberal Democratic Party (LDP), which came with economic liberalization, was responsible for the demise of the developmental state and the decade-long stagnation in Japan. He even blames the liberal political order, as it was the main cause of the economic meltdown in East Asia that began in Thailand in 1997.

While conceptually it is possible to argue that Asian cultural factors were important contributors to East Asia's economic modernization, there is no easy way of empirically gauging their relative significance. If one argues as Lee Kwan Yew and Mahathir do that certain Asian cultural values were at the root of East Asia's remarkable post-war success, there is little one can say about replicability of the East Asian development paradigm in other developing regions unless one is prepared to advocate cultural changes. This is because there is no reason to believe that countries with different value systems cannot grow.

# 3

# Development Policies and Governance

## 3.1. Market Friendly Policies

In its overview of the economic progress achieved by East Asia over the last three decades before the crisis, the World Bank miracle study (1993) concludes that East Asia's success can be attributed, in large part, to a market friendly policy or getting the basics right. Some of the basics or economic fundamentals are presented below:

- *Development of Agriculture*

Most East Asian economies had traits of interventionist regimes, but their policymakers exercised restraint in intervening in areas where the markets can be relied upon. This basic strategy of espousing a market friendly approach is often credited with the success in keeping price distortions within reasonable bounds, as in agriculture. At an early stage of development, a structural transformation from agriculture to manufacturing was a key to sustainable growth. East Asian emerging market economies were able to increase productivity of agriculture through land reform, investment in infrastructure, introducing more efficient farming technology, and deregulating prices of farm products. Rising productivity in rural areas therefore allowed large migration of labor from agriculture to manufacturing, which in turn brought about a concomitant increase in manufacturing employment and generated a large agricultural surplus to be transferred for industrialization. Between 1965 and 1990 the share of agriculture fell to 9 from 38 percent in South Korea and to 4 percent from 24 in Taiwan.

- *Social Risk Management*

In line with the market friendly approach, East Asia's strategy for social protection placed an emphasis on creating employment opportunities and raising real wages through rapid growth. The European model of social welfare with various entitlements to government transfers including publicly funded retirement programs was considered inconsistent with East Asia's outward looking development strategy as it was bound to undermine the competitiveness of their export performance. As a result, East Asian policymakers resisted organized labor's demand to legislate a minimum wage and unemployment insurance and suppressed the formation of industry and economy-wide unions with the belief that labor markets would perform their allocation role if left to themselves. That is, they avoided intervention in the labor markets to the extent possible so that wages and employment were determined largely by supply and demand factors.

- *Technology Openness*

The fundamentally sound development policies included the active imitation and assimilation of foreign technology through foreign licensing, and liberalization of capital good imports and foreign direct investment. One might question whether this liberalization constitutes a market friendly policy. Most East Asian economies did not take any significant steps to liberalize their trade regimes until the late 1990s, only doing so under foreign pressure. They needed foreign technology to maintain the competitiveness of their exports in global markets. Liberalization of foreign capital imports and foreign direct investment was therefore dictated by an export-led development strategy; it was not part of a market friendly strategy.

- *Accumulation of Physical and Human Capital*

Rapid growth could not have been sustained had it not been backed by high rates of investment and domestic saving. To secure a foundation for high and rising saving rates, East Asian governments managed their spending programs within the revenues available so that they could be net savers. The bulk of budgetary surpluses were then used to finance public investment in basic infrastructure. This spending discipline restrained large increases in social expenditure and gave East Asian policymaker's moral latitude to extol virtues of saving and to introduce various voluntary and involuntary savings schemes.[1] In addition, political stability, low rates

---

[1] In many East Asian economies, for example, the expansion of the financial system network through postal savings systems successfully increased the accessibility of financial savings instruments to non-traditional savers (Stiglitz 1996).

of inflation, and stable exchange rates together with the control of labor market disruptions created incentives and an environment favorable to undertaking long-term investment and financial savings. Large investments for improving and expanding primary and secondary education were instrumental in rapid accumulation of human capital. This emphasis, together with post-secondary education, which focused on vocational and technical skill training, nurtured a better-educated labor force suited for an outward looking development strategy.

Yoshitomi (2003: 15), however, points out that high rates of saving and investment in physical and human capital are not sufficient, though necessary, conditions for economic transformation. They are not because unless there exists entrepreneurship that is capable of learning and innovation that can maintain high returns on capital, a high rate of physical investment cannot be sustained. In Yoshitomi's view, effective interactions between investment and innovation are 'at the heart of what happened in East and Southeast Asia.' Although the region's export-oriented policy was a critical vehicle for promoting capital investment and assimilation of advanced foreign technology, Yoshitomi argues that without those able and forward looking entrepreneurs, with managerial skills to transform new ideas into practice and to create new firms to absorb the growing number of skilled workers, the outward looking strategy may not have succeeded. While no one disputes the importance of entrepreneurs capable of taking risks, innovating, and imitating, an important question is how East Asia was able to foster an efficient entrepreneurial class. How the region came to develop those able entrepreneurs remains unanswered.

## 3.2. Interventionist Policies and Export Promotion

• *Interventionist Policies*

While espousing a market friendly strategy, in reality East Asian policy-makers did not hesitate to intervene in various markets in a systemic fashion and through multiple channels to encourage savings, subsidize exports, and allocate resources to desired sectors. Interventions were not confined to traditional areas in which significant externalities were present such as developing technological capabilities by building research and development centers and industrial parks and supporting all levels of education. They comprised industrial policies for import substitution of a wide range of intermediate products; the promotion of strategic industries such as heavy and chemical industries in South Korea; government owner-ship and control of banks and nonbank financial institutions; mechanisms for mandatory saving; and even setting export targets at firm and industry levels.

Of these market interventions, contribution of industrial policies to the development of strategic and infant industries has been the subject of intense debate. All East Asian economies installed and operated a system of industrial policies. How effective was East Asia's industrial policy regime? Although there is extensive literature on industrial policies in Asia, it has so far thrown little light on whether they were effective in developing the desired sectors largely because of the difficulty in conducting counter-factual exercises on whether East Asian economies could have done equally well in the absence of government intervention. In general, the evidence on efficiency of industrial policy is mixed during the earlier periods of industrialization, in particular before the 1990s when a market-oriented reforms were launched.

The ADBI study (Yoshitomi 2003: 37) claims that, in the early stage of development, policymakers in South Korea were able to identify the indus-tries they needed to promote at each level of comparative advantage by aligning incentives that produced appropriate industrial policies. The same report also points out that Korean industrial policy was not effective after the 1960s as it ran into moral hazard problems. In contrast, Southeast Asian economies were not as successful as South Korea was even at the early stage of development. The reason was that unlike in South Korea, industrial policy in the Southeast Asian subregion was heavily influenced by political considerations rather than economic efficiency.

Despite the conflicting evidence, both the World Bank (1993) and Stiglitz (1996) maintain that the market interventions were not as inefficient as often claimed; in fact, they were instrumental in inducing high rates of investment and high productivity growth in many industries and in first promoting exports of labor-intensive manufactures and then a decade later moving up to those of more capital-intensive heavy and chemical industries. Nor did the interventions necessarily increase the incidence of rent seeking and corruptive behavior, at least during the earlier periods of development.[2]

---

[2] There is no hard evidence supporting this argument, however. It is difficult to prove empiri-cally whether corruption had increased or decreased during the catch-up process before the cri-sis. As we argue in Chapter 7, however, corruption has become more obvious and hence emerged as a serious social issue since the crisis as the demand for public disclosure and information has increased with political democratization and market liberalization.

Financial policies were generally repressive in that they kept bank deposit rates below a market clearing level and maintained ceilings on lending rates. As will be pointed out in Chapter 6, financial repression and the weakness of the financial regulatory system were some of the critical risk factors for East Asia's emerging economies, eventually touching off the crisis. Writing before the crisis, however, Stiglitz and Uy (1996) and Stiglitz (1996), for instance, did not see that financial restraints or repression would present a danger of exposing these economies to a crisis.[3] Instead, repressive policies such as deposit rate controls contributed to stabilizing the financial system as they increased the franchise values of banks and, hence, discouraged banks from taking excessive risks. Were the efficiency costs associated with financial restrictions more than offset by the gains from greater financial stability? Going one step further, did the removal of financial restraints make these economies vulnerable to external financial shocks?

If anything, Stiglitz represented a minority view; the mainstream view was that before the crisis, repressive financial policies were to blame for financial retardation in East Asia. Stiglitz (1998b) himself changed his view after the crisis, saying that the weakness of the financial regulatory system was a risk factor that increased the probability of a crisis.

Assuming they were effective, what were the factors that ensured the positive outcomes of the interventionist policies? One explanation suggests that East Asian policymakers were following clear and relatively well-defined performance criteria for, and monitoring the consequences of, their interventions. Another claims that policymakers were prepared to halt or change their interventionist policies whenever they became excessively costly or when they were threatening macroeconomic stability. A third explanation points to a high level of institutional capacity backed by strong bureaucracies capable of administering interventionist policies as in Johnson's developmental state (1983). Policymakers knew where to find market failures and when and how to intervene to rectify them.

- *Export Orientation*

The most conspicuous feature of the East Asian development model was its espousal of an export-led growth strategy. South Korea and Taiwan shifted their development strategy from import substitution to export orientation

---

[3] Hellmann et al. (2000) distinguish financial restraint from financial repression. The former is used to improve the efficiency of financial markets whereas the latter is designed as a mechanism for the government to extract rents from the private sector. In reality, however, such a distinction cannot easily be made.

in the early 1960s. Southeast Asian economies followed the same strategy about a decade later. By the middle of the 1980s, the share of exports in GDP shot up to more than 30 percent from about 10 percent in the early 1970s in South Korea. The increase was more pronounced in Taiwan where it rose by almost 20 percentage points to 48 percent during the same period. Export orientation had also progressed at a high speed in some of the Southeast Asian economies in the 1980s. By 1990, the ratio of exports to GDP surged to 76 and 34 percent in Malaysia and Thailand respectively. Even a large country like China saw its ratio climb up to almost 20 percent by the early 1990s from less than 8 percent a decade earlier.

As previously noted, the agrarian reform released a steady supply of surplus agricultural labor to be employed in manufacturing and other industries in the urban sector. In order to absorb these migrating workers, East Asia's emerging economies had to generate demand for the goods and services produced by these workers. In relatively small countries with a limited size of the domestic market and a foreign exchange constraint, their choices were either producing those imported goods and services domestically or seeking the required demand in foreign markets through export promotion. Many manufacturing sectors exhibited increasing returns to scale of which exploitation required access to large markets, and an outward looking strategy was one that could allow the East Asian economies to gain access.

There were other advantages of an export push over import substitution. The export-led strategy loosened up the foreign exchange constraint on investment by increasing the availability of foreign exchange for importation of foreign capital and intermediate goods. The export push did not allow unnecessary or costly interventions largely because to be successful, it had to meet the efficiency standard of global markets. The high rate of capital accumulation combined with the availability of low cost of labor then put the East Asian economies on a path of rapid growth once the strategy was put into effect. More important, the export-oriented strategy provided the channels through which foreign technology could be imported and new knowledge acquired as exporters had to keep up to date with state-of-the art technology to remain competitive. The foreign technology and knowledge that export-oriented firms and industries accumulated were not subject to diminishing returns. Specialization along side comparative advantage and greater access to more advanced foreign technology then set in motion dynamic interactions between assimilation of new technology and capital deepening that in turn, brought about the further expansion of export-oriented industries. The success in export promotion also produced a range of other spillover and demonstration effects on nontradeable sectors of the economy.

The traditional view on the relative superiority of export-led development is that the strategy moves the economy inside the production possibility frontier closer to the frontier. On reaching the frontier, the strategy could also move the economy around the frontier until the domestic marginal rate of substitution is equal to the international price ratio, thereby approximating a free trade outcome. Some of the more advanced East Asian economies such as Singapore, Hong Kong, Taiwan, China, and South Korea might have reached the frontier by the early 1990s at least in their export-oriented industries. By this time, they were competing with advanced economies in global markets of those goods and services intensive in sophisticated technology and knowledge such as information and communication technology (ICT). ICT industries were, however, regarded as infant industries and again promoted as future sources of export growth as had occurred with labor-intensive manufacturing industries in the early 1960s. East Asia's emerging economies still have a large technological gap to be closed vis-à-vis advanced countries. This gap has continued to be the rationale for adhering to the export-push policy. However, as will be discussed in Chapter 11, this traditional view has been challenged and in fact many empirical studies show that exporting does not improve the efficiency of the economy.

Until the mid-1990s, before the crisis, there was a consensus that East Asia's economic success was in no small part attributable to an export-led growth strategy. Discussion therefore focused on identifying those factors, in terms of both policies and institutional changes that contributed to the successful implementation of the outward looking development strategy. Many studies on East Asia's export push suggest that one such factor was the firm commitment of East Asian governments to the strategy. The commitment was then backed by eliminating the bias against exports and instituting export subsidies that included protection of the home market, tax concessions, low cost credit, state support for research and development, and provision of infrastructure facilities such as the export processing zone. In addition to this preferential treatment, Stiglitz (1996) notes that preferential access to capital and foreign exchange, the active role of government in developing new export markets, and licensing and other regulations designed to enhance the reputation of the country's exports were also important for the success of the strategy.[4] It may also be true that

---

[4] However, Stiglitz argues that these support mechanisms would not have worked without the close and long-term relationships that were continually nurtured between exporters and governments.

before the crisis, avoiding overvalued exchange rates and sustaining a stable and predictable path for the real exchange rate were the export push. Export promotion policies were also successful because they worked in a way that induced significant competition through the contest scheme in Japan, and the performance-based incentive scheme that linked subsidies in the form of preferential interest rates and tariffs on imported goods to export earnings in South Korea (Pack 2000). To the authors of the World Bank study (1993), the success of the export push is an example of a winning combination of fundamentals and interventions. The strategy proved to be a winning combination because the expansion of manufactured exports did not impinge on allocative efficiency, certainly not to the degree of an import substitution strategy.

## 3.3. The Role of Government and Governance

- *The Role of the Government*

Most of the East Asian emerging countries that escaped from third world poverty through rapid growth had authoritarian, or even dictatorial, regimes. Many observers, though they disagree on the specific role of the government, agree that these nondemocratic regimes were effective in leading economic development by managing industrial policies, promoting exports, providing infrastructure to support production activities, and investing in education. Governments of other emerging developing economies were also engaged in similar activities and followed similar strategies, but they were not as successful. The question on the difference in performance of the government in different regions defies a ready answer largely because it is in general contingent on societal and political developments as well.

Even in East Asia, there are three different views on the role of the government. One is the market friendly approach in which the government complements rather than substitutes the market. Another is the developmental state view, and a third is a market enhancing view, which lies in between the two. All three views recognize inefficiencies of existing markets in developing economies as a result of numerous market failures related to public goods, nonexistence of several markets, technological and marketing spillovers, and coordination problems. There is therefore little disagreement on the rationale of government intervention in various markets; the disagreement is on the extent and mode of intervention.

According to the market friendly view, East Asian policymakers structured their interventions in a way that complemented rather than replaced markets. That is, they limited their role to improving the efficiency of markets in mobilizing and allocating resources. In contrast, the advocates of the developmental state view (Johnson 2001) argue that market failures in developing economies are so entrenched and pervasive that only active state intervention such as getting relative prices wrong were able to mitigate most market imperfections including those of capital markets that may not allocate adequate amounts of resources to strategic industries. As Aoki, Murdock, and Okuno-Fujiwara (1997) note, a fundamental difference between the market friendly and developmental state views rests on the differences in the perceived degree of market failures and perceived ability of the government to manage successful intervention. According to Aoki et al., the government's responsibility is not to solve the market failure problems; instead it is to support the development of private sector institutions such as financial intermediaries, labor unions, and trade associations that can overcome some of the failures such as the coordination problems associated with the asymmetric distribution of information. This is the market enhancing view.

In reality, East Asian governments did more than facilitate private sector coordination. For all practical purposes, they were active in producing various public goods, subsidizing strategic industries, pursuing egalitarian distributions, fostering public–private sector coordination, and even picking the winners. The different nuances of the three views on the role of East Asian states may not be as important as the questions of how effective East Asian governments were in ameliorating market failures and why they were effective compared to other governments of developing economies, if indeed they were.[5] Studies on East Asia's economic development sought answers from East Asia's effective bureaucracies, which were meritocratic and insulated from political pressure. But then these answers in turn, raise more questions as to why and how East Asian economies were capable of establishing effective bureaucracies resistant to political pressure; the same studies often invoke the Confucian cultural setting where state bureaucracies attract the cream of the crop of society and are accorded public respect, a claim that cannot be proved or disproved.

Whichever view is closer to the reality, however, what remains indisputable is that East Asian governments set economic growth and industrialization

---

[5] Krueger (1995: 24) raises the possibility that growth would have been even faster in the absence of government interventions.

as their first priority. They were also consistent in pursuing policies and strategies required to sustain rapid growth. Indeed, of all factors that underlie East Asia's economic ascendancy it was their dedication at the expense of social objectives that set apart East Asian governments.

- *Private and Public–Private Sector Coordination:*
  *Deliberation Councils*

At an early stage of development, nondemocratic governments of East Asia's emerging economies sought to establish their political legitimacy as well as to limit their discretion over economic policies to remain in power. Legitimizing their rule required the support and cooperation of a wider private sector. To this end, they created operated governance systems of consultative polities rather than representative regimes based on written constitutions, elected legislatures, and formal institutions of checks and balances (Campos and Root 1996: chapter 4).

In order to secure broad support from the private sector in general, and business elites in particular, Campos and Root argue that East Asian regimes guaranteed economic rights to economic agents and introduced many wealth sharing mechanisms, such as land reform, rural infrastructure development, promotion of small and medium sized enterprises, and public housing programs. The ADB study (1997: 18) agrees with this assessment: basic property rights as well as the rule of law were established much more securely in East Asia than in most other developing countries. This study goes on to argue that 'contracts were enforced and legal institutions were set up to settle disputes' and 'legal stability fostered the rise of a vigorous private sector and gave long-term confidence to foreign investors.'[6]

In their efforts to draw as many groups into the decision making process as possible, the East Asian economies also instituted various mechanisms and practices of cooperation, not only between the government and businesses, but also between workers and employers, small and large businesses, and between businesses and financial institutions.

One such institutional device they chose was known as deliberation councils, which Japan had organized for the management of economic

[6] The authors of the ADB study may wish to retract these statements now that it is generally recognized that weak legal institutions with the prevalent disregard for the rule of law were one of the major fragilities that provoked and deepened the East Asian crisis. It is instructive to note that autocratic regimes can easily override both property rights and law. Property rights may have been strong in East Asia, because authoritarian governments were prepared to, and in fact did, form all types of alliances with the private sector. The author owes this point to Haggard.

policies. They were active in and essential to the formation of policies, rules, and regulations that govern a sector, industry, and, in some cases, the entire economy.[7] As they participated—indirectly at least—in policy-making, the councils were able to overcome many of the private sector's reservations about the commitment to shared growth. Various formal and informal deliberation councils provided opportunities to businesses in the nondemocratic regimes to learn about and make suggestions on govern-ment policy. They also offered various types of rewards to participants who cooperated. For example, the Japanese government solicited the counsel of participants from many types of councils in supporting ailing firms to reduce the incidence of bankruptcies, inducing mergers when there were too many small firms and approving the formation of recession cartels. Through these coordinating activities, the councils served as a means of improving cooperation between government and business during the early post-war period (Stiglitz 1996).[8] Once trust between government and business was established, deliberation councils could reduce transactions and monitoring costs, uncertainties and lengthen time horizons for busi-ness investment.

There were other arrangements developed by Japan for the management of industrial relations and emulated to varying degrees by East Asia's emerging economies, such as: lifetime employment; the productivity council, which compressed the wage structure by limiting the salaries of top managers; and the practice of setting wages on the basis of the group rather than individual performance.[9]

According to Stiglitz (1996), these labor market arrangements cultivated long-term relationships between workers and employers and elicited labor's cooperation in adapting to technological changes by instilling the conviction that their interests were the same as those of the firm. It is known that similar labor market practices were widely accepted in the

[7] For a detailed analysis of deliberation councils, see World Bank (1993), Campos and Root (1996: chapter 5), Chang and McIntyre (1994). Chang and McIntyre are quoted by Haggard (2000: 21).

[8] Although other East Asian economies did not necessarily copy the Japanese pattern of coordination, the industrial organizational structure in which a small number of large, family-owned industrial groups dominated manufacturing and exports in East Asia may have facilitated the government–business cooperation at an early stage of the development through delibera-tion councils. This government–business relationship became collusive, earning notoriety as crony capitalism, as will be discussed in Chapter 5.

[9] On the lifetime employment system, Stiglitz (1996) and Campos and Root (1996) may not be right in that the system was not emulated throughout East Asia except in Korea. In most East Asian economies labor relations were more authoritarian and less cooperative than depicted by Campos and Root (1996). A rapid increase in real wages in part pacified labor unrest and moderated labor activism.

manufacturing sector in South Korea and Taiwan, throughout the 1970s and 1980s. If these arrangements were ever the norms of employment in South Korea, they did not appear to have contributed to industrial peace. Like other arrangements, they have also not survived economic and political liberalization.

Relationship banking has been and still is to some extent another cooperative arrangement between the government and businesses as well as between banks and their borrowing clients. In Japan, each firm, especially a large one, established a long-term relationship with a single bank, which was known as the firm's main bank. The main banking system was also introduced in other East Asian economies. As will be shown in Chapter 15, the main banking system could help reduce the severity of information asymmetry between lenders and borrowers. To the extent that this was possible, the long-term relationship enabled the main banks to increase the availability of long-term finance to, and allow them to play a larger role in determining investment and other decisions of, their client firms. East Asia's business relationships were in general based on long-term and repeat business. These characteristics contributed to improving the government–business and worker–employer levels of cooperation. But repeat business can easily be abused as a mechanism for favoritism, nepotism, and corruption, as it was in many East Asian economies before the crisis.

In the absence of a checking mechanism, cooperation and coordination between the government and businesses can easily slide into collusion. Discretionary and between bank and bank borrower powers exercised by authoritarian governments often result in fertile ground for rent seeking and regulatory capture. These problems were largely avoided in Japan and to some extent in other emerging economies in the region by establishing various types of contests among firms that followed nonmarket allocation rules (Stiglitz 1996). In South Korea and Japan the contest schemes were also utilized to coordinate private investment and to promote exports. The contests were geared to enhancing competition by rewarding firms with good performance and behavior relative to the others. For example, in the export industry, exporters were rewarded with subsidized credits, foreign exchange, and other benefits on the basis of their performance evaluated mostly in terms of their export earnings. This export contest scheme, according to many studies[10] provided strong incentives for domestic producers to develop new export products and to cultivate new foreign markets. Stiglitz (1996) also argues that the contests were able to mitigate

---

[10] For references, see World Bank (1993) and Campos and Root (1996).

corruption by clearly setting the rules and rewards of the game and ensuring transparency of the evaluation process.[11] In this respect, licensing requirements did enhance, rather than restrict, competition.

The contest schemes were effective so long as the authoritarian regimes were able to hold the private sector at a political distance and exercised their regulatory control indirectly through the banking sector and administrative guidance. However, once this regulatory discipline weakened, the actual contest schemes lost much of their credibility.

---

[11] Other contest examples in the labor market include the Japanese practice in which firms may hire a cohort of workers, who advance together. Since the mobility of labor is limited, workers are forced to work hard signaling that they are committed to their firm. In other words, they remain in contest (Stiglitz 1996).

# 4

# Failures of the East Asian Development Model: An Overview

The recent controversy on the viability of the East Asian development paradigm centers on questions of whether, and to what extent, financial and corporate sector frailties (together with government failures arising from regulatory capture and rent seeking) were masked by rapid growth and how seriously they will act as constraints on economic development in the twenty-first century. To answer these questions, this study first attempts to identify some of the critical failures of the model that drove some East Asian economies to the brink of collapse and that bode ill for post-crisis development in East Asia, before turning to the failures of the corporate, financial, and public sectors.

Even before the outbreak of the crisis, the East Asian economic system had been showing many structural strains. During the five-year period preceding the crisis, the system had been unable to forestall a massive increase in capital inflows that set off an asset market boom and the associated current account deterioration. When it came under a speculative attack, the system could not cope and simply broke down.

What was surprising about the 1997–98 crisis was that the crisis countries— Indonesia, Malaysia, South Korea, and Thailand—were so helpless in the face of the onslaught of a speculative attack despite the fact that by the mid-1990s they had already ushered in Western democracy and migrated toward the Washington Consensus reforms. Voluntarily or involuntarily, most countries in East Asia's emerging economies were prepared to accept the main message of the Washington Consensus that private markets are able to ensure the efficient allocation of resources and generate robust growth (Stiglitz 1998b) and therefore, to embrace the policies of the Washington Consensus: macroeconomic stability, privatization and market deregulation (including the labor market), flexible exchange rates, emulation of Western institutions, and increased education spending (Williamson 1997). The liberal ideology has in fact reached every corner of East Asia, including China. Advocates of the Washington Consensus reforms were confident that the reform would improve economic efficiency and resistance so that East Asia's emerging economies would become less vulnerable and, if they occurred, better manage financial crises. It did not, and financial market deregulation and opening made these economies more susceptible to financial turbulences than before, eventually touching off the 1997 crisis. What went wrong with the fundamentally Western reform in emerging East Asia? Was the paradigm shift premature, or engineered in an incorrect sequence? Did East Asian policymakers err in sequencing regime change?

Over three decades of rapid growth vested interests built structural rigidities into many sectors of the economy and policymakers of these economies did not fully appreciate the severity of local constraints on Washington Consensus reforms. As a result, the reforms were cosmetic in many instances and as such failed to restructure the systems in line with and to create institutions requisite for democratization and market liberalization to be credible with the global economy. This study identifies four such critical failures.

The first was benign neglect of the inherent conflicts between East Asia's governance mechanism, on the one hand, and the democratic polity and market liberalization on the other. By the early 1990s, it was clear, at least in some of East Asia's emerging economies, that the consultative mechanisms of coordination and cooperation between the government and the private sector and between different groups in the private sector were crumbling and degenerating into collusion, political cronyism, and corruption. Yet the East Asian economies were slow in developing democratic governance at various levels of the economy in place of the consultative polity that was the legacy of authoritarian regimes. Another failure was the inability to restructure the financial system that left intact the bank-based bias, outdated market supporting infrastructure, inefficiency of the regulatory system, and banking standards and risk management out of place with global realities.

A third failure of the system was the closed and non-transparent corporate sector that did not fare well with market liberalization and opening. In the early 1990s major corporations from East Asia were beginning to raise funds on global capital markets and were expanding their direct investment throughout East Asia, and even in Europe and North America, as part of their global strategy. Although these corporations were becoming more active on the global scene, they were slow in accepting the global norms and practices in accounting, disclosure, and corporate governance. Western investors were attracted to the growing economies of East Asia and owning a stake in these large corporations, which looked invincible and with a global reach. Up close, however, these corporations were riddled with poor accounting and auditing irregularities, non-transparent management, and a governance system that accorded minority stockholders little protection for their interests. Once again, East Asian economies failed to build a modern corporate sector that was transparent and accessible to foreign investors.

The fourth failure of the East Asian model was its fixation on an export-led development strategy. Although the strategy was the most conspicuous and successful feature of the East Asian development model, it was liable to a number of serious domestic risks, as it was predicated on a rigid industrial policy regime. The success of the export-led strategy bred many downside risks: underdevelopment of the nontradeable sector, the rise of large industrial groups as dominant players, an inflexible exchange rate system prone to overvaluation, and pervasiveness of market intervention. These risks were overlooked or improperly addressed.

When East Asia's emerging economies were embarking on an export-led development strategy—South Korea in the early 1960s and the Southeast Asian economies a decade later—they had to overcome a formidable array of structural and institutional problems that interfered with export promotion. One such problem was the limited pool of entrepreneurs, managers, and traders who could initiate and lead development of export-oriented industries. In many cases, the efficiency of export industries required adoption of increasing return technologies, but the small and unstable financial systems could not allocate large amounts of financial resources to these industries, because the risks in lending to exporters were perceived to be too high. These institutional constraints together with the limited availability of domestic and foreign resources meant East Asia's emerging economies could support only a small number of large producers—in some cases one or two—in each of the industries promoted for exports.

These firms grew to be successful exporters and to organize themselves as large family-owned or -controlled industrial groups. As they grew in number and size, large industrial groups created a monopolistic or oligopolistic market structure in many industries and were skewing wealth distribution. With a protected trade regime and a closed financial system, the pricing and supply behavior of these groups in domestic markets had to be regulated. And the emerging economies chose to rein in these powerful groups indirectly through the banking system. Since banks were vulnerable to domination and takeover by industrial groups, controlling these groups therefore necessitated and justified government control of the banking system. That is, the emergence of powerful industrial groups built barriers to financial deregulation and market opening. However, the banks did not oversee the large industrial groups very effectively.

In Southeast Asia, the bank–commerce separation was not strictly enforced, and as a result many banks and other financial institutions were owned by powerful families which also owned manufacturing and other firms. Although ownership of banks and in some cases nonbank financial institutions by any single shareholder was limited to enforced separation of commerce from banking in East Asia's NIEs, the industrial groups could easily dominate the management of banks and other nonbank financial intermediaries through cross-ownership. Short of direct government control of bank management, there was little the government could do to prevent industrial groups from dominating the banking industry. Given the dominance of industrial groups in many industries, it was also argued that domestic financial deregulation per se would not improve allocative efficiency of the economy, while it was bound to increase concentration of power in the hands of a few family-owned industrial groups.

Many of the structural problems that surfaced after the 1997 crisis have greatly undermined the viability of the East Asian development model in the twenty-first century. Even so, they may not necessarily signal the end of the system, although they certainly demonstrate that it is in need of repair, if not a complete overhaul. Needless to say, not one but many new models will evolve over time with political, societal, and economic changes that will take place in both East Asia and the rest of the world—democratization with economic liberalization, globalization in parallel with regionalization, and the emergence of a new economy driven by information and communication technology. Will they have distinct features in terms of institutions, economic structure, and policies that separate them from the Anglo-American or the European corporatist or social welfare system? What are the sectoral reform requisites that will help East Asia's emerging economies to regain their pre-crisis dynamism? To answer these questions the next two chapters will delve into the failures of the governance system and of the financial and corporate sectors before the crisis.

# 5

# Failures in Governance and Institution Building

## 5.1. The Breakdown of the Governance Mechanism

The East Asian governance of consultative polities has lost its place in the process of political and economic liberalization. In retrospect, the effectiveness of deliberation councils as a coordination and cooperation mechanism was vastly exaggerated, and more so in the Southeast Asian economies where they were loosely organized and operated, compared to those of Japan and South Korea. The ubiquitous councils were, in many cases, structured and managed to serve an advisory role for the government and also as a channel of communication with the private sector on the rationale of national economic policies. In South Korea, only in rare cases did policymakers take recommendations made by the councils seriously; they were seldom swayed by the councils' objections.

Toward the latter part of the 1980s when the democratization process got under way, cracks began to appear in the consultative governance structure in emerging East Asia. The system simply did not provide a social net large enough to accommodate the interests of many underprivileged groups, such as urban labor, small and medium sized firms, farmers, and various professionals groups, which found themselves left out of the decision making process. Growing popular demand for direct political participation in fact made the system unworkable. Democracies also provide consultative and risk sharing mechanisms. It is debatable whether democratic polities would have been effective in the early stages of development in East Asia, as the consultative governance occupied the space where democratic mechanisms could have grown.

The demise of consultative polities unveiled serious coordination problems at the national, industry, and enterprise levels. Large family-owned firms or industrial groups were growing more politically powerful to the point of dictating national economic policy. Their predatory pursuit for a large share in many markets, including financial ones, brought on a further concentration of both economic power and the industrial structure. Yet, many of the governments of East Asia's emerging economies literally did not care to know what the large family-owned enterprises and their main banks were doing. They acted as if they should not be involved in monitoring the behaviour of banks and corporations, lest it be misunderstood as interfering with market liberalization, although the liberal reforms should have been complemented by more effective rule-based supervision and regulation. On this part, banks did not seem to know what their client firms were doing.

The failure of the consultative mechanism was most obvious in managing industrial relations. Labor movements became more militant, disrupting not only workplaces but also at times entire national economies, yet governments could no longer mediate disputes between labor and management.

Democratization ushered in a new labor movement era in which labor began demanding a greater voice in economic and social policy choices and organized a variety of new trade unions and their federations. Labor unions were asking not only for the right to freedom of association and collective bargaining, but a political role in the national decision making process. With the growing assertiveness of labor unions, the consultative mechanism, which often left out labor, became irrelevant to managing industrial relations. At the same time, the labor movement brought forth new issues such as employment guarantees, unemployment insurance, the provision of publicly financed retirement pensions, and other benefits. East Asia's emerging economies were therefore ill prepared to meet the challenge of maintaining a balance between meeting labor's demands including its political participation, on one hand, and keeping labor market flexibility on the other. The region is still struggling to find a more effective conflict management system involving labor at both the national and enterprise level without sacrificing labor market flexibility.

The increasing concentration of production, exports, and corporate ownership in large family-owned enterprises and industrial groups also weakened the balancing role of the consultative polity. As their political influence grew, the industrial giants were not discreet about colluding with the ruling party or government bureaucracy to pursue their own interests. The growing influence of the industrial groups therefore eroded both the credibility and effectiveness of the consultative system. The political democratization process eventually brought an end to the role of the councils. As of the late

1980s, many of the deliberation councils in emerging East Asia had been dissolved and replaced by legislatures and political parties. Since then, the democratic polity has increased the demand for changes in the political and economic systems that are interlinked, yet distinct. However, the multiparty systems in many of East Asia's emerging economies have failed to establish ruling majorities and remain fractured and weak.

In Indonesia, the Philippines, South Korea, and Taiwan, the opposition parties have controlled the legislative branches. This division of power has led to a cohabitation arrangement between the ruling and opposition parties. As expected, this system has not worked well as the government and opposition parties have often failed to compromise on setting the national agenda. The result has been a political impasse, which has in turn, aggravated political instability and undermined the public trust of political parties and politicians. This political instability has invariably spilled over into the economic bureaucracy making it difficult to develop a predictable and credible policy framework and implement a coherent long-term development strategy. As a result, a new democratic system capable of building consensus and accountability has yet to evolve after a decade of democratization, creating a vacuum in conflict management and coordination. In the meantime, labor unions and other interest groups have mounted increasingly serious challenges to the government in a bid for greater participation in the policymaking process. In order to obtain the support of labor and interest groups, political parties, regardless of their ideological orientation, have been liable to give in to populist policies.

Rodrik (2000*b*) argues that in democratic societies, labor, business, and other social groups are more willing to cooperate and compromise in the political sphere, generating greater stability as a result, because liberal democracies entail constitutional rules and the separation of power, and also espouse the rule of law and protection of minorities. Although it is too early to judge, East Asia's experience so far does not appear to be supportive of his argument. East Asia's young democracies have been struggling to develop the institutions that tolerate political opposition and allow greater public participation. Most of these incipient democracies are far from building an institutional base for democratic polities, though the trend toward deeper democratization is irreversible in emerging East Asia. Even in communist states as China and Vietnam, some political liberalization has occurred. This development may be seen as a normal accompaniment to the increasingly open and growing role of the market economy. However, it remains to be seen whether this development will continue and improve the quality of institutions and governance in East Asia.

## 5.2. Institutional Quality

As argued in Chapter 2, the key to successful implementation of development policies in East Asia was the presence of a reputable and efficient economic bureaucracy capable of imposing discipline on private actors as well as deflecting external pressures from the power elites and interest groups, such as labor and industrial conglomerates. There is also empirical evidence to suggest the importance of a high quality bureaucracy in economic development. Radelet, Sachs, and Lee (1997) show that the quality of institutions, such as bureaucracies, is one of the most critical factors that determine long-term growth performance across regions and economies. Before the 1997–8 crisis, there was also the presumption that East Asia's emerging economies had developed many market supporting institutions that were efficient. Rodrik (1996) supports this presumption by showing that differences in the economic performance of the East Asian economies he chose for his study are in part explained by differences in the quality of their institutions.

In the aftermath of the 1997 crisis, the high quality of East Asian institutions has come into question. Yusuf (2001) argues that the biggest lesson learned from the East Asian crisis is that, contrary to the widely held belief, East Asian planners essentially did not know what they were doing. To many skeptics of the East Asian miracle, rapid growth (as was the case for other structural weaknesses) hid much of the government's ineffectiveness in policy management and coordination, the overzealousness in market interventions, and corruption. To these critics, the crisis has clearly brought to light many failures of public sector institutions, and they constitute prima-facie evidence that vindicates the skeptics' long-standing critique of East Asia's strong regimes. Was the quality of East Asian governments as bad as it is made out to be?

Contrary to popular belief, the technocratic elite of East Asia's strong states was not always insulated from political pressures and they often succumbed to the pressures of intervention by various interest groups.[1] In Southeast Asia, government officials forged close ties with private entrepreneurs to pursue their own interests. These ties made them highly susceptible

---

[1] During the pre-democracy period, the legislative branches in many East Asian economies were nominally involved in making and implementing policies. Much of policymaking power remained in the hands of bureaucrats, and the bureaucratic elite did not limit itself to playing an efficient functional role; it rose to assert itself to exercise political influences as well. However, no effective mechanism was in place to check their power, discretion, and abusiveness in their policy management. Like any other pressure group, they were bent on protecting their vested interests as in the case of their muted support for market deregulation and opening in the 1990s.

to corruption.[2] As in the case of Indonesia, relationships between politicians and business constituents were too close to be free of corruption and collusion. What is surprising is that corruption has increased in all four crisis countries and in the Philippines even after the 1997 crisis.[3] These developments may support Yusuf (2001) in saying that the heyday of the technocratic bureaucracy at the helm of a developmental state, pursuing long-term goals through industrial policies and a carefully measured opening of the economy, may be past.

If the quality and effectiveness of the East Asian bureaucracies deteriorated before the 1997 crisis, how serious was it? A World Bank measure of governance (2000*b*), which combines perceptions of voice and accountability, political instability and violence, government effectiveness, regulatory burden, rule of law, and corruption shows that the governance ratings of East Asian economies are, more or less, average by international standards. This measure also suggests that a country's institutional quality is highly correlated with its level of development. It concludes, noting that 'Unqualified praise for East Asian government institutions is surely overstated' while the argument that 'crony capitalism is more pernicious in East Asia than in other regions of comparable income is no less misguided' (p. 103).

---

[2] See Haggard (2000: 38–45), on the politics of business–government relations and corruption.

[3] A recent survey of corruption trends in Asia by Political and Economic Risk Consultancy, Ltd., 2001s shows that corruption in all four crisis countries has been rising. See also Kaufmann, Kraay, and Zoido-Lobaton (2002), and the Corruption Perceptions Index by Transparency International (2002).

# 6

# Weaknesses of the Corporate and Financial Sector

## 6.1. Corporate Sector: the Fall of East Asian Corporations

Two of the most distinctive characteristics of corporations in East Asia's emerging economies are that ownership is concentrated among a few large families and many corporations are affiliated with an industrial group. Such affiliations occur because an individual, a family, or a coalition of families controls a number of firms or because firms have extensive interlocking ownership (Claessens, Djankov, and Lang 2000). Diversified conglomerates, or Chaebols in South Korea and the overseas Chinese tycoons in Southeast Asia and Hong Kong, are closely held, controlled, and managed by families.

The diversified conglomerate form of organization has a number of advantages compared to other forms, particularly in developing economies. As Khanna and Palepu (1999) point out, large business groups provide important institutional services such as those of investment banks, accounting firms, and business schools. These services are often absent or of poor quality in many emerging economies. The East Asian industrial groups also have the capacity to pool internal resources and information to create internal capital (including venture) and labor markets. Unlike smaller corporations, they have the advantages of size and diversity to develop a common group brand that stands for world-class quality and customer service, advantages particularly valuable to export-oriented economies. Because of these advantages, at an early stage of development when institutional and legal foundations for a market-oriented economy are underdeveloped and capital markets are moribund, industrial groups or large family-owned corporations are able to economize on transactions costs. Before the crisis, these advantages were believed to be some of the reasons for the success of East Asian corporations.

As noted in Chapter 6, industrial conglomerates had to rely on bank financing for much of their investment; it was therefore no surprise that their leverage was higher than that of foreign conglomerates with easy access to capital markets. The debt–equity ratios of these groups rose gradually, and then shot up during the first half of the 1990s, making these conglomerates highly vulnerable to cyclical fluctuations. However, many thought that the high levels of debt at these groups did not pose any serious default risks as they were buffeted by the long-term relationship with banks and as the government stood ready to provide support to both these groups and the banks in the event of systemic shocks (Veneroso and Wade 1998). In fact, the high debt strategy, according to a World Bank report (1998), propelled East Asia through a meteoric rise in technology, productivity, and a standard of living that surpassed virtually all other countries. Wade (1990) makes the same point and argues that the high leverage was an important component of East Asia's success.

The Asian crisis has dramatically altered the positive assessment of the role and contribution to economic development of East Asia's large corporations. Many of the industrial groups were poorly managed, as they took excessive and unwarranted risks and unprofitable investment with borrowed funds. And they ignored the interests of small stockholders and stakeholders.[1] The principal owners' emphasis on personal objectives rather than profits meant that these groups were also prone to serious agency problems. Together with being highly leveraged, the pervasiveness of cross-debt guarantees among group affiliates created a systemic risk in which the failure of a member firm instigated the collapse of other firms, risking the downfall of the entire group. Contrary to popular belief, the groups were not an ideal training ground where a professional class of managers could be trained. Most of the senior managerial positions were held by members of the controlling families and were eventually passed on to their offspring. The increasing number of bankruptcies, excess capacity, the growing debt burden, and non-transparency during and immediately after the crisis, manifested the ills of the East Asian industrial groups.

What were the factors then that brought about the dramatic fall of East Asian corporations, particularly of large groups such as Daewoo in South Korea? How did these industrial groups allow themselves to be so reckless in diversifying their business and taking unwarranted risks? How did their

---

[1] Claessens et al. (2000) find that higher cash flow rights (dividend rights) are associated with a higher market valuation of corporations whereas higher ownership rights (voting rights) correspond to a lower market valuation in East Asia. This finding suggests that family control leads to a lower valuation and expropriation of small stockholders.

internal control become so weak, financial reports unreliable, disclosures inadequate, and audits so poor? One answer to this corporate malaise is that in the process of market deregulation and opening, the old system of corporate governance in which banks, or main banks in the case of large corporations were the monitors, broke down while a new system of Western corporate governance was not put in place. In relationship banking, banks obtain much of the information they need directly from their client firms rather than relying on firms' public disclosure, because the firms' specific information is not available to the general public. In a bank-oriented financial system, therefore, corporations have less incentive to improve corporate governance and transparency. To make matters worse, although barred from owning a controlling stake in financial institutions, large industrial groups were able to control a large number of banks and nonbank intermediaries through a scheme of cross-ownership. Even without ownership control, they could exercise a great deal of influence on the lending decisions of banks and other nonbank financial intermediaries, simply because at these institutions these groups were the most creditworthy customers.

Compared to German and Japanese banks, the main banks in other East Asian emerging economies were much more accommodating to financial needs, while less scrupulous in monitoring the investment and funding behavior of large family-owned industrial groups. Unlike their counterparts in the West, therefore, East Asian corporations were immune to market discipline. To be sure, capital markets were liberalized and partially opened and an increasing number of corporations, large ones in particular, were migrating to the stock and bond markets, but these markets were hardly able to perform external monitoring properly and they were in fact weakened because of their own structural weaknesses.

Institutional investors such as insurance companies, mutual funds, pension funds, and investment banks in advanced economies provide market incentives for the adoption of good corporate governance practices in the corporate sector. In emerging and developing East Asia, these institutions were, and still are, scarce and underdeveloped. Although the presence of foreign banks has been growing in terms of their assets and branch operations in the region, they seldom impose international standards of accounting, disclosure, and auditing on their clients; instead, they often assimilate into local markets, adopting local norms and practices.

A large number of foreign institutional investors have taken advantage of East Asia's opening of domestic financial markets and added a growing variety of East Asian stocks to their portfolios. However, they do not appear to demand the same high standards of accounting, disclosure, and audit-ing for East Asian corporations as they do in their home countries. Instead, they minimize the credit risks of their investments by diversifying their East Asian portfolios to the point where their holdings of different East Asian assets become almost perfect substitutes for one another. There is also little evidence indicating that foreign subsidiaries or joint ventures in East Asia set the standard for corporate governance through abiding by international rules and norms. So long as these foreign institutions were able to obtain insider status and inside information they had no incentive to improve the system since that would benefit their competitors.

While the development of Western rules, norms, and institutions that govern corporate behavior and protect the rights of shareholders was lag-ging, East Asian policymakers were refraining from intervening in bank management, beginning in the early 1990s. With this hands-off policy, they were letting loose much of their control over large corporations and industrial groups. This lack of monitoring by banks meant that large industrial groups were free to pursue whatever they believed was in their interest.[2] With so many foreign lenders pushing for loans at reasonable rates, it was no surprise that East Asian corporations invested heavily in real estate and built huge capacity in manufacturing with financing they obtained from the short end of the market, thereby lifting their leverage above an acceptable level and exposing themselves to balance sheet mis-matches of currency and maturity. Banks were making short-term foreign currency loans to East Asian corporations, but neither banks nor govern-ments were willing or able to restrain the increase in the corporations' external borrowing in the midst of a campaign for liberal reform.

## 6.2. Financial Sector Fragility: Financial Repression and Crony Capitalism

• *Bank-based or Market-based?*

There is a general consensus that East Asian financial systems have been dominated by banks and other financial institutions (Aoki 2000, Eichengreen 1999*b*, Park 1993). It is also widely accepted that for more than three decades preceding the 1997 crisis, most East Asian economies includ-ing Japan had relied on the banking system as instruments of industrial

---

[2] This argument does not suggest that government monitoring through the deliberation council was desirable or needed after the democratization process got under way.

policy—as a means of mobilizing savings and allocating them to strategic industries and favored projects (Haggard 2000: chapter 1). This strategy was successful in sustaining rapid growth and industrialization before being phased out in the 1990s. According to critics of the East Asian financial system, however, such a policy exacted a heavy toll: it resulted in a very weak and inefficient financial system that became increasingly vulnerable to a crisis (Eichengreen 1999*a*).

Before taking up the structural weaknesses of the East Asian financial systems, this chapter examines whether East Asian systems can be characterized as bank based, because by the mid-1990s, equity markets had become an important source of corporate financing in many of East Asia's emerging economies. Demirguc-Kunt and Levine (2001) constructed a conglomerate financial structure index for the 1990s in terms of size, activity, and efficiency of the financial system to gauge the relative importance of banks and capital markets. The index is a simple average of the time series of the three indicators of which means are removed. The three indicators are: the ratio of market capitalization to bank assets (size), the ratio of total value of equities traded to bank credit (activity), and the ratio of total value of equities traded to GDP multiplied by overhead cost (efficiency).

The simple ratios of assets or liquid liabilities of banks and non-bank financial institutions to GDP in Table 6.1 suggest that financial intermediaries held a dominant position in Indonesia, Japan, Korea, and Thailand in the 1990s. But Demirguc-Kunt and Levine's (2001) financial structure

**Table 6.1.** Overall Size and Financial Structure Indices in East Asia (1990–1995)

|  | Size of financial intermediaries[a] | Market capitalization/GDP | Financial Structure Index[b] | |
|---|---|---|---|---|
|  |  |  | Bank-based | Market-based |
| Indonesia | 0.49 | 0.18 | −0.50 | |
| Korea, Rep. | 1.15 | 0.37 | | 0.89 |
| Malaysia | 1.13 | 2.01 | | 2.93 |
| Philippines | 0.41 | 0.52 | | 0.71 |
| Thailand | 1.16 | 0.57 | | 0.39 |
| Hong Kong | — | 1.96 | | 2.10 |
| Singapore | 1.13 | 1.37 | | 1.18 |
| Japan | 2.72 | 0.79 | −0.19 | |
| Great Britain | — | 1.13 | | 0.92 |
| United States | 1.84 | 0.80 | | 1.96 |

[a] Domestic assets of deposit money banks and other nonbank financial institutions as percentage of GDP.
[b] The financial structure index is an average of the ratio of market capitalization to bank assets (size), the ratio of total value of equities traded to bank credit (activity), and the ratio of total value of equities traded to GDP multiplied by overhead cost (efficiency).
*Source*: Demirguc-Kunt and Levine (2001).

**Table 6.2.** Efficiency of the Financial Sector across Countries

|                | Overall efficiency[a] | Overall efficiency[b] | Overall efficiency[c] |
|----------------|----------------------:|----------------------:|----------------------:|
| Indonesia      | 1.85                  | 2.70                  | 10.76                 |
| Korea, South   | 19.77                 | 17.86                 | 54.93                 |
| Malaysia       | 44.24                 | 74.91                 | 19.45                 |
| Philippines    | 3.88                  | 3.15                  | 6.73                  |
| Thailand       | 13.70                 | 19.72                 | 26.35                 |
| Hong Kong      | 45.54                 | 44.90                 | 22.10                 |
| Singapore      | 32.20                 | 54.62                 | 23.04                 |
| Japan          | 15.84                 | 20.17                 | 19.80                 |
| Great Britain  | 26.97                 | 20.65                 | 23.54                 |
| United States  | 15.76                 | 16.95                 | 18.64                 |

[a] Total value of domestic equities traded as a ratio of GDP/bank net interest margin.
[b] Total value of domestic equities traded as a ratio of GDP/bank net interest margin.
[c] Total value of domestic equities traded/market value of domestic equities/bank net interest margin.
Source: Demirguc-Kunt and Levine (2001).

indices of the eight East Asian economies in Table 6.1 show that, except for Indonesia and Japan, all had developed a market-based system prior to the 1997 crisis, calling into question the assertion that East Asia had a bank-dominated financial system.

The high values of the Demirguc-Kunt and Levine conglomerate index for the six East Asian economies (excluding Indonesia and Japan) are accounted for by a sharp increase in the total value of equities traded as a share of GDP and hence reflect the increasing importance of capital markets. When the size of the equity market was relatively small as in the 1970s and 1980s, both the market capitalization and the total value of equities traded as a share of GDP remained relatively stable in all countries except for those with high incomes (Demirguc-Kunt and Levine 2001 and Table 6.2). In 1997, stock market capitalization as a percentage of GDP fell dramatically, whereas a similar ratio for money plus quasi-money did not, and has not returned to the pre-crisis level in Indonesia, Malaysia, and Thailand (see Table 6.3). The stock market capitalization ratios in Table 6.3 have been highly unstable compared to the money plus quasi-money indicator. This relative instability stems from the pro-cyclical features of the demand for equities.

Once the cyclical component is removed from the size and activity indicators, the part of changes in stock market capitalization that are explained by cyclical fluctuations becomes very large, whereas this is not observed in the case of the monetary indicator. What this means is that the demand for equities tends to be more sensitive and hence influenced by changes in investors' perceptions of economic prospects than the demand for bank

Table 6.3. Monetary Aggregates and Stock Market Capitalization

| | 1990 | | 1996 | | 1998 | | 2000 | | 2002 | | 2003 | |
|---|---|---|---|---|---|---|---|---|---|---|---|---|
| | I[a] | II[b] | I | II | I | II | I | II | I | II | I | II |
| Indonesia | 7.1 | 40.1 | 40.0 | 52.2 | 23.2 | 59.5 | 17.8 | 54.2 | 17.3 | 54.9 | 26.2 | 53.4 |
| Korea, Rep. | 42.5 | 38.4 | 24.9 | 42.6 | 35.1 | 58.2 | 33.6 | 71.1 | 45.5 | 75.8 | 54.5 | 76.7 |
| Malaysia | 110.4 | 64.4 | 304.4 | 92.3 | 136.6 | 95.3 | 129.8 | 97.2 | 130.7 | 102.1 | 163.2 | 102.6 |
| Philippines | 13.4 | 34.2 | 97.4 | 56.3 | 54.2 | 61.1 | 68.0 | 60.2 | 50.0 | 58.7 | 29.2 | 56.1 |
| Thailand | 28.0 | 70.0 | 54.9 | 80.6 | 31.2 | 102.9 | 24.0 | 104.1 | 36.3 | 99.2 | 84.4 | 96.7 |
| Hong Kong | 110.6 | – | 287.0 | 176.0 | 207.8 | 201.3 | 377.0 | 226.8 | 286.7 | 238.9 | 456.1 | 259.1 |
| Japan | 96.1 | 115.1 | 65.6 | 112.2 | 63.2 | 120.8 | 66.3 | 121.9 | 53.2 | 133.5 | 70.7 | 136.0 |
| Singapore | 93.0 | 93.1 | 162.9 | 87.0 | 115.3 | 116.1 | 167.1 | 108.0 | 115.4 | 115.8 | 158.9 | 122.4 |

[a] I: stock market capitalization as a percentage of GDP.
[b] II: money plus quasi-money as a percentage of GDP.
*Source*: IFS various issues and World Bank Indicators 2004.

liabilities. In relationship banking, in which banks establish long-term relationships with their clients, it is expected that bank lending will be less procyclical.

The size and activity indicators tend to be volatile largely because of instability in the stock market. In order to eliminate this volatility, Park, Song, and Wang (2004) constructed trend measures of each of the two indicators by applying the Hodrick-Prescott filter to the data supplied by Demirguc-Kunt and Levine (2001).[3] The filtering of the size indicator produces surprising results: the UK had a market-based financial system, but the US did not in the 1970s and 1980s. In East Asia, Malaysia and Singapore had already developed a market-based financial system in the 1980s. By the mid-1990s, the Philippines had transformed its financial system into a market-based one.

The filtering of the activity indicator suggests a somewhat different development. When the UK is held as the norm for a market-based financial system, the activity indicator shows that South Korea had become a financial market-based economy by the mid-1980s. During the first half of the 1990s, Malaysia, Singapore and the Philippines, somewhat later, moved into the category of a market-based system. These conflicting pieces of evidence suggest that the Demirguc-Kunt and Levine indices may not be reliable indicators of the financial structure. Indeed, if the Demirguc-Kunt and Levine indices were to be accepted, then one could argue that the growing importance of financial markets that began in the 1980s rather

---

[3] A trend measure of the efficiency indicator cannot be estimated because of the unavailability of the data.

than the dominance of East Asia's banking sector had a greater bearing on the 1997–8 crisis. Since the Demirguc-Kunt and Levine conglomerate index does not appear to be a reliable measure of the structure of the financial system, this study uses the simple measure of the ratio of financial assets to GDP in Table 6.3 that shows that East Asian financial systems were bank or financial intermediary based during much of the period under discussion.

## • *Financial Frailties and Crony Capitalism*

To the critics of the East Asian development model, the financial system that was dominated by banks that became 'too big to fail' was one of the most serious systemic weaknesses that brought about the downfall of East Asia's crisis countries. The moral hazard syndrome stemming from the implicit government guarantee was bound to install an inefficient risk management system, causing a massive deterioration in the quality of bank assets. The second weakness was the failure of introducing and enforcing global accounting and auditing practices that made bank balance sheets non-transparent. The lack of transparency, in turn, created fertile ground for corruption. The cumulative effect of corruption and the inefficient allocation of credit eventually manifested itself in poor economic performance.

A third weakness was that the dominance of banks left little room for the development of capital markets, which requires detailed information on the financial positions and legal structures of firms that is needed to protect minority stockholders. Except for Malaysia and Hong Kong, most East Asian economies do not have a common law tradition; they have French, German, or other legal foundations. Countries without common law tend to emphasize the rights of creditors more than the rights of stockholders and hence to develop a bank-based financial system.[4] Insofar as they were relying on banks for financial intermediation, East Asian economies including Japan had less incentive to improve accounting, auditing, disclosure, and corporate governance than they otherwise would have.

During the early 1990s, the bulk of foreign capital inflows were channeled to domestic firms through a poorly managed and inefficient banking system. Ensconced in a closed and regulated market environment, banks, which were placed under the direct control of the government in many

---

[4] Non-common law countries such as those with a French civil law origin are also likely to have underdeveloped, corrupt, and bank-based systems (Demirguc-Kunt and Levine 2001).

East Asian economies, did not have incentives to improve their risk management capabilities demanded in a deregulated financial environment. The banks were slow or negligent in complying with global standards on capital adequacy, loan classification, loan-loss provisioning, and lending restrictions, including those on investments in stocks and bonds. They certainly did not care to monitor their client firms, not nearly as carefully as privately owned and deregulated banks would do. Since they were in control of banking, East Asian governments had developed the complacency of delaying the building of a prudential supervisory and regulatory system for monitoring the banks that were increasingly exposed to new and greater risks. In the relationship banking that characterized the East Asian financial system, banks were supposed to play an important role in monitoring corporations, but it was unclear who was to monitor the banks. In the end it was the government.[5]

The critics of the East Asian model also argue that financial liberalization should have been carried out in parallel with the reform of accounting, auditing, and disclosure of financial institutions and firms, but it was not. Advanced market-supporting institutions such as competent accounting and securities law firms, investment banking, credit rating agencies, corporate restructuring specialists, and fund managers were understandably slow to develop. In the absence of these institutions, it was questionable whether incipient capital markets could have buffered against speculation or served as stable sources of investment financing.

Finally, government control of banking created opportunities for collusion between bank owners and managers, on the one hand, and politicians and large businesses, which were favored borrowers at the banks, on the other. During the early periods of economic development, Eichengreen (1999b) argues, when high return investments were abundant in East Asia, the industrial policy of using banks as an instrument of resource allocation did not pose serious efficiency problems. Once these opportunities were exhausted, sustaining rapid growth required a more efficient allocation of resources, which, in turn, dictated liberalizing and opening domestic financial markets. Instead, East Asian governments stuck to the old strategy of bank-dominated control, disregarding market signals in intervening in credit allocation. Eventually, nonperforming loans began to pile up at

---

[5] As a group of monitors, depositors are too diversified, numerous, and unorganized to be effective monitors. Shareholders are either diversified or the bank itself may be owned by some of its major borrowers, disqualifying them as effective monitors. For the public good, the government assumes the role of the monitor-regulator. Financial reform has shifted the system of governance from relationship monitoring to one that is rule-based.

banks risking the solvency of these institutions. Krugman (1994) was the first to point out that East Asia was reaching the point of diminishing returns and that rapid growth was only being sustained by a massive infusion of capital, much of which came from abroad in the form of short-term credit. Eichengreen (1999a) also makes the same argument that East Asian governments chose to liberalize the capital account to facilitate borrowing from abroad instead of improving the efficiency of the economy. Unfortunately, he argues, they did it backwards by deregulating short-term borrowing first.

# Part II

# The Asian Crisis: Causes and Consequences

# 7

# The Buildup of the Crisis

## 7.1. Capital Inflows and Investment Boom and Bust

In the early 1990s, induced by the region's economic success and financial liberalization coupled with low interest rates in advanced economies, a large volume of foreign capital began to flow into East Asia. Much of the inflow went to finance investment in the real estate sector in Indonesia, Malaysia, and Thailand and to manufacturing in South Korea. The ensuing investment boom built up strong inflationary pressures, in particular in the non-tradeable sector, resulting in overvalued currencies and growing current account deficits.

Banks and other financial institutions in the Southeast Asian economies, freed from many lending restrictions in the process of financial liberalization that began toward the end of the 1980s, became increasingly aggressive in financing real estate investment, in part because their real estate loans were collateralized with physical assets, which increased in value with the onset of the investment boom. Inflation was gaining while large capital inflows kept the currencies of these countries relatively strong, resulting in a large appreciation of the real exchange rate. This real appreciation undermined their export competitiveness, unfortunately at a time when the Japanese yen was depreciating vis-à-vis the dollar.

Foreign reserve holdings of these countries were falling to a dangerous level as deficits on current accounts soared. In order to finance the growing deficits, these countries had to attract more foreign capital, which required higher domestic interest rates. The higher interest rates coupled with the mistaken expectation that nominal exchange rates would remain stable created strong incentives for both financial institutions and corporations to borrow heavily from international financial markets.

Except for a few large, state-owned enterprises and banks, most East Asian corporations and financial institutions had limited access to the long-term end of international capital markets due to their inability to obtain an investment grade rating on their bond and equity issues. It is also plausible that foreign lenders curtailed the maturity of their loans as a means of reducing the risk involved in their lending, stemming in part from non-transparency and poor governance, both in corporations and at banks (Rajan and Zingales 1998). This inability to raise long-term capital forced banks and other financial institutions to turn to the interbank market for short-term loans. At East Asian commercial banks, the volume of short-term foreign currency loans, the bulk of which were then relent to domestic firms for their long-term investment, soared beyond the prudent level, thereby causing both serious currency and maturity mismatches in their balance sheets.

Apparently, foreign lenders believed that since the government would not let these financial institutions fail, their loans were guaranteed. On their part, the domestic banks, long accustomed to relationship banking, operated under the mistaken assumption that their loans from the interbank market would be rolled over continuously. To make matters worse, most of these short-term loans were not hedged due to the high cost and limited availability of hedging instruments.

In the financial sector, higher interest rates were deteriorating the quality of assets held by and cutting into the profits of a growing number of banks and other financial institutions, as many of their clients were unable to service their debts. The absence of an efficient system of prudential supervision and regulation and the implicit bailout guarantee were adding to the financial woes at these institutions as they created serious moral hazard problems. Faced with falling profits and deteriorating cash flows, these financial institutions were investing more and more in risky assets to bolster their income statements and thereby increase their franchise values. Stability, as well as soundness, of these institutions was clearly at risk, and the situation was getting untenable.

As the number of business bankruptcies grew, however, monetary authorities in the crisis-affected countries had to increase liquidity to contain the volatile situation in the banking sector. At that point, speculators wasted no time in attacking the currencies. The moment they saw the crisis countries were losing large amounts of reserves they simply left the markets of these countries. Large, unhedged, short-term foreign currency debts of both financial institutions and private corporations then made many East Asian economies helpless in the face of a speculative attack, to which they eventually succumbed.

As Thailand and Indonesia failed to defend their currencies, foreign investors and lenders began to reassess the problems of currency and maturity mismatches in the balance sheets of financial institutions and corporations of other East Asian economies. Once these problems were perceived to be serious, key foreign actors recalled their loans and liquidated their holdings of East Asian securities, and so did domestic banks and other financial institutions, precipitating a crisis even in countries with no current account problem such as Hong Kong and Taiwan. By the time the Thai crisis reached the shores of Hong Kong, Taiwan, and South Korea, it had developed into a capital account crisis and self-fulfilling prophecy.

The preceding discussion on unfolding of the 1997 crisis raises an important question as to whether the crisis-affected countries could have mounted a credible defense of their currencies had they pursued a different set of macroeconomic policies, including an exchange rate policy. Here again, the economic profession is sharply divided. Eichengreen (1998), Corsetti, Pesenti, and Roubini (1998), and many financial industry analysts argue that pegging their currencies to the dollar was a serious mistake. Combined with laxness in financial regulation and supervision, in their view, the pegging led to a large increase in unhedged short-term foreign currency loans. The consequent currency mismatch set off a massive exodus of foreign investors and lenders from East Asia at a time when a host of structural weaknesses had made these economies highly vulnerable to a crisis.

Should the crisis-countries then have responded to the build-up of the crisis by floating their exchange rates and tightening monetary and fiscal policies to prevent the sudden reversal of capital flows? In retrospect, it is not clear whether such a policy prescription would have worked. In fact, floating could have further exacerbated financial instability because the real asset boom, which was gathering momentum and building up pressure for currency appreciation.[1] A higher interest rate would not have stabilized financial markets as it might have induced more short-term capital inflows. And, given the rigidities of fiscal policy, it could hardly have been an effective means of defending the currency.

Before the 1997 financial crisis, praise for East Asia for its economic achievements was effusive. The crisis suddenly reduced a region that had been proud of rapid growth with declining inequality and macroeconomic stability to a haven of reckless investors, insolvent financial institutions, and cronyism. Many argued that the major culprits of the crisis were the

---

[1] See Furman and Stiglitz (1998) and also Chapter 12.

structural weaknesses plaguing the financial and corporate sector. After the dust settled and the initial shock from the crisis wore off, however, more serious analyses of the crises appeared, disputing the conclusions of earlier studies. Also, the recent recovery in the region, which was much faster than the previous episodes in other countries would have predicted, renewed interest in the re-examination of the East Asian development paradigm from more positive perspectives (Park and Lee 2003 and Figure 7.1). As a result of these developments, there is growing doubt as to whether the alleged causes of the crisis have sound theoretical or empirical grounds for repudiating the East Asian development paradigm.

## 7.2. Structural Reform and Recovery

Post-financial crises in other countries suggest that it takes an average of two to three years for an emerging market economy to return to the pre-crisis trend rate of growth. Thereafter, GDP growth rates do not rise above the pre-crisis level, so that the level of GDP remains permanently below the pre-crisis trend (Lee and Rhee 2000). As shown in Figure 7.1, the East Asian crisis countries were able to bounce back in a V pattern adjustment, certainly much faster than expected, after a year and a half of severe recession. Since then they have again seen a slowdown in their growth rates. In particular, the Korean recovery stands in sharp contrast to the stylized patterns of adjustment. The initial GDP contraction and its subsequent recovery have been far larger than expected and then the cross-country evidence predicted.

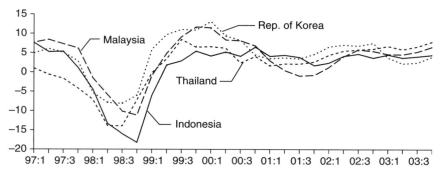

**Figure 7.1.** Quarterly GDP growth rates (percentage and year-on-year)

*Source*: ADB Regional Economic Monitoring Unit (ARIC) http://aric.adb.org/indicators/ino/peia.asp and International Financial Statistics, IMF, various issues.

At the beginning, the prevailing view on managing the crisis was that the crisis countries' commitment to structural reforms would be critical to their recovery. The IMF proposed reforms, which essentially espoused the development of a market-oriented economic system or an Anglo-American system of free capitalism, were expected to help East Asian economies emerge from the crisis with more stable, transparent, and efficient financial and corporate sectors and improve their long-term growth prospects. More important was the belief that the reforms would restore market confidence, thereby inducing the return of foreign lenders and investors to the region. The IMF reform program received strong endorsement because nothing short of a crisis would have forced the countries to undertake much needed and overdue reform (Rubin 2004).

In 2000, when the worst of the crisis was over and the crisis countries began to register substantial growth, the World Bank (2000b: 7) argued, 'assertive structural adjustment helped restore credit flows and boosted consumer and investor confidence.' Goldstein (2003: 370) expressed a similar view; 'Korea could not have regained market confidence without making a good "start" on structural reform.' However, there is little empirical evidence that the commitment to implementing various reform measures sufficiently improved the confidence of foreign investors and lenders to assist the crisis countries in recovering from the crash. Only when they saw a substantial increase in the current account surplus and signs of a resumption in growth did foreign investors begin to return to these countries (Park 2001).

Most of the serious structural weaknesses that were identified as the major causes of the crisis in Indonesia, South Korea, Malaysia, and Thailand could not have been removed in a span of two years. The evidence available does not support the contention that market-oriented reforms contributed to restoring market confidence during first two years of the crisis. International credit rating agencies reported that reforms in the banking sector in the crisis countries were not durable and extensive enough to ensure prevention of future crises. Only toward the end of 1999, did Moody's and S&P upgraded the sovereign credit ratings of South Korea and Malaysia to the lowest investment grade from speculation grade. By that time, the recovery was in full swing in East Asia. Journalistic accounts abounded with similar concerns and continued to raise doubts about the effectiveness of reforms in the crisis countries. Numerous publications put out by the World Bank and the IMF seldom failed to stress the need to speed up the pace of financial and corporate restructuring in the crisis countries. Under these circumstances, most foreign investors would find it too risky to return to the crisis countries, but did. Many of the foreign investors appear to have been lured back by signs of rapid recovery and substantial improvements in external liquidity resulting from large surpluses on the current account.

Reflecting recovery rather than ratings improvement, capital inflows in East Asia began to surge again, although they were below the pre-crisis level. Since policy changes and structural reforms are subject to many uncertainties and require a lengthy period to take effect, international banks and global institutional lenders do not appear to have either the patience or ability to monitor and assess the effects of structural reforms. This is particularly true in light of their preoccupation with the short-term performance of their portfolios.

Seven years into the reform process, the crisis countries have managed to restore the soundness and profitability of financial institutions and to alleviate corporate distress. But banks are still holding large volumes of non-performing loans and remain undercapitalized in all four crisis-hit countries (see Table 7.1). Many corporations in the region are still unable to service their debts. The progress in institutional reform has been less sanguine as it has been lagging that of balance sheet restructuring of banks and corporations. Admittedly, it is not easy quantitatively to measure progress in institutional reform, but pieces of anecdotal evidence suggest that new banking and accounting standards, disclosure requirements, and rules for corporate governance have been introduced, but are not rigorously enforced. It will take many years for the new system to take root.

Echoing the need to step up institutional reform, a World Bank update of East Asia in 2002 (World Bank 2002:2) urges the East Asian economies to advance reforms that reduce vulnerability to shocks and calls for actions to 'improve law and order . . . completing the restructuring agenda left over from the financial crisis, improving financial sector supervision and regulation . . .' There has not been much improvement since then.

Only recently have new banking regulations and supervision including tighter provisioning rules been introduced in Indonesia and Thailand. Reform of the central bank and the deposit insurance corporation, proposed to enhance compliance and to take prompt corrective action in troubled banks, has been mired in bureaucratic delays in the Philippines. State-owned banks still dominate the banking sector in Indonesia. Corporate restructuring through the legal and market system, which was expected to take over the direct government workout, has been slow throughout East Asia (World Bank 2004a). In view of this assessment, the crisis countries do not appear to be even halfway to the goal of restructuring their financial

**Table 7.1.** Nonperforming Loans (NPLs) in the Commercial Banking System of the Crisis-Affected Countries (% of total loans)

| | 1997 | 1998 | 1999 | 2000 | 2001 | 2002 | | | | 2003 | | | | 2004 | |
|---|---|---|---|---|---|---|---|---|---|---|---|---|---|---|---|
| | Dec | Dec | Dec | Dec | Dec | Mar | Jun | Sept | Dec | Mar | Jun | Sept | Dec | Mar | Jun |
| Indonesia[a] | — | — | 64.0 | 57.1 | 48.8 | 50.3 | 48.5 | 40.7 | 31.1 | 30.3 | 27.7 | 24.4 | 18.1 | 18.9 | 17.9 |
| (Excl. IBRA) | 7.2 | 48.6 | 32.9 | 18.8 | 12.1 | 12.8 | 11.8 | 10.5 | 7.5 | 7.6 | 7.1 | 6.7 | 6.8 | 6.3 | 6.2 |
| South Korea[b] | 8.0 | 17.2 | 23.2 | 14.0 | 7.4 | 6.6 | 5.0 | 4.8 | 4.1 | 4.2 | 4.7 | 4.9 | 4.4 | | |
| (Excl. KAMCO&KDIC) | 6.0 | 7.3 | 13.6 | 8.8 | 3.3 | 2.9 | 2.5 | 2.5 | 2.4 | 2.6 | 2.6 | 2.6 | 2.7 | 3.1 | 2.6 |
| Malaysia | — | 21.1 | 23.4 | 22.5 | 24.4 | 24.6 | 23.7 | 23.1 | 22.4 | 22.1 | 21.9 | 21.1 | 21.2 | 21.0 | 20.1 |
| (Excl. Danaharta) | — | 16.7 | 16.7 | 13.4 | 16.3 | 16.7 | 15.7 | 15.3 | 14.7 | 14.6 | 13.9 | 13.3 | 13.1 | 13.0 | 12.3 |
| Philippines[c] | 4.7 | 10.4 | 12.3 | 15.1 | 17.3 | 18.0 | 18.1 | 16.5 | 15.0 | 15.5 | 15.2 | 14.5 | 14.1 | 14.0 | 13.8 |
| Thailand | — | 45.0 | 41.5 | 29.7 | 29.6 | 29.7 | 29.9 | 29.6 | 34.2 | 34.1 | 34.1 | 33.5 | 30.6 | 29.6 | 29.6 |
| (Excl. AMCs) | — | 45.0 | 39.9 | 19.5 | 11.5 | 11.4 | 11.3 | 11.7 | 18.1 | 17.8 | 17.6 | 16.8 | 13.9 | 13.0 | 13.0 |
| China | — | — | — | — | — | — | — | — | 20.0 | | | | 15.0[d] | | |

[a] Only includes IBRA's AMC.
[b] The NPL ratio increased in 1999 due to the introduction of stricter asset classification criteria (forward liking criteria).
[c] From September 2002 onwards, the NPL ratios are based on the new definition of NPLs (as per BSP Circular 351) which allows banks to deduct bad loans with 100% provisioning from the NPL computations.
[d] Based on the four-tier classification (IMF 2004).
*Source:* World Bank (2004b).

institutions and corporations; it would be presumptuous to argue that the reform efforts have established a foundation for sustainable growth in East Asia. Nor would it be correct to assert that the gain in efficiency through the restructuring, difficult to measure even at this stage, has been one of the principal factors driving the recovery because the improvement in efficiency is likely to be realized and translated into high growth over a longer period, certainly longer than several years. In view of the preceding discussion, on might argue that the IMF structural reform programs were so misguided that they exacerbated the crisis, ignoring institutional and other local constraints to which the crisis countries were subject. In light of this continuing controversy, this volume will first turn to what went wrong with the IMF reform program before proposing an alternative reform program needed to construct a new development paradigm for East Asia in Part III.

# 8

# Causes of the East Asian Crisis: Structural Weakness vs. Liquidity Panic View

## 8.1. Structural Weaknesses

Immediately after the 1997 financial crisis, critics of the East Asian miracle and many experts from international financial institutions were quick to blame structural weaknesses together with misguided macroeconomic policy as the main causes of the crisis, although they did acknowledge, rather grudgingly, that sudden changes in market sentiment played a role as well. A typical characterization of the crisis is provided, for example, by Lane et al. (1999): the East Asian crises were rooted mainly in financial sector frailties, stemming in part from weaknesses in the corporate and government sectors, which made them increasingly vulnerable to changes in market sentiment, a deteriorating external situation, and contagion.

As discussed in Chapter 6, the list of financial sector weaknesses in East Asia that came to light after the crisis is so long and daunting that one wonders whether there was anything right in East Asia and whether the economic miracle was not, in fact, a mirage. To enumerate a few weaknesses, governance of firms and financial institutions was non-transparent. Inadequate and inaccurate economic and financial data prevented foreign investors and lenders from making informed decisions and risk assessment of their investments. The financial regulatory system was woefully weak and inefficient. Banks simply did not have an effective risk management system. The absence or underdevelopment of domestic bond markets, which made these economies rely on short-term foreign loans exacerbated the crisis because it was easier for foreign lenders to withdraw their loans, triggering a massive reversal of capital flows once a financial panic set in. There is a vast and ever growing body of literature on the causes and consequences of the East Asian crisis.[1] At the risk of repetition, this study reviews some of the alleged or actual causes of the crisis as they provide a starting point for identifying structural frailties of the East Asian model.

Most of the financial sector weaknesses analyzed in Chapter 6 were widely known and extensively analyzed even before the 1997 crisis,[2] and it is arguable whether they were any more serious than similar problems in other parts of the world. In fact, a recent study by Demirguc-Kunt and Levine (2001) shows that there had been a great deal of improvement in the soundness and efficiency of East Asian financial systems before the 1997 crisis. There is little doubt that financial weaknesses exacerbated financial instability and economic contraction once the East Asian economies came under a speculative attack but they might not have been serious enough to trigger the financial crisis.[3] First of all, there is no clear evidence that by the mid-1990s East Asian economies were crumbling under the inefficiencies of crony capitalism, bringing the period of rapid growth to an end. Table 6.2 (above) presents three measures of efficiency of East Asia's financial sector. Except for Indonesia and the Philippines, the overall efficiency of the financial systems of the other East Asian economies was more or less comparable to that of either the United States or Great Britain in the 1990s.

## 8.2. Were they the Direct Causes?

In analyzing the phenomenal growth experience of East Asia, Young (1995) and Krugman (1997) argue that much of the rapid growth before the 1997–8 crisis had been supported by the growth of inputs and very little by efficiency improvement measured by total factor productivity (TFP). Over time, the supply of low-cost labor declined and the rate of return on capital also fell, bringing an end to East Asia's miraculous performance. According to the TFP research during the 1990s, the productivity gap between the East Asian emerging market economies and industrial economies was as wide as before. East Asian growth was the result of working harder, not smarter (Krugman 1997).[4]

---

[1] For the latest account of the East Asian crisis, see Stiglitz (2002), Chapter 4.
[2] See Patrick and Park (1994).
[3] See Furman and Stiglitz (1998) for a detailed analysis on this issue.
[4] It should be pointed out that TFP estimates do not necessarily indicate whether investment rates are excessive or not. That is, the findings of low TFP growth in East Asian economies by Young (1995) and others do not necessarily prove that capital investment was excessive in

Was TFP growth as low as the estimates of these studies? A new study (Yoshitomi 2003) shows that measured growth rates of TFP in East and Southeast Asia were higher than in other developing countries and also higher than TFP growth rates in the US in the 1970s and 1980s, implying that East Asian economies were converging towards the international best practice production functions.[5] The contribution of measured TFP growth to income growth was low simply because capital accumulation was so high. A World Bank report (2000c) also suggests that East Asian economies managed to invest their savings productively, so that the return on capital investment remained higher than in most other developing countries, at least until the mid-1990s (p. 17).[6] Hsieh (2002) presents a different story however. TFP estimates based on data from national income accounts are subject to a large margin of error because of the inaccuracy of national income statistics on capital-output ratio and factor payments. To overcome the data problem, Hsieh (2002) estimates TFP using factor prices instead. According to his estimation, there are no significant differences between the growth accounting and price-based approaches for South Korea and Hong Kong (very low). However, the price-based estimates were higher for Taiwan (1 percent a year) and Singapore (more than 2 percent a year).

One could also question whether East Asian economies were intent on borrowing heavily from abroad to meet the ever-increasing volume of capital needed to compensate for losses in efficiency that were slowing economic growth. Data show that these economies did not have to liberalize their capital accounts to attract more capital inflows. Even before capital account transactions were liberalized and increasing volumes of foreign capital began to flow into East Asia, most East Asian economies were already growing at rates much higher than the rest of the world. In fact, it is this success and the potential for future success that had attracted

these countries. Furthermore, there are clear limits to the conventional growth-accounting method because it does not clearly distinguish between different sources of growth. If capital and technology cannot be separated, then TFP is not a true measure of technological progress. The distinction between capital and technology is often ambiguous. If technology is embodied in an imported capital good, then, it is hard to separate capital from technology. Growth accounting is a mere mechanical calculation; it does not explain a causal relationship. For example, technology grows at an exogenously given rate of $x$ at the steady state. Then, capital and output will also grow at the same steady-state rate $x$. Growth accounting will then attribute $\alpha \cdot x$ ($\alpha$ = capital share) of output growth to capital growth. Thus, although the true contribution of technology to output growth is 100%, growth accounting underestimates it by $(1-\alpha)$ 100% (Easterly and Levine 2000).

[5] The contribution of TFP growth to the region's miraculous output growth was relatively low compared to the experience of the currently developed countries when they were developing (Yoshitomi 2003).    [6] On the question of efficiency, see also Park (2001).

foreign direct investment and portfolio capital into the region. Not only had there been both rapid growth and domestic stability, but the rates of return on capital had been high before the crisis.

In most East Asian economies, the national budget was balanced or generating a surplus. As of the mid-1980s, all of the countries in the region had pursued policies of trade and financial liberalization. Given these sound fundamentals and the region's commitment to liberalization, foreign investors saw enormous opportunities for profit and moved vast sums of money into the region. Because of this massive inflow, investment as a proportion of GDP in all of these countries was significantly higher than it had been in the 1980s. At the same time, savings rates were stable, resulting in large increases in current account deficits.

East Asia's emerging economies were very reluctant to liberalize the capital account and trade in the financial services in the early 1990s. None of these economies enjoyed any comparative advantage in exporting financial services. As such, Anglo-American financial institutions could easily have dominated their domestic markets for financial services once they were allowed market access. By the mid-1990s, for instance, American and European financial institutions had already established a dominant position in international investment banking in Asia (Park 2002).

East Asian policymakers knew quite well that the deregulation of capital account transactions could be bound to increase volatility of capital movements, the exchange rate, and interest rates, complicating macroeconomic management when financial markets are shallow and illiquid. The small East Asian economies simply did not have the capacity to absorb large increases in capital inflows in the short run and their systems for financial supervision and regulation were hardly effective to moderate capital inflows. The increases were bound to fuel speculative asset demand. More important, their regulatory and supervisory systems were hardly comparable to those of advanced countries in terms of standardization and effectiveness. Few of the East Asian economies were able to meet the necessary information and disclosure requirements for capital account liberalization. Despite this weak capacity in prudential supervision and regulation, Western governments were increasing pressure to secure their financial firms' rights of access to East Asia (Park 1996).

The perils of pell-mell financial market opening were well understood before the crisis. Indoctrinated by the Washington Consensus view, however, advanced countries and international institutions ignored these risks and put increasing pressure on developing countries to open their financial markets. According to Rubin (2004: 256) 'there is a danger that arguments for opening financial markets slowly, or in stages, can become excuses for not opening them at all.' Even if a well-functioning system of supervision and regulation had been in place, the system would not have been able to minimize the disastrous consequences of large capital inflows, although such a system would have made the crisis less painful. One possible reason for this is that if banks were restricted in their real estate lending, domestic borrowers could have gone directly to international financial markets, as they did in Indonesia.[7]

It is also incorrect to argue that prior to the crisis, foreign lenders had limited access to much of the information needed for their investments, including reliability of the balance sheets of banks and corporations of East Asia's crisis countries. Foreign investors and lenders had plenty of information on financial markets and corporations but they either ignored or were not able to process what was available. In fact, many small foreign banks found it too costly to analyze financial as well as borrower specific information. If large and reputable banks were lending, then they thought they could lend safely as well. Likewise, they left the East Asian financial markets immediately when they saw their leader banks were making a hurried exit, creating confusion and panic in financial markets of the crisis countries.[8]

Crony capitalism and widespread corruption in East Asia were also well known to foreign investors. As noted before, however, several measures of corruption suggested that the risk of corruption had declined or remained unchanged before the crisis. As a matter of fact, corruption cannot be an important cause of a crisis. The Nordic states—Sweden, Norway, and Finland—which did not suffer from corruption, were unable to fend off the crisis in the early 1990s (Rodrik 1999). In a number of East Asian economies foreign lenders became close to government and government projects. Before the crisis, they understood the political economy and were willing to participate in it. There is also the suspicion that they were engaged in corrupt practices with the expectation that their government protectors would remain in office and to protect them.

---

[7] For further discussion on this issue, see Radelet and Sachs (1998), Furman and Stiglitz (1998), Hellmann, Murdock, and Stiglitz (2000), and Park and Song (2001).

[8] If indeed the lack of transparency and the inadequate disclosure of information made East Asia vulnerable to financial crises, how serious was the problem? Furman and Stiglitz (1998) show that increased transparency in the form of disclosure requirements was not needed, since markets can and do provide optimal incentives for disclosure. They also argue that under certain circumstances, information disclosure could exacerbate fluctuations in the financial markets and precipitate financial crisis (you do not cry fire in a packed theater).

Finally, the dominance of the banking sector per se was not a cause of the crisis, but non-transparency, poor risk management, and cronyism may have been responsible for touching off the crisis. In a bank- or intermediary-oriented financial system, it is only natural that the debt–equity ratios of firms are likely to be much higher than those in a capital market dominated financial system. Before the crisis, foreign lenders apparently did not consider that the balance sheet weaknesses would pose serious default and liquidity risks. Once the crisis erupted, however, the high leverage suddenly came up as one of the major vulnerabilities of East Asian corporations.

Many structural weaknesses were, and still are, found in East Asia's bank-based financial systems, but the Asian financial crisis does not prove that the Anglo-American market-oriented financial system is superior and more resilient to speculative attack. Indeed there is little empirical evidence suggesting that a bank-oriented system is exposed to a higher likelihood of a banking crisis than a market-based system. Barth, Caudill, and Yago (2000) show that there is no clear empirical evidence on which types of the financial structure—bank based or market based—are more likely to reduce the likelihood of a financial crisis. Recent studies also present evidence showing that restricting the ability of banks to diversify tends to increase financial fragility and crisis probabilities and that the financial structure has little bearing on long-run economic performance (Levine 2003).

One of the lessons of the Asian crisis is that the cost of a banking crisis is higher in a bank-based than a market-based system. When banks are cut off from the interbank loan market, as they were during the height of the 1997 crisis, many of them were not able to provide even short-term loans to their business clients. When the banks became insolvent, so did many of their client firms, both small and large, simply because these borrowers did not have access to other sources of financing. In a bank-oriented open financial system, therefore, a banking crisis can quickly become an economy-wide crisis, as the failed banks are likely to drag the entire real sector of the economy into insolvency.

In conclusion, as far as the financial system is concerned, the failure of the East Asian development model was not so much its bank domination, as it was poor management and regulation of the banking sector. Why did East Asia's emerging economies not realize and address these institutional problems for so long? As long as the economies were growing as rapidly as they did in the 1970s and 1980s, these potential problems never surfaced as serious issues and hence were conveniently ignored.

## 8.3. The Liquidity Panic View

In challenging the structural weakness view, Furman and Stiglitz (1998), Feldstein (1998), Radelet and Sachs (1998), and Chang and Velasco (1998) focus on the panic and herding of international investors as the more serious causes of the crisis. At the time of the crisis, the current account deficits measured as a proportion of GDP were large, but could have been financed had international lenders and investors not panicked and withdrawn their investments and loans. If the Thai crisis had been a current account crisis, Thai authorities could have minimized the severity and duration of the crisis, although they might not have avoided it altogether, by putting in place a system of basket, band, and crawl (BBC) for exchange rate management (Williamson 2000). But the panic turned a current account problem into a capital account crisis and made it at the same time contagious, spreading to other neighboring countries which had not experienced any serious current account problems, spiraling the current account problems that were manageable into a full blown capital account crisis. In a capital account crisis, a well-managed BBC system would not have been able to stave off the speculative attack.

According to Furman and Stiglitz (1998), the crisis was triggered by a panic, or a sudden change in the market's perception of risk, in part provoked by extensive criticism from a chorus of Western governments and international financial institutions, proclaiming that East Asian economies were suffering from profound problems. Although these problems were known before, this new emphasis deepened the crisis and damaged the prospects for recovery. When financial institutions are weak, corruption is widespread, and corporate governance is opaque, as it was in East Asia at the time of the crisis; Furman and Stiglitz (1998) argue that the probability of this kind of external shock being translated into a crisis increases. To proponents of the liquidity-panic view, opening financial markets in the absence of an effective system of prudential regulation and supervision of financial institutions was a mistake.

A close examination of the recovery from the crisis gives further credence to the liquidity-panic view. For example, Park (2001) singles out changes in macroeconomic policy and market perceptions as the two most important developments that have contributed to the recovery in East Asia. Beginning in 1998, the widespread condemnation that the crisis countries had profound, previously unrecognized, structural problems gave way to the realization that the crisis would, in fact, be temporary. Within six months of the crisis, a measure of stability returned to domestic capital and foreign exchange markets and all of the crisis countries began amassing large current account surpluses. With these developments, some of the foreign credit facilities were restored and foreign investors began to return to East Asia. Thereafter, the recovery had accelerated for three consecutive years before losing momentum as a result of the burst of the IT bubble in 2001.

To the extent that the Thai crisis had its origin in the capital account, a large measure to support liquidity organized by international financial institutions at an early stage of the crisis could have averted contagion of the crisis. Banks, nonbank financial institutions, and other institutional investors of advanced economies were clearly not taking prudent steps in managing the risks involved in their lending to the East Asian economies. Yet, the regulatory authorities of the European Union and North America did not sound the alarm, perhaps because of the lack of information on the riskiness of the loan portfolios in the institutions they supervised. Many smaller banks and institutional investors from other regions were following the lead of major multinational banks and other institutional investors in lending to East Asia on the assumption that these large institutions knew what they were doing.

The process of recovery for the last seven years in East Asia has also revealed failures and imperfections of international financial markets, deficiencies of the international financial system in providing the institutional role of a lender of last resort, and inadequacy of financial supervision and regulation of financial institutions of advanced countries investing in emerging market economies.

In conclusion, our analysis supports neither the structural nor liquidity-panic view in accounting for causes and consequences of the crisis. Indonesia, Malaysia, Thailand, and South Korea all fell victim to the speculative attacks in part, because they had failed to reform and improve efficiency of their financial and corporate sectors. At the same time, they can justifiably blame panic and herding of financial market participants for the severity of the crisis or the losses of income and employment. It is also true that none of the alleged causes of the crisis may have been as critical as originally thought, although there is no denying that most of the structural weakness in the financial, corporate and public sectors had converged to make many East Asian economies susceptible to speculative attacks even before the 1997 crisis. Undoubtedly, these weaknesses were some of the factors that increased the probability of a crisis, that is, the probability of translating internal and external shocks into a crisis. Therefore, from the perspective of this study, identification of those central factors that were serious enough to have led to such a high probability of disaster will throw light on the future viability of the East Asian paradigm.

# 9

# A Re-evaluation of the IMF Reform Program: Wrong Diagnosis and Wrong Prescription[1]

## 9.1. The IMF as a Manager and Lender of Capital Account Crises

From the outset, the IMF reform programs for the crisis countries did not have a well-defined road map to guide the formulation and implementation of stabilization policies, financial and corporate restructuring, as well as institutional reforms, except for the general policy prescription of the Washington Consensus (Lane et al. 1999). The IMF should not be criticized for its failure to develop a comprehensive framework *ex post facto*, however. After all, the IMF did not have the luxury of spending many months in designing a coherent program as the crisis was deepening every day, threatening the total collapse of the crisis countries. The program packages, therefore, had to bring in various reform measures that were presumed to help restore market confidence, reduce the likelihood of a recurrence, and improve the long-term economic performance of these countries without due consideration of possible conflicts between different reform objectives.

IMF conditionality included, in addition to traditional stabilization policies, a wide range of different measures for short-run operational restructuring as well as medium-term institutional reform, which numbered 73 in Thailand and 140 in Indonesia. Even with a well-laid plan, such an elaborate and complicated program was bound to run into a host of implementation problems. The IMF programs simply lacked coherent

---

[1] The most scathing attack on IMF policies can be found in Stiglitz (2002: ch. 4).

plans for recovery through structural and institutional reform. Therefore, it is not surprising that their effectiveness suffered from confusion in setting appropriate targets for restructuring, inconsistencies between different reform measures, and a misguided sequencing of financial and corporate restructuring.

The single most important cause of the ineffectiveness was that the IMF did not recognize that the crisis was a capital account crisis. Recent studies leave little doubt that Indonesia, Malaysia, Thailand, and South Korea all suffered a severe capital account crisis (IMF 2003). According to the evaluation report by the independent evaluation office of the IMF, 'The crisis was triggered by massive reversal of capital flows, short-term flows played a prominent role, and contagion was an important factor' (IMF 2003: 1) With little experience in managing such a crisis, however, the IMF treated these countries as if they were experiencing serious current account problems. Instead of stressing the need to supply a large amount of liquidity to avert the run on financial institutions and depletion of reserves, the IMF prescribed a set of restrictive monetary and fiscal policies and institutional reform to restore market confidence. In retrospect, the IMF would have been more successful in containing the crisis if it had played the role of a lender of last resort, but it had neither the resources nor the mandate to play such a role. At best, the IMF, as Fischer (2001) puts it, is a crisis lender and manager mostly for emerging market and developing economies with the financial backing of its major stockholders.

One piece of evidence of the limited ability of the IMF as a capital crisis lender and manager is the failure of the second line of defense in the IMF program for South Korea. Foreign lenders and investors who were panic stricken on learning that South Korea was running out of its reserves set off a bank run by recalling their loans and withdrawing their investments all at once despite the IMF's repeated assurance that the country's economic fundamentals were strong and it was committed to structural reform. Nevertheless, it was clear then that they would not stop their liquidation short of receiving a guarantee that their loans would be repaid. And there was not enough money. The amount provided by the IMF was not enough even to repay foreign currency loans maturing before the end of 1997. A number of countries including the G-7 committed themselves to erect a second line of defense with additional resources of more than US$20 billion in the event there was a need to supplement the initial funding provided by the IMF. But market participants were highly skeptical about whether the additional money would be available if needed.

In retrospect, the buildup of the crisis required the intervention of a true lender of last resort, and it became evident that only the major shareholders of the Fund could assume such a role. Major international financial institutions with large exposures in South Korea agreed to a coordinated rollover of their short-term loans to Korean banks on Christmas Eve 1997 only after they learned of the US government's willingness to intervene. To many foreign financial institutions and other market participants the US was the only country that could conceivably guarantee repayment of their loans. Without the intervention of the US, which managed to persuade other G-7 countries to put pressure on their banks to restructure their short-term claims on Korean banks, the coordinated rollover would not have succeeded. The series of events leading to the rollover demonstrates that the Fund did not have either the credibility or confidence of market participants to organize such a debt-restructuring scheme.

The wrong diagnosis of the crisis produced the wrong prescription. One issue, which is dealt with in the next section, is whether it was desirable to subject the East Asian crisis countries to a myriad of structural reform measures when they were faced with a serious capital account crisis. The patterns of recovery in East Asia since 1998 suggest that the crisis countries, South Korea in particular, did not suffer from insolvency problems as initially diagnosed. The emphasis on structural reform may therefore have deepened and prolonged the crisis, even if the distinction between an insolvency and a liquidity crisis cannot be made easily and, in fact, may not even be useful in crisis situations.

Another controversial element of the Fund programs was the high interest rate policy that proved to be ineffective as a measure for stabilizing financial markets in a capital account crisis. Ineffectiveness of the policy stemmed in part from the IMF's failure to articulate the objectives of the policy. Pushed to the brink of default, authorities in the crisis countries had to do something, but neither the Fund nor the authorities could properly assess the consequences of the high interest rate policy, simply because they could not decide whether stabilization of the nominal exchange rate or targeting inflation should be the policy priority.

In the depths of a bank-run crisis, when foreign lenders are recalling their loans all at once, it is difficult to forecast expected exchange rates in three to six months' time, and with a high probability of debt default, risk premiums added to these countries could have been anything at that time. Under these circumstances, it was impossible to determine the level of interest rates that could stabilize the foreign exchange market with or without an exchange rate target. In the end, the Fund veered to inflation targeting as the nominal anchor. Since many firms in the crisis countries were heavily leveraged, they were vulnerable to the high interest rate policy. Even those firms that could have survived with lower interest rates could not stay in business. The large increase in business failures together with the Fund's indecision on the timing of monetary policy relaxation delayed the recovery.

## 9.2. Multiplicity of Reform Programs

There is a large body of literature on the analyses and reviews of country experiences with the IMF's structural reform conditionality.[2] For example, Goldstein (2003) levels several criticisms of IMF conditionality for East Asia's crisis countries: the scope of the individual country programs for Indonesia, South Korea, and Thailand was too broad to be implementable, the quality of specific measures was unproven, and sequencing of short-run liquidity management and long-term institutional reform was not made clear. Haggard (2000) shows that most of the structural reform measures imposed by the IMF had been previously acknowledged and also appeared on the priority list of reform in the crisis countries, but they were stalled due to domestic opposition before the crisis. For this reason, Goldstein (2003: 370) claims, 'Fund gaitsu—warts and all—may still be the best option out there for jump-starting structural reform.'

The effectiveness of structural reform will depend critically on public support, but equally on local ownership of the reform program. Stiglitz (1998a) was the first to raise the question of viability of structural reform that is imposed from outside through the process of conditionality; such a reform could not be sustainable because it could discourage recipients to develop their own analytic capacity and to gain confidence in their ability to utilize it. Secrecy involved in conditionality negotiations also increases the risks of shirking or policy reversals (Branson and Hanna 2000).

To many, 'conditionality is viewed as a crude attempt to generate policy change in return for grants or loans' (Branson and Hanna 2000: 3). Conditionality can take several forms, and those imposed on the East Asian crisis countries could be characterized as coercion or hard core concepts 'that have lost credibility' (Branson and Hanna 2000: 4). Branson and Hanna argue that to be effective, conditionality should be an instrument of

---

[2] See Goldstein (2003) for a review.

mutual accountability rather than imposition of policy changes. According to this view, conditionality should commit lending institutions, such as the IMF and World Bank, to lend, and their borrowers to borrow, under jointly determined conditions, because it is 'a process of signaling and nurturing mutual commitment' (Branson and Hanna 2000: 13) between lending agencies and borrowing countries, 'a concept that is consistent with ownership by and partnership with borrowers' (Branson and Hanna 2000: 3).

A second criticism of the Fund programs laid out for the three East Asian crisis countries is that the number, scope, and detail of structural policy conditions were overwhelming. As recounted by Goldstein (2003: 400) 'the number of structural policy conditions included in these programs with the three Asian crisis economies is very large . . . many more than you can count using all your fingers and toes.' At their peak, the numbers were 140 in Indonesia, 94 in South Korea, and 73 in Thailand (see Table 9.1).

Particularly striking is the case of Indonesia. The Fund program included a surprising number of nontraditional areas of conditionality. 'There were, inter alia, measures dealing with reforestation programs; the phasing-out of local content programs for motor vehicles; discontinuation of support for a particular aircraft project and of special privileges granted to the National Car; abolition of the compulsory 2 percent after-tax contribution to charity foundations; appointment of high-level advisors for monetary policy; development of rules for the Jakarta Clearing House; the end of restrictive marketing agreements for cement, paper, and plywood; the elimination of the Clove Marketing Board; the termination of requirements on farmers for the forced planting of sugar cane; the introduction of a micro credit scheme to assist small businesses, and the raising of stumpage fees' (Goldstein 2003: 400–1). Goldstein speculates that these reform measures were included 'for anti-corruption reasons, to instill confidence in private investors that the system was changing, to facilitate monitoring of commitments, and (for some commitments) to reflect the

**Table 9.1.** Number of Structural Policy Commitments in IMF Programs with Three Asian Crisis Countries, 1999–2000

| Indonesia | 10/97 | 1/98 | 4/98 | 6/98 | 7/98 | 9/98 | 10/98 | 11/98 | 3/99 | 5/99 | 7/99 | 1/00 | 7/00 |
|---|---|---|---|---|---|---|---|---|---|---|---|---|---|
| | 28 | 31 | 140 | 109 | 96 | 68 | 62 | 74 | 35 | 33 | 29 | 42 | 41 |
| South Korea | 12/3/97 | 12/5/97 | 12/24/97 | 2/98 | 5/98 | 7/98 | 11/98 | 3/99 | 11/99 | 7/00 | | | |
| | 29 | 33 | 50 | 53 | 51 | 39 | 53 | 83 | 94 | 68 | | | |
| Thailand | 8/97 | 11/97 | 2/98 | 5/98 | 8/98 | 12/98 | 3/99 | 9/99 | | | | | |
| | 26 | 24 | 21 | 73 | 50 | 69 | 8 | 9 | | | | | |

*Source:* Goldstein (2003).

structural policy agendas of either other IFIs (the World Bank and the Asian Development Bank) or certain creditor countries' (p. 401).[3]

A third problem of the Fund's conditionality stemmed from the multiplicity of reform measures, making it difficult to define the strategy and operational targets of structural reform. Since the IMF programs did not anticipate the sharp downturn in the economy, massive currency depreciation, and the full extent of problems in the financial and corporate sector, the reforms had to be implemented in a reactive manner. Modifications had to be made as new information about the effects of the initial measures and the depth of the financial institutions' unsoundness and corporate distress became available (Lane et al. 1999).

With this reactive process of implementation, the required strategy and operational targets for restructuring and institutional reforms could not be clearly defined, nor could a consensus be easily obtained beforehand; they had to be adjusted repeatedly. Therefore, the reactive process raised the fundamental question of what would constitute realistic targets for operational restructuring and institutional reforms, sufficient to regain the confidence of private investors and to reduce the vulnerabilities of the crisis countries in terms of bank capital adequacy, the size of NPLs, and loan provisioning. Financial reformers, for instance, could not reach an agreement on whether the operational definition of NPLs should be inclusive of all loans overdue for three months or longer or if they should eschew the old mechanical classification in favor of a set of new forward looking criteria. In the end, the crisis countries adopted an international best practice of forward looking criteria, though the new loan classification has not made it any easier to determine a reasonable level of NPLs, and hence, the amount of public funds needed for resolution.

The rationale behind the reform mandate of raising banks' BIS (Bank for International Settlements) ratios to over 10 percent (and large corporations in South Korea to lower their leverage below 200 percent before the end of 1999) was never made clear. Immediately after the crisis broke out, there emerged a consensus that insolvent financial institutions must be closed, and in fact, many were suspended or liquidated. The programs, however, did not present a clear picture as to whether it was desirable to close all of the money losing institutions at once or in some sequence. The programs did not indicate which types of institutions, new or old, should replace those liquidated institutions in such a way that stability of the payment

---

[3] In the case of South Korea, the creditor country was the US. Blustein (2001: 143) quotes a remark made by an IMF official, which says 'the U.S. saw this (crisis) as an opportunity . . . to crack open all these things that for years have bothered them.'

system and credit flow could be maintained, existing customers would be served, and a large number of skilled professionals shed by the failed financial institutions could be re-employed elsewhere. Confusion and dissension in the process of setting targets and strong resistance by the affected groups created uncertainties in domestic financial markets on the pace and extent of required reforms. To many foreign market participants, these changes were viewed as evidence of backtracking on the part of domestic policymakers.

# 10

# The IMF Structural Reforms: Inconsistencies in the Program

## 10.1. Conflicts between Structural Reform Measures

By following a reactive process of implementation, authorities in the crisis countries may not have given due consideration to the question of whether the prescribed reforms were appropriate or consistent with one another. That is, the IMF programs did not fully appreciate possible conflicts between different reform measures and objectives as the following cases demonstrate.

• *Conflicts between Stabilization Policy and Structural Reform*

Execution of operational restructuring, defined as resolution and recapitalization of financial institutions and corporate debt workout, and institutional reforms do not automatically guarantee recovery and resumption of growth. As the experiences of the crisis countries elsewhere suggest, the restructuring and reforms could deepen the economic downturn in the short run unless they are complemented by expansionary macroeconomic policies. In each of the crisis countries, the IMF was indecisive as to when reflation of the economy should begin and what instruments—monetary and fiscal—should be employed.

Furthermore, programs for all three countries saw the need to upgrade loan classification, loan loss provisioning, and capital adequacy at banks, but the IMF failed to examine whether the planned regulatory upgrading could be completed within a three-year period as mandated and the extent to which it could disrupt the recovery process. In many cases, banks were trying hard to reduce their exposure to weak but viable borrowers, while policy authorities were busy providing special credit facilities and credit guarantees to the very same borrowers to speed up the recovery process.

• *Conflicts between Operation Restructuring and Institutional Reform*

The injection of public funds into banks for recapitalization led to government ownership of a growing share of corporate assets, banks, and other nonbank financial institutions. Whether intended or not, this was clearly against the spirit of the IMF programs, which essentially espoused a market-led approach in financial and corporate restructuring. By mid-1999, the state had amassed a large share of banking assets, ranging from 18 percent in Malaysia to 78 percent in Indonesia (World Bank 2000*b*). Few knew how to deal with this nationalization problem; that is, how, to whom, and at what prices, these assets would be sold in the future. Since selling government-owned financial institutions is politically sensitive and often a lengthy process, the government-led privatization, as it was being procrastinated, would come under undue political pressure, create opportunities for corruption, and most of all perpetuate intervention in the banking industry.

Many of the institutional reforms required by the IMF programs, including the reform of government bureaucracy and the legal system, were to address the underlying structural weaknesses of the economy and hence were medium- or long-term priorities. At the beginning of the crisis, however, the institutional reforms were perceived to be so critical to stabilizing domestic financial markets by winning back the confidence of foreign lenders, they were put into effect simultaneously with operational restructuring without setting a priority between short-run liquidity management and building a strong foundation for a stable and efficient market-oriented economy. In the end, this failure of prioritizing reform objectives interfered with the implementation of institutional reforms in two ways.

First, the rush to introduce new corporate governance, a new regulatory and supervisory structure, and new accounting standards, and even to initiate legal and judicial reform suffered from poor planning and the limited institutional capacity to establish a set of alien institutions, and has therefore resulted, in many cases, in cosmetic reform. Second, once recovery was under way, it became difficult to maintain the momentum of reform, because recovery itself improved foreign investors' confidence. For the past several years, foreign investors and lenders have been losing interest in monitoring whether these countries are keeping the promise of their planned reform. Little market pressure has been exerted on these economies to stay the course of the initial reform program. In adjusting the sovereign ratings of the crisis countries, for example, the rating agencies appear to attach more weight to improvement in the external liquidity position and macroeconomic variables than progress in restructuring. This lack of foreign pressure has given a false impression to the crisis countries that the international community is satisfied with their economic reform.

## 10.2. Wrong Sequencing in Financial and Corporate Restructuring

As far as financial restructuring is concerned, the IMF and the policymakers of the crisis countries knew what should be done, drawing on the experiences of other countries that had suffered a similar crisis. However, there was no known 'best practice' for corporate restructuring when practically all of the corporations in manufacturing were suffering from liquidity problems, as in South Korea, and when all of the real estate, construction, and infrastructure sectors were lying in ruins as in Southeast Asia. The London Rules was chosen for the workout of corporate debt but neither debtors nor creditors understood why such an alien approach was introduced and why reducing the debt–equity ratio so drastically in the short run was critical to the success of the IMF programs. Opinions were also divided, and remain so to this day, on the advantages and disadvantages of a government-owned, centralized asset management company (AMC) versus privately owned, decentralized AMCs in the management and disposal of NPLs at banks.[1]

The adoption of the London Rules, procedures for voluntary, out-of-court settlements for corporate restructuring, was to some degree dictated by the absence of market and government institutions specialized in merger and acquisition, and a well functioning court-based resolution procedure. In this framework of out-of-court workouts, the government was supposed to play

[1] In order to deal more effectively with the management of non-performing assets, South Korea, Malaysia and, more recently, Indonesia established centralized AMCs while Thailand chose a decentralized process in which each commercial bank is encouraged to establish its own AMC. AMCs could be effective in restructuring insolvent financial institutions and selling their assets, although they are not expedient vehicles for corporate debt workouts, in particular for those in manufacturing (Klingebiel 2000).

A centralized AMC is often more effective in forcing the operational restructuring of insolvent financial institutions and has the advantage of centralizing scarce skilled personnel. It could, however, become a place where NPLs and collateral are parked for a long period instead of liquidation (Baliño et al. 1999).

the role of mediator, facilitating an orderly debt resolution, and banks the role of creditors managing the workout of corporate debt. But, in most cases, the government ended up dictating the entire process.

Corporate structuring should have been treated as an integral part of financial restructuring. However, the crisis countries were to restructure banks first by cleaning up their balance sheets and building up their equity base and then letting the banks take up corporate debt workout. To this end, a large portion of banks' nonperforming loans was transferred to the state-owned asset management company and then, to varying degrees, the banks were put in charge of restructuring ailing but viable corporations. The rationale for such an approach was, in the wake of rehabilitation, that the structure of governance and prudential framework of banks would provide powerful levers to bring about corporate restructuring (Baliño et al. 1999). Contrary to such expectations, this strategy was ineffective because of the moral hazard syndrome at the state-owned banks, which dominated the banking industry, and of banks' inability to resume normal lending operations. These problems held up the recovery as well as corporate restructuring. The bank-first strategy, therefore, posed a serious danger of necessitating repeated bank recapitalizations as evidenced by the experiences of Thailand and South Korea.

Moral hazard problems at public enterprises are not new, but they turned out to be more serious in a crisis situation. The state-owned banks wanted to maintain the status quo. They certainly had little incentive either to collect overdue loans or to engage in the workouts of weak, but potentially viable, corporations to which they lent money. In restructuring corporate debt, the banks were to follow a set of forward looking criteria, which included the prospects of recovery of troubled corporate borrowers at the banks. It is difficult to separate out potentially viable ones from a group of troubled firms because the separation requires forecasting of their survival after a debt workout; that is, estimating accurately how many of the restructured firms would regain their financial soundness and profitability. Since the banks were lacking in their ability to forecast and assess credit risk, their corporate restructuring did not necessarily restore soundness of their balance sheets. This meant that the success of corporate restructuring very much depended, among other things, on the speed of the economic recovery.

Since the banks had limited experience in forecasting cyclical developments in various industries, in credit risk management and investment banking, identifying nonviable corporations was difficult, contentious, and time consuming. These problems were further compounded by the unreliability of corporate financial statements. Under these circumstances, the restructured banks took the easy way out: they avoided corporate workout as much as possible, so as not to increase their holdings of NPLs or to lower their BIS ratios and profits. As a result, the banks kept many weak or near bankrupt corporations, which should have been either liquidated or subjected to workout, in their loan portfolios for longer than necessary. Supporting many of their nonviable loan customers meant that they were squeezed in catering to the credit needs of healthy borrowers. The moral hazard problem at banks, which has persisted to this day, therefore delayed corporate restructuring and resulted in a deterioration of asset quality of the banks, which, in turn, has undermined their long-term viability.

Another development that complicated the bank-led corporate workout was the introduction of international best practices in classifying and estimating the values of NPLs at banks. In order to assure the credibility of reform, the crisis countries sought at the onset of the crisis the services of the US and Europe-based accounting firms, consulting agencies, and investment banks for estimation and restructuring of NPLs, simply because there were no credible and reliable domestic counterparts. Understandably, these foreign firms followed Anglo-American standards in due diligence and restructuring, which were unfamiliar to and more stringent than those of the crisis countries. Furthermore, given the pessimistic outlook of the economy, they were inclined to overstate the size of their NPLs at the banks. Additionally, they were concerned about their potential liability in case they overvalued assets (Baliño et al. 1999). As a result, in many instances, foreign accounting firms and investment banks overestimated the bad loan problems at banks beyond a manageable level, thereby further reducing banks' lending capacity and deepening the credit crunch.

Once subject to these new and tougher criteria for loan evaluation and due diligence, the lead or main creditor banks and debtors found it difficult to reach agreement on the modality of their debt workout. Insolvent corporations objected to what they perceived to be a 'fire sale' of their assets. On their part, commercial banks did not have the staff experienced in managing corporate debt workouts. Instead of evaluating project viability and the debt service capability of workout candidates, banks in Thailand, for example, were more inclined to recover their loans as much as they could by foreclosure on their assets if the candidate clients had pledged sufficient collateral or guarantees from reliable entities. Failing this, banks would keep them on their books and continue to provide short-term emergency financing to prevent any further losses (Pakorn 1999).

As for banks' capacity to lend, the institutional reform in which banks were obligated to comply with the new, more rigorous regulatory requirements, including a capital adequacy requirement over 8 percent, interfered with their return to normal lending. Since most banks were unable to raise equity capital, they were forced to either reduce their holdings of risky assets (mostly loans) or to issue high cost subordinated bonds to replenish their capital. Whichever option was chosen, a higher capital adequacy requirement proved costly and worsened their earning prospects.

In order to improve profitability, they had to tighten up their credit risk management and did so by scrutinizing the creditworthiness of small and medium sized firms.[2] Once public funds, or taxpayers' money, were injected into insolvent banks, authorities in the crisis countries set a higher standard of performance for these institutions in terms of net profits and the volume of NPLs. Knowing that the government had a low tolerance of further losses or deterioration in the quality of assets, bank management withdrew further from lending, in particular to small and medium sized firms. The new capital adequacy requirement (CAR) together with stricter loan loss provisioning and risk management further reduced the capacity of banks to supply fresh loans.

The credit contraction was severe, and there is evidence that during the first two years of crisis management, it slowed recovery as well as corporate restructuring, particularly in Malaysia and Thailand. In Thailand, for example, the tightening of both regulation and supervision brought about a downward spiral by making banks more reluctant to lend, causing a credit crunch, more business failures, and in the end a deeper recession (Pakorn 1999).[3]

---

[2] Lower profits lower the franchise values of these banks, further limiting their access to the capital market. Hellmann, Murdock, and Stiglitz (2000) suggest that the lower franchise value could lower incentives for making good loans, increasing the moral hazard problem. There is no evidence that East Asian banks resorted to gambling in the face of the declining franchise values.

[3] At the same time, Thailand's stock exchange stipulated the prerequisites for new entrants, stringent minimum profits for several consecutive years, and a minimum number of shareholders, among other things. Most small and medium sized enterprises were hardly able to meet these requirements, while their access to commercial banks and finance companies was drastically reduced (Pakorn 1999).

Part III

# Institutional Reform: Challenges and Prospects

# 11

# Reform of Government and Industrial Policy

## 11.1. The Role of Government

At the beginning of the liberal reform in the early 1990s, there was a general expectation that democratic changes would subject the public sector in general, and the government in particular, to extensive market-oriented reform. It was clear that a developmental or strong state could not survive political democratization. Democratization also raised questions as to the viability of industrial policy and an export-led growth strategy in a new era of market liberalization and opening.

Whatever its merits, a developmental or a strong state has outlived its usefulness in more advanced emerging economies simply because actors participating in decision making at the national level have increased in both numbers and diversity and the government has assumed a greater role in social rather than economic development. However, the challenges facing less developed East Asian economies—Cambodia, Laos, Myanmar, and Vietnam—are likely to differ from those that are more advanced. These countries are years away from establishing a functional democracy. They suffer from other structural deficiencies. Bureaucracies are weak and inefficient; markets are segmented and fractured; the number of experienced specialists and professionals who could manage national policies is relatively small in number and often scattered, making it difficult to bring them into the government to form a technocratic elite. They need to develop a strong but limited government—a state, which is strong enough to resist political pressures for market intervention, but, unlike a strong state, is willing to accept market-led growth. Reform priorities in these countries include developing rules and norms that could provide government officials with incentives to act in the collective interest while controlling corruption and arbitrary actions.

As for economic reform, there is the question of how soon and in what sequence these developing economies should go about opening their markets. Since the burden of transition to a democratic and market-oriented regime is likely to be daunting, they may be given the freedom to exercise opt-outs in the event their local and political priorities conflict with a given obligation they may have with international financial institutions (Rodrik 2001). Within a framework of a strong but limited state, these countries may have a better chance of managing industrial policies needed, to facilitate technology transfers and to rectify market failures that require government intervention, and paving the way for integration into the global economy.

Is there a risk that a strong state strategy may support and perpetuate authoritarian regimes in these countries? There is. But the experiences of the other countries show that such a development can be avoided if political leadership is committed to democracy. If the political leadership articulates an encompassing interest in the overall performance of the economy and the public demand for democratization intensifies, as it has in more advanced East Asian economies, such leadership could develop an efficient bureaucracy insulated from pressure.

In charting a new development strategy for the twenty-first century, many of East Asia's emerging economies may find it unavoidable to operate in a framework of a mixed economy in which the market and government complement each other, although policies and reforms in East Asia have taken a decisive swing towards the market. As Stiglitz (1998 *a* and *b*) points out, the issue is not whether the government should intervene in the market, but to what extent the government can make the markets work better, correct market failures, and assume a catalytic role of political expediencies that is supportive of democratic transitions. To play this catalytic role, East Asia's emerging economies will be searching for a new modality of market intervention and a new industrial policy.

## 11.2. Industrial Policy and Export Orientation

- *Is Industrial Policy Dead?*

For almost four decades before embarking on liberal reform in the early 1990s, almost all East Asian economies, including Japan, of the early post-war period, had pursued some type of industrial policies as part of their growth strategies. They did so to develop targeted industries or to climb the ladder of comparative advantage. Since the early 1990s when the liberal ideology of market deregulation and opening started taking hold throughout East Asia, the reform has been directed to reducing the role of the state to that of producing essential public goods and providing macro-economic stability. In fact, market liberalization and opening has left little room within the WTO framework for developing infant or favored industries, export targeting, and state coordination of private sector investment and production through various subsidization schemes. The WTO rules are even restrictive in allowing state support for research and development for technical changes including the absorption and adoption of foreign technologies to the extent it involves subsidies.

Despite the setting and enforcement of WTO rules and widespread acceptance of the Washington Consensus, the recent past has seen more than its share of industrial policies. Indeed, the reality is that industrial policies have run rampant during the last two decades—nowhere more so than in those economies that have steadfastly adopted the agenda of liberal reform (Rodrik 2004). There is no shortage of arguments for industrial policy. Indeed, the case for industrial policy may have become stronger with rapid technological change and economic globalization. It may be reactivated to rectify some of the market failures caused by advances in information and communications technology, which have moved an increasing share of trade in goods and services and various types of financial transactions across national borders to cyberspace.

A variety of technologies, particularly those associated with the Internet, have been disrupting and reducing the share of many traditional industries while creating a host of new service-oriented ones and opening new opportunities for exporting technology related services in East Asia.

Over time, the ongoing information and communications technology (ICT) revolution will change East Asia's industrial structure as well as its comparative advantage. Many countries like India, which has not had any measurable comparative advantage in producing and exporting manufactured goods, may suddenly find new competitiveness in ICT-based service exports such as software, telemarketing, and data transcription.

In the new global economy driven by ICT, however, learning new technologies can be very costly without turning to some types of industrial policy (Lall 2003). This is because information and communication technologies are linked in the production chain in such a way that imports cannot substitute for local inputs; learning them has to be coordinated across firms and activities. Rapid technological change also calls for the creation of new institutions for setting standards for quality and productivity, as well as more advanced infrastructure in ICTs. It even requires changes in the legal system. In Lall's view, free markets cannot bring about all these structural changes without government intervention. As Sachs (2000: 90) puts it, successful technological innovation requires close cooperation among the government, academia, and industries, that is, industrial policy: 'America has a sophisticated industrial policy for the uptake of ICT: so should developing countries.'

In order to adjust to changes in their comparative advantage and competitive environment in global markets, East Asian economies have been increasing their investment in knowledge-based and ICT-oriented industries to develop them as export-oriented sectors in the future. Except for Japan, South Korea, and Taiwan, however, other countries in the region have not been able to move beyond the technology adopting stage. If East Asian economies fail to keep up with global ICT technology development, they may render themselves incapable of even maintaining their current living standards. Since information technology is less likely to converge than other forms of technology, East Asia may find it difficult to narrow the current technology gap vis-à-vis advanced countries. A World Bank report (2000b) goes so far as to say that whether East Asian economies could create a second miracle may depend upon their ability to tap into the new economy. How then should the East Asian model be modified or adjusted to accelerate the process of catching up with terms of advanced countries in technological sophistication?

According to another World Bank study (2000c), a development model that capitalizes on the technology and knowledge revolution would require the following components: economic and institutional policies that facilitate a quick response to technological changes; a dynamic information technology infrastructure; and a highly skilled and creative population. Have most East Asian economies (excluding Japan) developed these fundamentals? Would the East Asian development model, deprived of industrial policy, be able to help create an environment conducive to technological innovation, as well as adoption?

The World Bank miracle study (1993) points to the region's ability to adopt new technologies. The study also highlights the region's well-educated population as one of its main strengths. In the 1970s and 1980s, many East Asian economies were highly successful in expanding their capacity to adopt new manufacturing technologies in such sectors as automobiles, semiconductors, household electronics, shipbuilding, and machinery. These sectors were then transformed into export-oriented industries. These experiences together with their relatively strong fundamentals suggest that East Asian economies will be able to catch up with Western information technology in the twenty-first century, given all crucial steps are successfully completed. The question is whether the East Asian economies could take these steps without government intervention.

- *Efficiency of Export-led Development Strategy*

In recent years, there has been a series of empirical studies that show that exporting itself is not valuable, as it does not improve the efficiency of the economy (Tybout 2001, Hahn 2004). After the publication of Young's paper on East Asia's low TFP growth (1995), it was expected that the efficiency of export-led development strategy would be scrutinized and challenged. The traditional view, which focuses on the learning effect of export-led growth, is that exporting improves productivity as it serves as a vehicle of diffusion of disembodied technology or knowledge across countries. If the learning and diffusion mechanism through exporting is in operation, the causality runs from exporting to productivity enhancement.

A number of papers using firm-level panel data from several emerging market economies show that exporting firms are more productive, capital intensive, and technologically sophisticated than domestic market oriented ones. However, their relative efficiency has little to do with the exporting activity itself, but that they are better firms to begin with in all respects in being able to, or choosing to export. According to these studies, exporting is a self-selection process: more productive firms enter the export market, because they are the ones which can bear, and later recoup, the sunken entry costs of transportation, setting up a distribution network, and design modification. In fact, these studies show that after entering into exporting, exporting firms do not realize any productivity improvements over nonexporters, leading to the conclusion that the causality runs from productivity to exporting.

If exports are not prone to positive externalities and spillover, then there is little justification for subsidizing exports and hence there is little that supports the superior performance of the export-led development strategy. Do these studies reject the traditional view of the learning effect through exporting? It is too early to make any judgment, but a recent study using annual plant level data on Korean manufacturing during the 1990–8 period shows that the learning effect cannot be ruled out: the positive and robust cross-sectional correlation between exporting and TFP is explained by both the self-selection and learning effect (Hahn 2004).

What is unconvincing about the self-selection view is that it does not provide a persuasive explanation on why better firms tend to choose exporting. It may be true that productive producers have the capacity to bear the cost of entry into exporting, but they also have the choice of remaining as domestic market-oriented firms. Their choice to export therefore means that they expect that exporting is more profitable than selling in domestic markets. If this is the case, then one can argue that there will be strong incentives for domestic market-oriented firms to improve their productivity to enter competition in international markets. Furthermore, exports were in general, heavily subsidized and still are to some extent in all East Asian economies. Given relatively higher profits and the incentives of exporting, more productive firms would be entering into exporting activity as they improve their cost efficiency over time. Subsidizing exporting can enhance the overall productive and technological capacity.

If developing countries need to acquire mastery over a broad range of activities, instead of concentrating on what one does best to sustain economic development, they can also benefit from following an export-oriented strategy. Global markets provide a wide variety of goods and services from which local firms can choose for their exports. Taiwan's experience shows that the export-led strategy can lead to diversification of exported goods and services. Rodrik also admits that conditioning subsidies on exports, which is an important aspect of performance-based incentive policies, has the valuable feature in that it ensures the incentives are reaped by winners rather than losers. This carrot-and-stick approach has proved to be highly effective in East Asia.

A rethinking of the relative superiority of the export-led strategy in recent years appears to have had little effect on the views of East Asia's policymakers. More advanced East Asian economies—South Korea, Singapore, and Taiwan—may have reached the stage of development when they can in fact grow out of the strategy, and perhaps they should as they are on the liberal reform track of trade liberalization. As noted in Chapter 4, they also realize that the strategy embedded many structural rigidities that left them at risk of exposure to financial crises. Yet they have been slow in and even averse to accepting a more balanced development strategy in which domestic demand is as important a source of growth as exports. They appear to be reluctant to part with export-led development as it had been the most effective strategy of sustaining rapid growth before the crisis and it helped pull them out of the crisis. Japan will continue to push exports as long as it is unable to recover from the recession that started a decade ago. China and other East Asian developing economies appear to be determined to replicate the success stories of other export-led economies in East Asia.

- *New Industrial Policy*

In view of the fact that the Washington Consensus reforms have yet to deliver the expected outcome and the potential benefits of industrial policy can be substantial, it is premature to propose that East Asia's emerging market economies do away with industrial policy in the belief of efficiency of the market. At the same time, however, it would be equally unreasonable to argue that East Asian economies can or should return to the old regime of industrial policy to adjust to the new economy. Indeed, few countries in the region should attempt to revive or emulate the narrowly defined industrial policy regimes of Japan in the 1950s and those of South Korea and Taiwan in the 1960s and 1970s in which government policies were focused on improving comparative advantage by identifying and subsidizing winner industries. The global community will simply not allow more advanced East Asian economies to return to the pre-crisis industrial policy regime while other developing countries in the region may not have developed the administrative and institutional capacities to manage such a regime.

Less developed East Asian economies could ignore the WTO rules and may demand a space for industrial policy in future rounds of multilateral trade negotiations. However, other East Asian economies will have to abide by the WTO rules if they do not want to risk losing their access to the markets of developed countries. Would there be a middle-of-the-road approach to industrial policy that may help East Asian economies in reducing the ICT gap vis-à-vis advanced countries without infringing on WTO rules? In order to operate within the confines of the WTO, East Asian governments are likely to move in the direction of allocating more resources to investment in education at all levels and funding for basic research and development. But investment in education and research and development may not be enough.

Rodrik (2004) proposes a new framework of industrial policy in which private initiative is embedded in public action that encourages restructuring, diversification, and technological dynamism beyond what market forces could generate. In this framework, industrial policy is a process through which the causes of information and coordination failures are identified and appropriate policy actions are taken to ameliorate

93

them. The appropriate policy action is directed to the activity or technology that produces coordination failures. As for information failure, the most effective response is to subsidize investments in new and non-traditional industries.

An ideal industrial policy process would operate in an institutional setting in which private sectors establish a flexible form of strategic collaboration. This could be achieved through constructing new and improving existing industrial clusters in order to exploit external economies associated with supplying a wide range of services, including financial ones, creating a pool of skilled workers, and knowledge spillovers.

Industrial clusters refer to regional concentrations of manufacturers and suppliers of intermediate inputs and various services including financial ones in one or multiple industrial sectors. They are generally supported by an infrastructure consisting of research facilities, business services, and a communications and transportation system. Industrial clusters are either vertically or horizontally integrated in terms of production and marketing. Strong linkages among firms and the supporting technological and business infrastructure, geographical proximity of firms, educational and research institutions, and financial and other service providers improve efficiency and hence competitiveness of the firms in clusters. Industrial clusters are ubiquitous throughout both developed and developing countries. In recent years they have multiplied throughout the global economy in response to supporting ICT and other technology-intensive industrial development.

There is now extensive literature on industrial clustering that shows it helps small and medium sized firms to overcome growth constraints and to improve their export prospects (Schmitz and Nandvi 1999),[1] as a concentration of firms engaged in similar or related activities can generate a range of external economies that lower the cost of production. The success of clusters for small and medium sized enterprises (SMEs) in Italy is often pointed out as evidence of successful clustering.

Clustering is particularly relevant to the early stage of development as it helps small enterprises grow by mitigating informational and other market failures associated with the provision of financial, technical, and market support. Since clustering can facilitate specialization and taking small investment continuously over time, it can serve as an effective framework for initiating industrialization in resource-constrained developing countries.

---

[1] See also the other papers on clustering in the same special issue of *World Development* (1999).

Once clusters are developed, they can relax the growth constraints on SMEs as they can create the opportunities for them to grow. If horizontal and vertical cooperation among the firms in a cluster can be expanded and strengthened, clusters have the ability to deal with the increased competition resulting from economic liberalization and globalization. This is because the ensuing efficiency can help firms that belong to clusters meet global standards for costs, quality, speed of response, and flexibility.

Recent studies carried out by the Institute of Development Studies (IDS), UK (**www.ids.ac.uk**) show that clusters can be more effective in terms of strategic responses to global competitive pressure if they complement their private joint actions with public sector support as catalysts or mediators. That is, successful clusters cannot be created in a vacuum: either central or local governments should help create a critical mass of firms around which educational, research institutions, transportation and communication systems, and financial and other business service firms can be built. In fact, many regional and local authorities have had a hand in shaping the development of clusters: many existing clusters throughout Europe and Asia have benefited from government support and intervention in their expansion. In fostering clusters, both developing and more advanced economies in East Asia may find room for an active industrial policy without violating WTO rules. The IDS studies show that as far as developing industrial clusters is concerned, industrial policy works better if it is decentralized and builds on public–private partnerships. South Korea, for example, attempts to duplicate the clustering success of advanced countries through expanding and enhancing public–private sector cooperation. It has begun construction of six high technology innovation industrial clusters specialized in robotics, automobiles, nanotechnology, and optical cables sectors with the objective of developing them for future exports.

# 12

# Institution Building for Governance

## 12.1. Governance

If industrial policy is viewed as a process of finding an intermediate position between market and public sector dominance, it will have to be democratically accountable and carry public legitimacy. It is then crucial to develop an institutional setting that will ensure the viability and accountability of the industrial policy regime. Industrial policy is fundamentally concerned with the provision of public goods for the productive sector. The capacity to provide these public goods requires good institutions.

The importance of institutions in economic growth is well known based on extensive theoretical and empirical literature on the subject.[1] As Rodrik (2000b) puts it, the question is no longer whether institutions matter, but which institutions matter and how to develop them. A recent World Bank study (2000b: 144) agrees: it shows that 'a 20% improvement in macroeconomic, trade, financial, and public institutions can add 1.2–2.0 percentage points to a country's per capita growth.' Of these institutions, those comprising a governance mechanism deserve the closest attention in East Asia (Yusuf 2001).

Governance may be defined as 'the traditions and institutions by which authority in a country is exercised' (Kaufmann et al. 1999: 1). According to KKZ, the traditions and institutions include (1) the process of selecting, monitoring, and changing governments, (2) the capacity to formulate and implement rational policies, and (3) the respect of citizens and government for the institutions that facilitate and mediate their social and

---

[1] See Mauro (1995), Knack and Keefer (1995), Temple and Johnson (1997), World Bank (2000b), and Rodrick (1995 and 2000b).

economic interactions. Each of these three qualities of governance is then summarized by a subset of two key indicators. The process of selecting and replacing those in authority is represented by 'voice and accountability' and 'political instability and violence.' The ability of governments to formulate and implement sound policies is captured by 'government effectiveness' and 'regulatory quality.' The third quality—enforcing the rules of society and preventing the abuse of public power for private gain—is measured by 'rule of law' and 'control of corruption.'

KKM (Kaufmann, Kraay and Mastruzzi 2003) then constructed indices of six governance indicators for both 1997/8 and 2002 using 194 different measures obtained from 17 different sources of subjective governance data compiled by 15 different organizations (see Table 12.1, reproduced from KKZ). Table 12.1 presents point estimates of the six indicators for the eight East Asian economies and of OECD averages for 1997/8 and 2002. In interpreting these indicator estimates over time and between countries, caution should be exercised as quantitative indices are subject to substantial margins of error. Even after allowance for these errors, changes in the indicators reveal significant governance trends in East Asia.

One of KKZ's findings shown in Table 12.1 reveals that the quality of governance in the East Asian economies is very low compared to an international norm represented by an OECD average in all six categories of governance. A more surprising result is that on average the quality of governance in the grouping of East Asia's crisis countries deteriorated despite their efforts to reform political, economic, judiciary, and regulatory institutions since the crisis. In Indonesia, the Philippines, and Thailand, control of corruption became less effective than before (Table 12.2). Similar developments can be found in the report by Transparency International (see Figure 12.1).[2] In all countries except for Thailand, political instability increased: in Indonesia, the Philippines, and Thailand, there was a decline in government effectiveness, rule of law, and regulatory quality. Malaysia, the Philippines, and Thailand suffered a setback in voice and accountability. The discussion on the East Asian government in Chapter 3 and KKZ's studies on governance leave little doubt, therefore, that the paramount priority of reform for a new East Asian paradigm is to improve East Asian institutions for governance.

KKZ (1999 and 2002) provide convincing evidence that governance matters for development: better development outcomes in terms of per

[2] KKZ indices show that there has been some improvement in the control of corruption in Korea. However, the 2004 Report by Transparency International shows a slight increase in the perception of corruption (see Figure 12.1).

**Table 12.1.** Estimates of Governance

| | Voice and Accountability | | | | Political Stability | | | | Government Effectiveness | | | |
| | 2002 | | 1997/1998 | | 2002 | | 1997/1998 | | 2002 | | 1997/1998 | |
| | Estimate | SE[a] | Estimate | SE | Estimate | SE | Estimate | SE | Estimate | SE | Estimate | Est. |
|---|---|---|---|---|---|---|---|---|---|---|---|---|
| *ASEAN 9* | | | | | | | | | | | | |
| Brunei | −0.82 | 0.22 | −0.92 | 0.29 | 1.10 | 0.35 | 1.32 | 0.41 | 0.96 | 0.30 | 0.01 | 0.77 |
| Indonesia | −0.49 | 0.17 | −1.13 | 0.25 | −1.37 | 0.20 | −1.29 | 0.26 | −0.56 | 0.15 | −0.53 | 0.25 |
| Malaysia | −0.27 | 0.17 | −0.09 | 0.25 | 0.51 | 0.20 | 0.55 | 0.25 | 0.92 | 0.15 | 0.71 | 0.23 |
| Philippines | 0.17 | 0.17 | 0.63 | 0.25 | −0.49 | 0.20 | 0.27 | 0.26 | −0.06 | 0.15 | 0.13 | 0.25 |
| Thailand | 0.20 | 0.17 | 0.22 | 0.25 | 0.55 | 0.20 | 0.25 | 0.25 | 0.28 | 0.15 | 0.01 | 0.23 |
| Cambodia | −0.56 | 0.25 | −0.91 | 0.36 | −0.25 | 0.39 | — | — | −0.56 | 0.29 | — | — |
| Laos | −1.73 | 0.25 | −1.05 | 0.36 | −0.12 | 0.39 | — | — | −0.80 | 0.29 | — | — |
| Myanmar | −2.05 | 0.17 | −1.75 | 0.25 | −1.38 | 0.22 | −0.97 | 0.3 | −1.29 | 0.18 | −1.46 | 0.32 |
| Vietnam | −1.36 | 0.17 | −1.45 | 0.25 | 0.49 | 0.20 | 0.65 | 0.26 | −0.27 | 0.16 | −0.3 | 0.26 |
| *Asia NIES* | | | | | | | | | | | | |
| Hong Kong | 0.15 | 0.18 | 0.01 | 0.25 | 1.03 | 0.22 | 0.92 | 0.27 | 1.44 | 0.17 | 1.25 | 0.25 |
| Korea, Rep. | 0.63 | 0.17 | 0.91 | 0.25 | 0.49 | 0.20 | 0.16 | 0.25 | 0.84 | 0.15 | 0.41 | 0.23 |
| Singapore | 0.51 | 0.18 | 0.13 | 0.25 | 1.28 | 0.21 | 1.39 | 0.25 | 2.26 | 0.16 | 2.08 | 0.23 |
| Taiwan | 0.89 | 0.17 | 0.71 | 0.25 | 0.71 | 0.20 | 0.94 | 0.26 | 1.00 | 0.16 | 1.29 | 0.25 |
| Japan | 0.99 | 0.17 | 1.14 | 0.28 | 1.20 | 0.20 | 1.15 | 0.29 | 1.07 | 0.16 | 0.84 | 0.31 |
| China | −1.38 | 0.17 | −1.29 | 0.25 | 0.22 | 0.20 | 0.48 | 0.26 | 0.18 | 0.15 | 0.02 | 0.25 |
| OECD | | | 1.40 | 0.24 | | | 1.11 | 0.26 | | | 1.35 | 0.27 |

[a] SE: Standard Errors.

*Source:* Kaufmann, Kraay, and Zoido-Lobaton (2002) and Kaufmann, Kraay, and Mastruzzi (2003).

**Table 12.2.** Control of Corruption

|  | 2002 | | 2000 | | 1998 | | 1996 | |
|---|---|---|---|---|---|---|---|---|
|  | Est. | SE | Est. | SE | Est. | SE | Est. | SE |
| *ASEAN 9* | | | | | | | | |
| Brunei | 0.32 | 0.33 | −0.15 | 0.66 | 0.06 | 0.76 | 0.34 | 0.61 |
| Indonesia | −1.16 | 0.15 | −1.09 | 0.16 | −0.99 | 0.17 | −0.44 | 0.17 |
| Malaysia | 0.38 | 0.15 | 0.18 | 0.17 | 0.75 | 0.16 | 0.48 | 0.17 |
| Philippines | −0.52 | 0.15 | −0.49 | 0.16 | −0.35 | 0.17 | −0.37 | 0.17 |
| Thailand | −0.15 | 0.15 | −0.34 | 0.16 | −0.12 | 0.16 | −0.30 | 0.17 |
| Cambodia | −0.90 | 0.23 | −0.57 | 0.28 | −1.27 | 0.27 | −0.87 | 0.47 |
| Laos | −1.25 | 0.23 | −0.91 | 0.27 | −0.70 | 0.27 | −0.87 | 0.47 |
| Myanmar | −1.37 | 0.20 | −1.25 | 0.25 | −1.30 | 0.32 | −1.09 | 0.27 |
| Vietnam | −0.68 | 0.16 | −0.75 | 0.18 | −0.62 | 0.18 | −0.60 | 0.22 |
| *Asia NIES* | | | | | | | | |
| Hong Kong | 1.52 | 0.16 | 1.44 | 0.18 | 1.66 | 0.18 | 1.40 | 0.17 |
| Korea, South | 0.33 | 0.15 | 0.45 | 0.16 | 0.18 | 0.16 | 0.51 | 0.17 |
| Singapore | 2.30 | 0.16 | 2.50 | 0.17 | 2.52 | 0.18 | 2.04 | 0.17 |
| Taiwan | 0.81 | 0.15 | 0.72 | 0.17 | 0.91 | 0.18 | 0.69 | 0.17 |
| Japan | 1.20 | 0.15 | 1.38 | 0.17 | 1.32 | 0.18 | 1.14 | 0.17 |
| China | −0.41 | 0.15 | −0.34 | 0.16 | −0.20 | 0.17 | −0.01 | 0.17 |

*Source:* Kaufmann, Kraay, and Zoido-Lobaton (2002) and Kaufmann, Kraay, and Mastruzzi (2003).

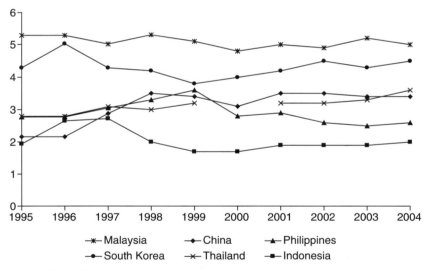

**Figure 12.1.** Transparency International Corruption Perceptions Index
*Source*: Transparency International (www.transparency.org).

capita incomes, infant mortality, and adult literacy depend on better governance.[3]

If institutions are as important as they are believed to be, what types of institutions do East Asian economies most need to develop better governance? If the needed institutions are identified, how could they be fostered in the East Asian cultural setting? Our conclusions to be drawn from the discussion in Chapters 5 and 6 suggest that the main thrust of institutional reform should be directed to building legal, social, and political institutions for governance indispensable for the working of an effective democratic political regime with deregulated and open markets.

As for the political system, it has been extensively documented, both in theory and in evidence, that democracy fosters good governance in the economic sphere: it is more effective in managing shocks, less prone to randomness and volatility, and produces more desirable distributional outcomes (Rodrik 1997). Democratic rule stabilizes expectations, provides the institutional foundation for monitoring government and private sector misconduct and a self-correction in the form of elections.[4]

Democratic transitions improved economic performance in the Philippines whereas they did not bring about any noticeable change in growth and stability in Thailand and South Korea before the crisis. Most important of all, the nascent democracies in East Asia proved to be durable and robust in the face of severe economic and social distress (Haggard 2000: 221–2). According to *The Economist* magazine, democratization has been so successful that it should be viewed as yet another Asian miracle.

Democracies must be complemented and supported by other institutions that make markets function properly. Rodrik (2000*b*) identifies five such institutions. They are: property rights, an independent central bank, and institutions for regulation, social insurance, and for conflict management. A regulatory framework should include: rules for contracting, bankruptcy proceeding, and regulations and laws governing financial institutions and markets. These institutions are essential in that they enhance market competition, while protecting the rights of shareholders and creditors.

---

[3] In order to establish the causality from better governance to better development outcomes, KKZ (1999) ran a series of cross-sectional regressions of developmental outcomes on each of the six indicators by instrumenting governance.

[4] According to Yusuf (2001), democracy has the potential for promoting good governance if certain procedural and constitutional rules are in place. These rules specify the division of responsibility between the central and subnational entities and between different branches of the state. Further divisions determine representation by different groups and regions of the country by legislative bodies and the formation of parties and specific election times.

Despite its urgency, building of these institutions has been a slow and uneven process. The old regime has been phased out, but a new system has yet to emerge. Policymakers of the young East Asian democracies have been under pressure to accept global standards and codes in managing economic, social, legal, and regulatory institutions while liberalizing and opening their markets. Just like policymakers elsewhere, they are accountable to the electorate, not to the market, and hence have not been able to ignore local constraints. East Asia has been hardly an exception to the dictum that politics are local, whereas economics are global. That is, 'markets are straining to become global, while the institutions that are required for their effective functioning—legal, social, and political—remain largely parochial and national' (Rodrik 2001: 1). This conflict would be more amenable if markets were driven by economic fundamentals and long-term considerations. They are not: they are often swayed by purely short-run financial concerns and, as a result, display excessive volatility, more so with economic globalization. This disjuncture between globalization of markets and the national scope of market supporting institutions has been more pronounced in tradition-bound East Asia.

In emulating Western rules and institutions, it would be a mistake for the East Asian economies to abruptly graft them onto their societies. Those imported rules and practices must be filtered through local practices and needs, as Japan did in introducing a legal system based on a German model (Rodrik 1999). Without proper indigenization and assimilation of Western reforms, there is the danger that new institutions can be disregarded or circumvented. Indeed, the force-feed approach of reform has begun to show its limits in East Asia: there is growing evidence that the old system of governance may resist itself in Indonesia and Thailand where the vested interests of existing asset ownership and the advantageous connections of large businesses have been protected and favored over reformers.

Ignoring the constraints imposed by local politics could deprive the crisis countries of the benefits of the signaling function of Western reform. Efforts at institutional reform in emerging market economies may often serve as a signal to foreign market participants that the crisis countries are indeed transforming themselves and capable of developing institutions compatible with those of Western societies. During the non-crisis period, market participants will most likely be indifferent to the quality of those institutions. However, once the emerging market economies are perceived to be vulnerable to a crisis, foreign participants seize the opportunity to scrutinize institutional quality and the ability of these countries to implement reform.

If foreign investors discover that the reforms are rather superficial, they may withdraw their investments. In this event, the reforming countries lose the signaling function of and past investments in institutional reform (Pistor 2000). This possible loss of credibility has thus far not been a serious problem in East Asia, principally due to the robust recovery since the crisis. If, however, foreign investors discover that East Asian economies have been procrastinating in their reform efforts, making them vulnerable to external financial shocks and their contagion again, their reaction will likely be much more unpredictable than before.

Western reforms have not been progressing in a straightforward and monotonic fashion: it has come to a halt in many parts of East Asia. East Asian reformers will therefore be better off if they let the outside world know that they will take into consideration local constraints and rely more on local knowledge in their reform rather than blindly following the so-called best practice model of Western and foreign advisors (Rodrik 2000a). Obviously this process will take many years, if not decades and, more importantly, the world outside of East Asia may not be patient enough to wait that long. Herein, then, lies the crucial role for international institutions: instead of blindly forcing the East Asian economies to comply with the Western governance, they should help these countries to develop a more indigenized system and make foreign investors and lenders understand why such a system is more appropriate to East Asia in general.

## 12.2. Public Sector Malfeasance

When it comes to reform of the public sector, combating corruption has always been one of the most important problems in East Asia. It is such a difficult and politically sensitive issue that fighting it goes beyond implementing liberal economic policies and enacting better laws.[5] Although they realize the urgency of at least reducing, if not eradicating the incidence of corruption, many East Asian political leaders have been slow or even reluctant to undertake many anti-corruption measures and campaigns. Anti-corruption efforts have invariably ended in failure in many parts of East Asia, largely due to the lack of political will or capacity, including proper strategies and structures. In many parts of East Asia, reformers are

[5] For a review on corruption and development, see Bardhan (1997). The World Bank has a long list of publications on corruption posted on its website (www.worldbank.org/publicsector/anticorrupt/readings.htm).

often those who have been corrupted or those close to corrupted government officials.

International cooperation could assist individual East Asian countries to develop the necessary will and capacities. In this regard, the World Bank has been supporting various anti-corruption measures since 1996 and the UN has also joined in an anti-corruption campaign (United Nations Convention against Corruption). In December 2000, seventeen Asian and Pacific countries agreed to join forces to develop a regional anti-corruption compact in collaboration with the OECD and ADB.[6] An action plan was produced and endorsed by participating countries a year later. The plan has three pillars: developing effective and transparent systems for public service; strengthening anti-bribery actions and promoting integrity in business operations; and supporting active public involvement. The action plan contains legally nonbinding principles and standards of policy reform, which the participating countries commit to implement in a voluntary manner. The implementation of the action plan is also designed to offer participating countries regional and country specific policy and institution building support. A progress review made in implementing the action plan in each country is based on self-assessment reports by participating countries. These reports are then assessed in regular meetings of the steering group represented by all signatory countries, a mutual plenary examination procedure.

The implementation of the action plan is voluntary, which means that governments in participating countries shoulder the primary responsibility for addressing corruption-related problems in their countries. International organizations and governments of advanced countries are expected to provide financial support for capacity building as well as meeting the policy objectives of the action plan. At this stage, one can only conjecture the future course of development of the regional anti-corruption compact in that it is the first regional effort for combating corruption in Asia-Pacific. The success of the compact will, in large measure, depend upon the level of determination shown by participating countries to reach out for outside assistance in the eradication of corruption.

The desirability of international cooperation in combating corruption underscores the importance of and the potential benefits from economic integration in the region. The disjuncture between local politics and economic globalization could be eased through transnationalizing the production of some of the public goods such as economic and political

---

[6] www.OECD.org/daf/Asiacom/Actionplan.htm

governance that individual countries cannot efficiently supply. However, global federalism, in which global democratic institutions could harness global markets, is at present beyond imagination. A second best solution then may be to deepen economic integration at a regional level, much as the EU has done. If economic integration proceeds as expected, East Asian countries could render support to one another and organize a region-wide campaign to bring under control the region's public and private sector malfeasance.

# 13

# Corporate Sector Reform: Governance

## 13.1. Corporate Debt Workout

Corporate reform in the crisis countries in East Asia has focused on the (i) resolution of ailing and bankrupt firms, (ii) strengthening of the legal system for bankruptcy, (iii) restructuring of large family-owned corporations, and (iv) improvement of overall corporate governance. After four years of corporate restructuring following the crisis, a World Bank review (2001a: 4–5) reported that 'major segments of the corporate sector have been subject to little or no meaningful restructuring' and 'the difficult part of corporate restructuring appears to lie ahead.'

In particular, the review points to the ineffectiveness of the London approach of voluntary out-of-court settlements. Owing largely to this voluntary feature, difficult cases involving politically powerful or obtuse debtors have been either sent to the court or remain unresolved. The approach has also resulted in low quality restructuring: instead of addressing fundamental structural problems—governance and balance sheet improvement—it has focused on temporary easing of debt servicing. Although an increasingly large number of cases have been sent to the court, weak judicial capacity has delayed the court-supervised resolution of debt collection and bankruptcy, resulting in a significant backlog of cases.

Three years later, the World Bank's East Asia update (World Bank 2004b) reported that progress in corporate debt restructuring in East Asia's emerging market economies lowered leverage ratios to a level in line with international standards, although in most countries firms with interest rate coverage ratio below one still hold about 10–15 percent of total corporate debt. But the progress in reform of the legal and judiciary framework for bankruptcy has been disappointing.

One of the major problems of corporate restructuring has been the extraordinary weakness of the judicial system in dealing with potential bankruptcies. Initially bankruptcy laws did not exist in a number of countries, and even now where they do exist, it is very difficult to implement them. The London approach was designed to find some practical way of getting around the reality that the courts were very slow and inadequate, and at times corrupt, in their handling of these problems. The key is legal reform, including good bankruptcy and restructuring laws, good protection of creditors, and mechanisms to force the process through.

The weak capacity of the judiciary has overburdened the court system with the effect of holding up corporate operational restructuring. However, strengthening the effectiveness of the court system is, at best, a long-term reform objective and, regardless of how desirable it may be, cannot be achieved in a short period of time. The lack of experience and the shortage of skilled personnel in the legal profession, investment banking, and areas such as bank regulation and accounting have acted as severe constraints on corporate restructuring.

Despite the urgency of reform, bankruptcy laws have not been promulgated in South Korea; they have been enacted but not implemented and civil courts are saddled with a case backlog in Thailand. Although Indonesia has adopted a new bankruptcy law, the commercial court has not been effective in resolving corporate insolvency because it has suffered from weak administration and lack of transparency and accountability. Only recently has China started the process of enactment of a new bankruptcy law.

Do viable alternative approaches to corporate debt resolution exist? The World Bank (2001a) supports the traditional approach of bank-led restructuring. However, this approach will succeed if there is a sound and efficient banking sector capable of managing the debt workout, write-offs, and bankruptcy management. And an efficient and sound banking sector is not on the horizon in many East Asian economies. In the meantime, market participants are not prepared to wait until East Asia puts its corporate sector in order. Should the government then intervene in the restructuring process, using banks as instruments? The answer must be no. Economic recovery will improve corporate profits and cash flows and also the opportunities to raise equity capital and hence ease corporate debt problems. Growth appears to be the most realistic option to the crisis countries when it is combined with government intervention to complement the court resolution proceedings and bank-led restructuring (Park 2001).

## 13.2. Restructuring of Family-owned Industrial Groups

The most striking characteristic of the East Asian corporate sector, in which a small number of large families control a large number of listed companies, continues to be an enduring feature. Industrial concentration in East Asia has indeed been overwhelming: ten of the largest families controlled more than half of the publicly traded companies in Indonesia, the Philippines, and Thailand. A similar figure for Hong Kong and South Korea was a third. In Indonesia and the Philippines, a single family controlled 17 percent of the total market capitalization (Claessens, Djankov, and Klingebiel 1999). Despite seven years of corporate sector reform, the predominant economic position of large, family-owned enterprises in Southeast Asia and the chaebol in South Korea remain largely unchanged.

Of more concern is that most of these large corporations and business groups in Southeast Asia maintain a controlling interest in banks and a large number of nonbank financial institutions. Given this type of ownership structure, it is difficult to imagine that these banks and other financial institutions could be entrusted with monitoring the financial and investment activities of large family-owned businesses. Nor would capital markets be capable of scrutinizing and watching over corporate malfeasance. In the absence of an institutional and legal infrastructure for protecting the rights of shareholders, replacing the family-based system with an equity market-based system can, at best, be a long-term solution.

What types of reform then will be able to improve East Asian corporate governance and restrain the collusive behavior among the government, financial institutions, and large enterprises? How could a policy regime that will discipline family-owned firms and reduce agency costs be developed? In view of their poor performances and structural deficiencies, should the Korean chaebol and financial dynasties of overseas Chinese tycoons be broken up into pieces?

One hasty solution was indeed to do just that in the wake of the crisis. Some East Asian governments, notably the Korean government, dissolved a number of the industrial groups that had overextended themselves to invite financial difficulties and mandated the surviving ones to lower the leverage, slim down their once sprawling operations, and improve the transparency of their operations. Khanna and Palepu (1999) on the other hand argue that since the East Asian industrial groups act as substitutes for the institutions that support effective markets in capital, labor, goods and services, the rapid dismantling of the groups could result in the weakened competitiveness of East Asian corporations and exacerbate East Asia's institutional void due to the absence of an alternative industrial organization. Instead of taking them apart, Khanna and Palepu therefore suggest that corporate reform should be directed to building investment banks, accounting firms, and a sound legal framework such as the SEC that supports well-functioning markets for capital, labor, management, and the transfer of foreign technology in the long run.

In the short run, however, they argue these industrial groups must be subjected to an internal restructuring that will upgrade their corporate governance, accounting methods, and disclosures in line with international standards. In South Korea, they have been subject to meeting a set of stringent requirements for transparency in corporate governance. After seven years of corporate restructuring, Chaebol reform remains a controversial and contentious issue. This corporate reform stalemate is not surprising, if one looks into similar experiences in other countries.

Chile took almost a quarter of a century to build efficient capital markets, and they are still far from completion. During this formative period, Chile took a wide range of reform of business groups in parallel with the building of capital market supporting institutions. Following on Chile's success, Khanna and Palepu suggest a number of internal reform measures for business groups that are shown to be effective in the short run: investing in internal information and incentive systems; learning to exit from money losing businesses; relying more on long-term equity capital from foreign as well as domestic sources; and adopting foreign holding company structures. In addition to these changes, the World Bank (1998) provides another list of long-term reforms that include: improving enterprise monitoring; enforcement of corporate governance regulation; improving the corporate governance framework; facilitating greater participation of credit rating agencies, securities analysts, and the financial media; and strengthening regulatory institutions.

At present, there is little disagreement on East Asia's need to catch up with advanced countries in managing shareholder value, and improving accountability and transparency of the corporate sector. This prevailing view also holds that management styles around the world will be locked into an Anglo-American trajectory, thereby becoming more homogeneous. Indeed, East Asian corporations operating in globalized markets may have no choice but to conform to this trend in the long run, but despite the apparent need, they will need time to adapt to the Anglo-American system.[1]

---

[1] Japanese companies now have the option of whether to maintain their traditional board system with an internal auditor (and an external auditor as well), or what's called a board committee system based on the Anglo-American Board of Directors model, with a majority of

Corporate governance is a set of mechanisms through which outside investors protect themselves against expropriation by insiders. In developing a new corporate governance, there appear to be two alternatives for East Asia: the bank-based system, à la the Japanese main bank, or the German universal bank and the equity market-based system. Contrary to the widely held belief, German banks did not provide effective governance (Baums 1994). As for the Japanese main bank, during the heyday of the Japanese economy in the 1980s, the bank-centered governance was regarded as superior to market-based governance (Aoki and Patrick 1994). After many years of stagnation and financial sector problems in Japan, much of the luster has disappeared from bank-centered governance. Japanese relationship banking remains susceptible to the soft budget constraint, i.e. banks continue supporting unsound firms that require radical reorganization (Kang and Stulz 2000). Japanese banks are also accused of colluding with enterprise managers to deter external threats to their control and collect rents on banks.[2] According to Aoki (2000), a crucial feature of Japanese main banks was the expectation that the banks would determine whether financially troubled borrowers would be bailed out at their own cost or liquidated. When this expectation was not met, the role of the main banks was greatly reduced.

These problems with bank-based governance suggest that East Asian economies should opt for a more market-centered corporate governance system, at least in the long run. However, for this system to function properly, it must be supported by a set of well-developed market supporting institutions that include accounting firms, law firms, rating agencies, investment banks, and bankruptcy courts. And it will take many years for these institutions to come into existence and mature. In the meantime, many emerging market economies in East Asia may have no choice but to rely on a bank-based governance system complemented by a regulatory system that is based on well-defined, neutral rules such as capital adequacy, loan classification, disclosure, and loan-loss provisioning requirements, which could minimize the potential risk of allowing industrial and commercial firms to control banks.

board members from the outside, or at least a majority of those on the three major committees (nomination, audit, compensation). It appears that Japan is moving toward a hybrid model which is not Anglo-American, with considerable retention of control within management. Note that for most of the East Asian economies the issue is not separation of ownership and control, but the dominant controlling shareholder (business group family) and the minority shareholders.

[2] See La Porta et al. (1998) for a further discussion and references on these issues.

Family-based corporate governance can be a workable form of govern-ance and thrive in such a market-oriented open economy like Hong Kong (Khan 1999) under certain conditions. These conditions include proper monitoring capabilities of the financial system, managerial expertise, and market competition. In the case of Hong Kong, insolvency and bankruptcy procedures are transparent, and accounting and auditing standards are higher than in other East Asian economies. These institutional features help reduce problems related to disclosure, corruption, and inefficiencies of Hong Kong's large corporations, suggesting that the family-based system could be 'an interim type of governance for some time to come,' provided, of course, that the monitoring role of banks can be strengthened beyond what it is today.

Although East Asian business groups have been slow in protecting the interest of minority stockholders and improving disclosures, they have been transforming their governance system into one with more Anglo-American features of corporate governance. Together with this transformation, institution building, though slow in progress, will strengthen market discipline and weed out inefficient groups. As East Asia's legal, regulatory, and financial systems mature, the hold of large industrial groups over the economy will weaken. Since the crisis, big business groups have sought to diversify their sources of financing by issuing bonds and equities and have come to understand the modern notion of shareholder value. Finally, the emergence of the new economy in East Asia, despite the fact that the region is lagging many years behind the US and Europe in its shift into e-commerce, will produce strong market forces that are bound to bear down on the management practices of East Asian industrial groups (*The Economist* 2000).

The widespread exploitation of the Internet will greatly reduce the advantages East Asian industrial groups possess in gathering and assessing information. As the cost of obtaining information has declined, owing to its sheer abundance and instantaneous accessibility to all, it has become easier for smaller and medium sized firms to move into knowledge-based industries and other territories traditionally dominated by the groups. Most of the Internet firms, 'dotcoms,' are small and tend to be financed with equity capital by venture capitalists or market investors. These businesses also rely much more on stock options as compensation to employees. As a result, the investors of dotcoms demand more transparency. In learning to exploit the Internet, most East Asian companies either forge alliances with Western companies or with Western venture capitalists, or most attempt to list their ventures. Greater exploitation of the Internet will yield more equity and listings, which will eventually lead to greater transparency and faster development of capital markets.

Seven years of institutional reform have so far received a mixed review and one may rightly question whether new rules and regulations governing Western corporate governance are being enforced rigorously enough to bring about changes in the behavior of East Asian corporations, particularly large ones. Now that the crisis-hit countries have recovered, there is the danger that East Asia's large industrial groups may start obstructing the reform process and colluding once again with politicians and government bureaucrats to protect their vested interests. In this regard, recent political developments in several Southeast Asian economies are not encouraging, as they have created opportunities for large business groups to slow down the reform process. Despite these relapses, business–government relations are likely to undergo fundamental changes in East Asia, largely because numerous social groups and more importantly, foreign investors, have emerged as countervailing forces powerful enough to block a return to the old regime of collusion between business, government and corruption.

# 14

# Social Welfare and Industrial Relations

## 14.1. Social Welfare

Since the economic take-off in the early 1960s East Asian societies have always been averse to the idea of introducing a European system of social welfare for equitable distribution of income and wealth and protection of the elderly and the poor. Before the crisis East Asia's emerging economies in general relied on a growth with equity strategy, an implicit social contract in which expanding opportunities for upward mobility are emphasized through investment in people and communities while avoiding large scale income transfers. Such a social contract may have been more compatible to some of East Asia's cultural values—the work ethic, respect for community and authority, and a tradition of paternalistic government. Within the framework of the implicit social contract, East Asian welfare policy placed its priority on investment in education, public health, land reform, and the support for small and medium sized enterprises for redistributive purposes. The growth with equity strategy was also an alternative to the expansion of social welfare for those who are left behind in the process of economic globalization.

Since the early 1990s, and in particular in the aftermath of the crisis, the viability of the strategy of growth with equity has been called into question largely because it has not been able to cope with social and political changes in East Asia. Most of all, democratization and market liberalization have brought about fundamental changes in the role of government in East Asia, changes that were not anticipated only a few years ago. The role of government is changing from that of leading economic development as in the 1960s and 70s to leading social development as a supplier of social services. The general public expects and demands, much more than before, governments to increase the coverage of and strengthen social policy to deliver health care and pension plans and to protect workers, low-income groups, and the elderly. These services were previously relegated to a category of secondary importance (World Bank 2000d).

A number of secular trends have also undermined the implicit social contract of the pre-crisis model of growth with equity (Haggard 2000: 187–9 and World Bank 2000a). Populations are ageing rather rapidly, while in some countries of East Asia the fertility rate is falling. Urbanization and globalization have reduced the capacity and weakened the willingness of the younger generation to assume intra-family income support for old age consumption. At the same time, inequality of income and wealth has risen throughout East Asia since the crisis.[1] These developments have put a heavy burden of expanding the social safety net, including unemployment insurance, on the government, when existing funded and unfunded public pension programs have a limited coverage of the population.

Governments of East Asia's emerging economies have been slow in making policy adjustments to these structural changes. They have not been able to increase the provision of social services because of the lack of fiscal resources for a consensus on the scope of social protection. Globalization has also complicated the formulation and implementation of social policy as it has created serious social tension by exposing a deep fault line between groups who have the skills and mobility to flourish in global markets and those who do not (Rodrik 1997). Economic globalization has made highly mobile capital, skilled workers, and professionals. This mobility has reduced the effective tax base in East Asian economies and weakened the influence of political coalitions that support a higher level welfare spending through tax hikes. Trade and capital account liberalization together with the expansion of e-commerce has further reduced the tax base. This tax base erosion often means that in order to support an enlargement of social insurance, governments end up taxing more heavily than before the very group of people they are seeking to protect.

Given this potential conflict of interest between those who are mobile and those who are not, Rodrik (1997) argues that market-opening policies should not be prioritized, since it makes little sense to sacrifice social cohesion for the sake of liberalization. However, most East Asian economies, including developing ones that will continue to seek the demand for their goods and services in foreign markets, cannot afford to be idle onlookers of the globalization process, and herein lies East Asia's

---

[1] A recent study (Yoo and Kim 2001) shows that there has been a noticeable deterioration in income distribution in Korea since the 1997 crisis, although Korea has managed a rapid recovery.

dilemma: to actively join in the globalization process, they have to provide more social services to facilitate structural adjustments than before while being squeezed on resources available for the supply of those services.

At present, social insurance systems for the financing of old age consumption in East Asia fall into two groups: the National Provident Fund systems of Indonesia, Malaysia, and Singapore and social security systems of South Korea, Philippines, Thailand, China, and other transition economies. The Provident Funds are defined-contribution systems with an emphasis on saving. Since they maintain a benefit-contribution link, they can avoid the financial unsustainability and other distortions of the pay-as-you-go financing of the social security system. In many of East Asia's emerging economies, in particular the more advanced ones, the ageing of the population and financing difficulties of pay-as-you-go systems caused by slow economic growth have entailed pension reform that has brought about a growing acceptance of a fully funded system.

The Central Provident Fund (CPF) of Singapore (established in 1963) is a mandatory, publicly managed, and defined-contribution system based on individual accounts rather than a benefit program. As a defined contribution, it is safeguarded from actuarial and deficit problems. However, the CPF is more than a pension scheme; it also provides financing for housing, health care, and tertiary education. Because of heavy financing of infrastructure and social spending, it is speculated that the real rates of return on CPF investment have been very low or even negative. Although contribution rates have been high and wage earnings have been growing rapidly in Singapore, the average balances for CPF members have remained relatively low, as a result of extensive pre-retirement withdrawals for housing and low real rates of return credited to members' accounts. Furthermore, the CPF scheme covers neither inflation nor longevity risks. Because of these structural deficiencies, the CPF does not adequately provide old age security, with the possibility of worsening pre-retirement inequalities. These defects may dissuade many countries in East Asia from adopting the Singapore scheme.[2]

The other type of the pension program in East Asia is the traditional social security system of advanced countries. East Asia's social security systems are publicly mandated and operated on the pay-as-you-go scheme with defined benefits. Like those of advanced countries most of the East Asian social security systems have fallen into serious financial problems and even those with a strong financial position are expected

---

[2] See World Bank (2000*a*) for the Singapore system.

to face financial unsustainability in the future. The Korean system is a case in point.[3]

South Korea has been at the forefront of developing a comprehensive social security system, in particular since the late 1980s. The overall system includes an employment insurance system (EIS) established in 1995, four publicly supported pension plans, and universal health care insurance in 1987. Of the four pension plans, the national pension scheme, introduced in 1988, has the most extensive coverage: it includes workers in workplaces with five or more employees, farmers, fishermen, and the self-employed. The total number of participants exceeds 16 million, almost 37 percent of the country's total population.

Fifteen years after its creation, however, the scheme has run into serious financial difficulties and its future financial viability remains clouded. As of the end of 1998, the gap between the amounts of reserves necessary for all future pension payments and the actual balance—the volume of net implicit pension debt—was estimated to exceed 120 trillion won (or approximately US$92 billion at the current exchange rate) largely because of the imbalance between benefit payments and contributions (Moon 2001). Since then the imbalance has widened further. If the current imbalance persists, Moon (2005) predicts that within twenty years the annual benefit payments will exceed annual contributions and the fund will likely be exhausted by 2031.

The three other publicly supported pension schemes have not fared any better in terms of financial viability. The government employees' pension scheme had run up a deficit of 3 trillion won by 1999. The private school teachers' pension scheme is likely to exhaust its reserves within a decade. The fourth publicly funded scheme for military personnel has been kept afloat by a huge amount of government subsidies. The structural weaknesses that pay out more benefits than received contributions, inefficient management of pension schemes and health insurance are well known in South Korea. Without drastic reform, which does not appear to be forthcoming, Moon (2005) argues that the pension schemes will impose huge economic and social burdens in the future. Conflicts of interest among various participants in the schemes have blocked much needed pension reform, and will continue to do so. Despite its relatively short history as a universal system since 1987, the national health plan has been plagued by financial difficulties of one kind or another. For all practical purposes it has gone bankrupt. By the end of June 2001, it had depleted its reserves.

---

[3] See World Bank (2000a) for the Korean pension system.

Social risk management in East Asia raises three related issues. One is the appropriate scope of social welfare, pertaining to whether individual countries in East Asia have developed political forces and the administrative capacity to mobilize resources needed for and to manage an elaborate social welfare system without impinging on their growth potential. The second issue is the choice of a pension system that is realistic in terms of cost and efficiency. Neither the National Provident Fund nor the traditional social security system appears to be viable in the long run and both require fundamental reform. A third issue is the question of whether there is any need for regional or even global cooperation for individual countries for supporting a full-fledged social welfare system in individual countries that includes publicly supported pension and health care plans in a globalized world in which capital and skilled labor have become increasingly mobile.

One of the major objections to introducing a comprehensive welfare system like the European system is that it could erode growth potential in countries pursuing an outward looking development strategy. Drawing on the experiences of the Nordic countries Kuhnle, Hatland, and Hort (2003), however, dispute the argument that comprehensive social security and welfare represent barriers to economic growth, because the system can be made work friendly and family friendly. They further claim that an elaborate social security system could serve as a shock absorber to countries suffering from a financial crisis and could even speed up recovery at a low social cost in terms of less poverty and social inequality.

In more advanced East Asian economies, where a substantial portion of the workforce is in the formal sector, conditions may be rife for introducing social security and other insurance programs as they have sustained high rates of savings and fiscal prudence. Haggard (2000) also argues that an unemployment insurance program can encourage job mobility and reduce resistance to temporary layoffs.[4] To Haggard (2000: 231), however, the European social welfare system is not necessarily a viable option for many East Asian economies, because of 'the absence of strong, unified labor movements and social democratic parties and nowhere in the region do such political forces currently exist' and that a realistic alternative

---

[4] A recent World Bank study on globalization (World Bank 2001a: 112) recommends institutionalization of unemployment insurance even though it acknowledges that unemployment benefits encourage the unemployed to stay out of a job. The rationale for such a recommendation is that a majority of the beneficiaries of the insurance are likely to be in the formal sector; therefore, unemployment insurance may create incentives to stay out of the informal sector but not to stay out of a job.

is some type of a middle way arrangement that could deal with the new requirements of those more exposed to external shocks than others. In countries such as Thailand, the Philippines, and Indonesia, where the prerequisites for unemployment insurance are lacking, the first priority of their social welfare programs is to alleviate poverty, and improving the design and administration of public works programs may be more effective than insurance in protecting the unemployed.

An in-depth discussion of the merits and demerits of the National Provident Fund and social security systems in the East Asian context is beyond the scope of this study. It is clear that without reform the National Provident Fund has too many structural deficiencies to be an effective social protection system. The sobering experience with social welfare policy in Korea should be an object lesson to other East Asian economies contemplating introducing a comprehensive social security system. In constructing a social protection system, therefore, East Asian governments cannot be too ambitious whether their choice is a National Provident Fund or a social security system. In nascent democracies, governments will find it extremely difficult to raise contributions while reducing benefits to maintain the financial sustainability of a pay-as-you-go system. Furthermore, since East Asian societies are moving toward a minimal state, it is unrealistic to expect that governments should and can be responsible for the provision of a whole gamut of social welfare services. Given the limitations in raising the necessary fiscal resources, they should limit their role to the provision of basic social insurance and assistance to the poor, elderly and the public. Mandated and managed pension funds that are partially funded should be complemented by private pension schemes, which should cover a growing share of social insurance arrangements for the active population.

At this stage of development, it appears that a vast majority of the elderly will have to rely on family and community support for their old age consumption in the future. Given this inevitability, social welfare policies regarding tax incentives, the legal structure, housing, and the targeting of social assistance should be adjusted to complement and strengthen the informal implicit contract system.

If they are targeting the poor, then one can make a stronger case for the growth-first strategy. As Dollar and Kraay (2002) argue, growth is good for the poor. Their empirical results show that overall economic growth leads to one-for-one growth in income at the poverty level. Furthermore, public social expenditure has little effect on either growth or distribution in poor countries because public expenditure is often not well targeted to the poor.

This new evidence underscores the importance of growth for the protection of the poor in East Asia.

Turning to the third issue of social protection, poor countries will increasingly lose their capacity to build a formal social welfare system in the future as a result of labor mobility. In a globalized world economy, once part of the globalization process, social protection may not be their sole responsibility in the sense that it will benefit advanced countries as well. For instance, a large increase in unemployment in the poor countries as a result of the decline in older industries (in part caused by their market opening) will develop pressure for large labor migration to advanced economies. If advanced countries are prepared to ease the burden of the transition of the workforce by providing relocation and training assistance to workers' economies, they will stay home. Every nation will then benefit from the assistance for industrial restructuring in developing economies. Development assistance for building the workforce capacity in the poor countries would therefore help promote indigenous development.

If globalization were to proceed in an uninterrupted fashion, social protection in individual countries would require global cooperation and assistance. Furthermore, globalization demands the adoption of common standards and codes as well as coordination of macroeconomic and structural policies. It follows then, that there is a need for pooling their efforts and resources to ease social tensions in any given country as a result of globalization for global welfare. At this stage of globalization, it is difficult to expect that such multilateral efforts could be realized, although they may be organized at the regional level. Developing collective social security by adopting common standards for social protection and organizing a region-wide support program, and harmonizing taxes in an effort to improve the quality of social services will provide incentives for poorer countries to participate in and strengthen cohesiveness of regional economic cooperation and integration in East Asia.

## 14.2. Democratization and Labor Participation

Up until the late 1980s, before inaugurating political democratization, most East Asian economies were able to maintain some measure of labor market flexibility through rapid growth. As long as the economy was growing 7 or 8 percent a year, generating a strong demand for labor, there was no apparent need to suppress wage increases. Rapid growth also fostered a highly integrated labor market with a compressed occupational structure of wages, and its benefits were shared as they reached the urban poor. Labor was, however, largely excluded from the political process and economic and social decision making at the national level. Most East Asian governments discouraged formation of unions among urban workers and often suppressed the activities of the economy- and industry-wide unions. As a result, a small percentage of the overall as well as the modern formal sector workforce participates in labor unions. Collective bargaining coverage is even lower than the degree of labor representation.

Democratic transformation has unleashed labor's demand for greater participation in political and social institutions, including the institutions for labor market governance at the national and enterprise level. Advocates of a more participatory approach believe that labor's participation is an overdue and desirable development in that the absence of democratic mechanisms had a role to play in causing the crisis and that the economic advantages of worker participation are unobtainable without independent and representative worker organizations. Subscribing to this pro-labor view, the tripartite procedures involving labor, business, and government are proposed as a means of improving economic performance and minimizing social instability through the resolution of conflicts that otherwise impede adjustments to external shocks (Campbell 2000). Rodrik (2000*b*) makes a similar point that greater and improved social dialogue at the micro level through participatory political institutions that mediate conflict among social groups, including labor and business, can facilitate policy adjustments and reform.

There are other advantages associated with labor participation. In a globally competitive environment, firms have to acquire the ability to adapt to changes in technology and product markets. This ability requires extensive communication between labor and management, which can be achieved more readily in a unionized setting. The problems of information asymmetry between labor and management may be another justification for the creation of democratic participatory mechanisms at the enterprise level. The interests of labor and management often diverge and, hence, relevant information is not identically perceived. Social dialogue or democratic participation can be a tool, solving the information problem, as it is a mechanism through which commitment is instilled and resistance minimized. In the end, better decisions are made, and they are better enforced.

The demand for labor participation has led to institutionalization of a large number of tripartite initiatives involving labor, management, and government in East Asia and the crisis appears to have given these initiatives a new impetus. Campbell (2000) argues that the Korean experience with its tripartite approach, which has been most extensive and influential in East Asia, is evidence that better social dialogue leads to better economic performance.

However, the prospects of the tripartite approach for industrial peace are not as promising as the Korean experience may lead one to believe. The new Korean government that came to power in 1998 placed the creation of a tripartite commission at the top of its reform agenda to restore industrial peace and to mobilize nationwide support for the economic reform it was about to undertake as part of IMF conditionality. The commission was inaugurated early in 1998 with the high hope that it would negotiate an agreement between labor and management on matters related to sharing the burden of restructuring. During the first year of its operation, the commission was successful in eliciting labor's support for a restructuring program that required a large labor shedding. A year later when the economy began to recover, however, labor was no longer prepared to cooperate, refusing to give tacit support to the government program. Two labor federations represented at the tripartite commission refused to accept any more layoffs resulting from restructuring and demanded wage hikes. When their demands were not met, one labor federation withdrew itself from the commission. Although the federation eventually returned to the commission, the work of the commission has been stalled in one dispute after another, and few in South Korea believe that the commission will gain its status or influence as a decision making mechanism for economic and social decisions comparable to those in Europe.

Many skeptics argue that in retrospect, the tripartite commission's ability to support restructuring was largely due to the timing of its formation, i.e. right after the crisis broke out. At a time when a national consensus emerged on the urgency of restructuring corporations and financial institutions, effectiveness of the commission might have not been due to its being an effective participatory institution for labor. They also point out that in a society where the tradition of social dialogue for consensus building does not exist, tripartite approaches would have their limits as an effective mechanism for labor participation.

One reason for this pessimistic view is often traced to the absence of political parties supported by labor. Worker organizations, which have a relatively short history in South Korea, have not had the opportunity to participate in and negotiate with other political groups in making economic and social policies at the national level. Partly due to this lack of experience and tradition, the government and management representatives find it difficult to conduct productive discussions at commission meetings. Frustrated at labor's inability to deal with policy issues, the government and management representatives have expressed their reservations about continuing dialogue with labor. Their earlier confidence in the tripartite machinery has been on the wane. Labor, unable to push through their demands, has often resorted to mass mobilization tactics. The fragile foundation for mutual trust among the participating members of the tripartite commission could not withstand the harsh realities of restructuring. This constitutes the second reason.

A third reason is that labor union federations participating in the tripartite commission represent the interests of a relatively small segment of the labor force. In South Korea, only 12 percent of the total labor force belongs to various unions. The corresponding percentage is even smaller in other East Asian economies. While so many workers are left out of the formal process of participation, critics argue that whatever decisions the tripartite arrangements may make, they are not likely to have significant effects on resolving labor issues.

Finally, in many East Asian economies, including South Korea, the formation of economy- and industry-wide unions is not allowed. As a result, loosely structured federations of enterprise unions represent the voice of labor at the tripartite commission. These federations find it difficult to control the rank and file at company unions due to the absence of a multi-tiered consultation mechanism at the industry and regional level; hence, they are constrained in enforcing many of the policy decisions they agreed to at the commission. Their relative inability to enforce commission decisions has rendered inconsequential whatever decisions the commission makes, as they are not enforced, bringing down the tripartite arrangement as a useful coordination and conciliation mechanism undermining the effectiveness of the tripartite approach in South Korea.

What types of labor market reforms are needed at this stage of development in East Asia? Labor experts as well as policymakers are divided over the choice between an Anglo-American system of flexible labor markets and a corporatist approach of labor participation favored by many European countries. The choice will be dictated in large part by the degree of labor mobility between industries and between firms (and eventually between countries) and the extent to which organized labor should be brought into the policy making process at the national level. After many decades of suppressive labor policies, and faced with the growing demand of labor for political participation, East Asian governments could no longer persuade labor or society as a whole of the rationale for discouraging union movements. They will have to find an appropriate place for labor in political and social institutions.

In a number of smaller European countries such as Denmark, Ireland, Norway, and Austria (Visser and Hemerick 1997 and Kock 2000) the tripartite mechanisms in the corporatist tradition are shown to be successful in promoting labor participation without sacrificing the flexibility of the labor market.[5] Although South Korea's experience with a similar approach has been less than encouraging, it is premature and unrealistic to argue that economic and political conditions are such that East Asia could not conceivably embrace the European tripartite approach and that the region should instead place greater emphasis on the Anglo-American tradition of labor market flexibility.

Nevertheless, strong unionism seeking political influence may not be compatible with East Asia's outward looking strategy. This is because together with a minimum wage, it will certainly reduce flexibility of the labor market. It may create dual labor markets that generate wait unemployment as people queue for the good jobs (Layard 2000). Workers should have some basic normal employment rights that include freedom of association, and freedom from forced labor and from discrimination in employment, but it is doubtful whether East Asian economies can afford artificial limits on working hours and schemes to promote an early withdrawal from the workforce and, by implication, unemployment insurance. If the goal of labor market policy is to create jobs and increase earnings of workers, investment in education will be the most effective strategy for improving the welfare of workers, as was demonstrated throughout the rapid growth period before the 1997 crisis in East Asia. With the increasing mobility of capital around the world, the earnings of the workforce of a particular country will increasingly depend more on its skills, and therefore education is the prime determinant of earnings and also an important factor contributing to a high level of employment.

---

[5] In Japan labor-management relations have been dealt with directly between companies and their employees. In some ways this was easier and more stable because of the management commitment to permanent employment for their regular employees. This made it possible to negotiate bargains not only over wage increases but particularly on job security. On the whole, Japan may not be a very good model, because of its unique political, labor and institutional characteristics.

# Part IV

## Financial Liberalization and Opening

# 15

# Progress in and Prospects for the Financial Sector Reform

Over the seven-year period since the crisis, it was not only the East Asian crisis countries that were subjected to IMF reform programs, but other emerging economies that made considerable strides in restructuring their financial sectors. As shown in 7.1, nonperforming loans as a percentage of total loans have declined in all five countries, most notably in Thailand. The quality of bank supervision, the availability of information, and the degree of private monitoring has shown uniform improvement.

In other areas of reform the record falls below earlier expectations. In particular in areas of governance, accounting, disclosure, and the legal process for liquidation or bankruptcy, all these countries have a large gap to fill before meeting international standards. The 2001 World Bank review (2001a) concluded that a complex set of institutional factors interfered with the reform process. The impeding factors include the political connections of major debtors, ownership of banks and other financial institutions by large family-owned conglomerates, and the lingering syndrome of too-big-to-fail. Inefficiency and corruption in the judiciary have further complicated restructuring.

Three years later, a similar report (World Bank 2004b) shows that despite continued restructuring efforts, there have not been any appreciable changes in the NPL ratios of Malaysia, the Philippines, and Thailand (see Table 5). In Indonesia, the financial position of state banks has become weaker than before. Although reforms have strengthened the effectiveness of the regulatory system, they have not necessarily reduced the vulnerability of the financial system in failing to prevent the rising household debt, particularly in the growth of credit card debt.

China is planning to open its banking sector to foreign participation after 2006. To prepare for the opening, Chinese authorities have stepped up their bank restructuring efforts. While progress has been visible in some areas, the financial conditions of the banking sector have continued to be weak. Most of all, the aggregate volume of NPLs reported as a proportion of banks' total loans stood at 15 percent at the end of 2003 (IMF 2004*b*). Reported NPLs under the four-tier classifications that include only overdue loans grossly overestimate the quality of banks' loan portfolios (IMF 2004*b*). Institutional reform of corporate governance and the ability to manage risk in the banking sector have been hampered by the historical legacies of the state-controlled loan allocation system. At the end of 2003, the Chinese government used part of its international reserves to capitalize two of the four state-owned commercial banks under its overall financial restructuring plan.

## 15.1. Banks vs. Capital Markets in Emerging Economies

The structural weaknesses of the East Asian financial systems were well known before the crisis. An intriguing question is why East Asian economies were so slow and nonchalant in attending to these problems. In retrospect, if these problems had been as debilitating as they were believed to be, they should have launched a wide range of reforms to open and diversify their financial systems. They did not in part because of the inertia and complacency bred over a long period of rapid growth before the crisis. The bank-dominated financial system, though heavily controlled, had supported rapid growth for three decades before the outbreak of the crisis. There were no compelling reasons to tinker with a system that was working well.

Policymakers in East Asia's emerging economies also subscribed to the theory that a bank-based financial system was more appropriate to developing countries where information asymmetry between lenders and borrowers is more severe than in advanced countries. Even repressive financial policies were rationalized. As the argument goes, problems of incomplete information, markets, and contracts tend to be more severe in the financial sector in any economy, whether developed or underdeveloped. These market deficiencies weaken and sometimes break down the functions of the financial system. And they can be more frequent and pronounced in developing economies, suggesting that imposing restraints on bank borrowing and lending may be necessary to improve efficiency in the financial sector.[1]

---

[1] Yanelle (1989) shows scale economies and Bertrand oligopolistic competition imply that unfettered competition in financial intermediation is not likely to be realized and hence, that deregulated banking may not lead to an efficient allocation of resources.

One of the implications of information theory of finance is that the more pronounced information asymmetries and the higher the transactions costs, the more preferable banking arrangements are to direct securities markets. In developing economies, where informational problems are severe because accounting and auditing systems are typically less reliable and shareholder rights are not adequately protected, banks have a greater advantage in monitoring lenders than capital markets. In the course of development, institutions specializing in gathering, assessing, and disseminating information appear, as do regulatory agencies that can enforce contracts and greater disclosure of firms and legal systems that protect the rights of investors. This institutional development makes it possible to nurture bond and stock markets. Even in advanced countries with well-developed legal and regulatory systems, however, banks have remained the dominant source of external financing.

Aoki (2000) argues for the desirability of relying on a bank-dominated financial system at an earlier stage of development on the grounds that much of the information critical to financial transactions cannot be digitalized nor disclosed because it is tacit. The role of banks, in contrast to that of capital markets, is to process information regarding borrowers and their conducts that are often tacit. In providing finance to enterprises in developing countries, lenders in many cases have to deal with less standardized and unquantifiable information on the quality and reliability of entrepreneurs and managers, which is an important element of the *ex ante* monitoring of borrowers. This *ex ante* monitoring dealing with tacit information is not easily substitutable by introducing capital markets.[2] Banks also have the advantage of entering into repeated transactions and relationships with borrowers in order to mitigate informational distortions by sharing information and building trust. This relationship banking, in turn, can facilitate the provision of long-term (or at least ongoing) credit much more than open securities markets. The disadvantage of relationship banking is of course that it may turn into mechanisms of collusion whereby bank and borrowing company managers alike hold the potential of extracting rents from their respective institutions.

In a number of recent papers, Demirguc-Kunt and Levine (1999) and Levine (2002) show that well-developed financial systems exert, independent

---

[2] Reliance on the banking system does not necessarily imply that the East Asian emerging market economies could ignore more specialized capital market activities, such as derivative transactions, securities underwriting and trading, and capital market monitoring. Aoki argues that this line of business should be developed in parallel with the monitoring of tacit information by banks, as they complement one another. To this end, Aoki advocates the development of a universal banking system in which the holding company controls the multiple subsidiaries.

of the degree of domination by banks and other financial intermediaries or capital markets, positive influences on economic growth. More specifically, their cross-country study indicates that neither intermediary-centered nor market-centered financial systems are associated with high growth in countries at different stages of economic development. That is, the financial structural characteristics pertaining to dominance, either by financial intermediaries or markets, are immaterial to promoting economic growth.

Instead, they argue that the legal environment and its development are more critical to financial development than financial structural characteristics. La Porta et al. (1999) suggest that the legal environment for investor protection and contract enforcement is the most critical determinant of the level and quality of financial services and, thus, of the development of both financial intermediaries and market. One implication of the legal approach is that protection of investor rights is a basic determinant of the financial structure. A legal system that provides strong protection of shareholder rights, such as the right to vote on key corporate matters, to select corporate directors, or to sue the directors and the firm, encourages the development of equity markets. On the other hand, a legal system that secures creditor rights such as the right to repossess collateral or to reorganize firms encourages lending. Such a legal system is therefore likely to be compatible with, and hence supportive of, development of a bank-based financial system.[3]

While the importance of the legal environment for financial development cannot be denied, it should also be pointed out that the legal approach has little to say on whether banking arrangements are less efficient in mobilizing and allocating savings and more prone to financial instability than direct securities markets. As shown empirically by Demirguc-Kunt and Levine (1999), national financial systems tend to become more market oriented as countries become richer and develop a well-functioning legal system. In view of the inefficiency of the legal system and accounting practices and disclosure that do not meet global standards, it follows that developing economies may have to rely on bank-based financial systems at least at the early stage of development. That is, given the elaborate institutional requirements for shareholder protection, many developing countries are likely to find that protecting the rights of both

---

[3] Corporate bonds are more like loans in terms of these rights and capabilities. The reason that corporate bond markets have not developed in Asia are precisely these problems of monitoring, poor quality of information and asymmetric information. When corporate bonds are issued in very large amounts, their cost (interest rate) is less than that which banks have to charge, or at least do charge. One of the reasons for this includes regulatory controls such as the holding of reserves required for banks.

banks as lenders and their depositors as creditors is relatively more expedient and less costly than shareholder rights. The legal approach therefore provides yet another explanation for the bank-based financial systems in developing countries.

## 15.2. Reform Agenda

The preceding analysis suggests that it is inappropriate to recommend less developed East Asian economies to invest more and initiate reform for capital market development when their banking systems remain unsound, unstable, and inefficient. This is particularly true for China. As far as China's reform priorities are concerned, they are: improving the quality of loan portfolios, transparency and accountability of the governance system, and risk management. A sound and efficient banking sector that ensures a stable payment system is a prerequisite to the development of unified and efficient financial markets.

Conditions of financial systems in more advanced East Asian economies such as Hong Kong, Singapore, South Korea, and Taiwan are different and may be rife for building and improving market, legal, and regulatory infrastructures and deregulating and opening capital markets to diversify sources of financing to meet the variegated portfolio preferences of investors. Relying on traditional banking is likely to constrain this growth potential.

The most important objective of financial reform is to have the market-based provision of finance, rather than controls over interest rates and credit allocation throughout East Asia. To the extent that credit allocation, whether through banks or capital markets, is done on the basis of market information and access rather than government direction, then interest rates should reflect market conditions. This reduces the rents that led to so much corruption in control systems. There will also have to be strong prudential rules about lending too much to any single company or to groups of related companies.

The agenda of financial reforms differs from country to country in emerging East Asia and is long and growing. At the top of the list is the strict separation of banking from commerce: the separation should be observed so that industrial groups or large enterprises are prevented from owning controlling stakes in banks and other financial institutions. There are other reforms that deserve close attention for building a more stable and competitive financial sector.

- *Privatization of State-Owned Financial Institutions*

There is little disagreement that financial reform should begin with the reprivatization of state-owned banks, nonbank financial institutions, and corporate assets in East Asia's emerging market economies. If ownership and management control of major banks and other financial institutions remain in the hands of the government, as is likely in these economies, the government will be unable to extricate itself from its extensive involvement in the reform process. This will delay institutionalization of market-oriented reform.

In a state-controlled economy like China, privatization has no meaning. At present China's prime concern is to restore soundness of its banks, and in this sense, its plan for recapitalizing the state-owned banks is a step in the right direction. After seven years of financial restructuring, however, the crisis countries can no longer postpone the selling of state-owned financial institutions back to the private sector: reprivatization holds the key to the successful reform of corporate governance, in general, and large, family-owned groups that dominate many industries, in particular. Reprivatization will also help ease the growing government debt burden from restructuring.

If the general principle of bank–commerce separation is to be upheld in emerging East Asia, then a single individual or family-owned conglomerate should not be allowed to own a large stake in banks and other financial institutions, and state-owned bank stocks will have to be sold to the general public for wider dissemination. However, ownership dispersion does not necessarily prevent large groups from taking over management control of financial institutions, because they can always command a large block of voting stocks by putting together a number of small shareholders through cross-ownership. Given the difficulty of regulating such collusive behavior, the government may choose to form its own group of small shareholders (usually other institutions it controls or owns) to thwart the efforts of the groups, as South Korea has done in the past. This may safeguard bank–commerce separation, but at a cost. It may perpetuate government control of banks and, hence, may not serve the purpose of reprivatization.

If a widely dispersed ownership of banks and other financial institutions is not a viable option, then privately owned investment funds can be created primarily for the takeover of these financial institutions. Another option would be to sell off shares of the nationalized banks to the public and then introduce fee-based representation of the dispersed owners to monitor bank management (World Bank 2001*a*). A third option is to create financial groups which are not subject to ownership restrictions are not related to industrial groups or do not own any industrial or commercial entities except for their stocks for financial investment. To encourage the formation of these groups, the government could provide tax and other incentives to large conglomerates to spin off their financial firms to establish an independent financial group or financial holding company.

- *Opening of domestic financial services industry*

In theory, foreign financial institutions—whether they are fully owned or joint ventures with local investors—can contribute to financial efficiency as they bring in capital and provide sophisticated financial management skills. In practice, this view is not necessarily backed by empirical evidence. Crystal, Dages, and Goldberg (2002) show that foreign banks in Latin America appear to have a greater capacity to make loans, absorb losses, and to make provisions for nonperforming loans than local banks. Since 1990, foreign ownership of banks and other financial institutions has risen substantially in East Asia. Foreign financial investors have also increased their stakes in many East Asian financial institutions. Despite the substantial inroads they have made in penetrating East Asia's financial intermediation industries, it is not altogether clear at this stage whether foreign-owned or -controlled financial institutions have contributed to recovery and restructuring of the financial systems of the region, and if they have, how much. Lardy (2001) argues that their contribution in Asia was below initial expectations and smaller than in parts of Latin America.

The role of foreign financial institutions in providing management skills is difficult to assess, but pieces of anecdotal evidence suggest that it has not been impressive. Foreign financial institutions are not going to serve as the vanguard of financial reform or upgrading financial efficiency of the financial systems of countries where they operate; they are there to earn profits. Their presence does not guarantee that these institutions will install highly paid managers and introduce the best management practices. In many cases, they cannot recruit top-class managers and have to work with the local staff. More importantly, they tend to assimilate into the local financial environment. Foreign buyers that come in and take over banks have different cultures and traditions. The contribution of foreign banks largely depends on whether the foreign owner is a banking institution that intends to exist in perpetuity, or a private equity investor that intends to turn the bank around and then sell it again.

It is also true that they often do not receive national treatment in their lending and borrowing operations. Accorded national treatment, they may be able to compete with domestic firms and serve as a catalyst for a broader reform of the financial system. Even if the contribution of foreign financial institutions is not clear or quantitatively significant, it is undeniable that economic forces driving the globalization of finance will bring pressure to bear on East Asian economies to adjust to this trend by opening their intermediation markets and providing a level playing field to foreign competitors. In China, opening financial intermediation industries to foreign participation will serve as a catalyst for financial modernization.

Policymakers from both emerging East Asia and China should consider taking advantage of their market opening as an opportunity to exert pressure on domestic financial institutions to improve their balance sheets and operations as well as consolidating themselves through mergers and acquisitions. Foreign competition will serve as a credible threat to domestic financial institutions in this context. Unless domestic financial institutions reform themselves voluntarily, they will not only lose their market share but run the risk of also being driven out of the domestic intermediation market.[4]

## • *Universal Banking and Capital Market Development*

By enacting the Gramm-Leach-Bliley (GLB) Act of 1999 the US repealed several Federal laws and overrode numerous state laws to permit the creation of new financial holding companies that establish separate but affiliated subsidiaries to engage in commercial banking, investment banking, and insurance business. The GLB Act has broken the wall separating commercial banking from capital market and insurance activities, thereby giving greater opportunities for diversification. Even before the GLB enactment, East Asian economies relaxed restrictions on commercial banks to conduct investment banking. It appears that the GLB Act has encouraged further relaxation.

---

[4] A recent study on foreign ownership of local banks (Crystal, Dages, and Goldberg 2001) does not find any major differences in soundness and stability between large foreign and domestic retail-oriented banks in Chile, Colombia, and Argentina. The same study, however, finds that in terms of loan growth, provisioning expense, and loan-loss provisioning, foreign banks in general outperform domestically owned banks. On the basis of these findings, the authors conclude that foreign bank entrants into emerging markets extend positive influences on the stability and development of local banks. Another recent study on the Korean banking sector development (Hwang, Kim, and Shin 2001) shows that branches of foreign banks in South Korea did not discriminate between sound and bad banks in their lending and their foreign currency loans did not display any cyclical pattern.

Recent empirical studies also show that removing restrictions on the ability to diversify bank activities is likely to increase banks' soundness (Barth et al. 2000). This expansion of universal banking has therefore made inconsequential the debate on the relative efficiency of the bank-based vs. market-based financial structure in more advanced East Asian economies and whether they should place more emphasis on capital market development. If universal banking is allowed, then reform of the legal and regulatory system should be geared to supporting the development of both the banking sector and capital market.

Along with legal reform, accounting and auditing rules are also in need of reform to conform to the global standards, and more importantly should be enforced so that information asymmetry between private investors and firms issuing equities and bonds can be mitigated. Private investors have the right to have accurate information on earnings prospects, debt service capacity, and the governance structure of issuing firms. For the development of the corporate bond market, a reliable bankruptcy law should also be established. In universal banking, banks are exposed to more risks than before and hence are required to improve their risk management and at the same time should be subject to greater restriction on their asset management. The ADBI report (Yoshitomi 2003) advocates universal banking as a capital market development strategy. Given their dominant position, high reputation, and information advantage, the report argues that banks should be encouraged to issue, underwrite, guarantee, and invest in corporate bonds.

Universal banking has many advantages, but also serious disadvantages that led to barring historically commercial banks from engaging in investment banking. The most serious problem is the conflict of interest between banks and private investors. It is possible that banks could underwrite bonds or stocks of troubled borrowers and to use the proceeds of the issues to pay off bank's loans to firms.[5] The mitigation of potential conflicts of interest arising from expanding the scope of bank activities will require strengthening prudential regulation in the banking sector.

---

[5] See Yoshitomi (2003: ch. 4) for a full discussion on the advantages and disadvantages of universal banking.

# 16

# Exchange Rate Regimes: Fear of Floating

## 16.1. Reluctant Floaters

Many studies have shown that an exchange rate fixed at an untenable level can be one of the major causes of financial crises, as was the case in Mexico, East Asia, and Russia. Intermediate regimes such as adjustable pegs have also proved to be unworkable over any length of time for those emerging market economies integrated or integrating into international capital markets and should not be expected to be viable (Fischer 2001, Velasco and Larrain 2001). The major part of the argument against nonfloating regimes is that they undermine monetary independence when the capital account is fully liberalized. Countries that adopt free floating, on the other hand, benefit from independent central banks, which provide seignorage as well as the services of lender of last resort; they are also able to make adjustments to changes in the terms of trade or export markets, even in the presence of wage-price rigidities.

Echoing the general support for exchange rate flexibility, Blinder (1999) argues that floats should be the accepted norm in the new financial architecture. Williamson (2000: 15–16), long an advocate of intermediate regimes for emerging market economies, concedes in his book that 'no country that had been allowing its currency to float reasonably freely has suffered a crisis anywhere near as acute as those experienced by the East Asian victims of the 1997 crisis,' although this evidence does not necessarily mean that crises are impossible in flexible exchange rate regimes.

While there has been growing acceptance of free floating for emerging market economies, intermediate regimes have, by no means, been hollowed out. Frankel (1999), Williamson (2000), Rogoff et al. (2003), and Reinhart and Rogoff (2004) still believe that a variety of adjustable peg systems, or managed floating, are likely to be more appropriate to a large segment of emerging market economies than the two corner solutions—pure floating and currency board. Using the Natural classification scheme devised by Reinhart and Rogoff (2004) and Rogoff et al. (2003: 54) show that intermediate regimes have been durable: there is no evidence suggesting the hollowing out of the spectrum of exchange rate regimes. In particular, according to the authors, few countries classified as emerging and developing economies adopt a free floating regime. The main reason for this persistence is that 'intermediate regimes deliver lower inflation, at apparently little cost in terms of lost growth or higher volatility.'

A number of East Asia's emerging economies chose free floating after the 1997 crisis, but they have been so heavily engaged in stabilizing their nominal exchange rates that to McKinnon (2003) they were de facto peggers. Malaysia decided to adopt a fixed exchange rate system in the midst of a crisis, China continues to adhere to what it calls a 'managed floating system,' and other East Asian *de jure* floaters intervene extensively to stabilize their nominal or real exchange rates. According to the classifications by the IMF and Levy-Yeyati and Sturzenegger (2004), the Philippines appear to be the only free floater among East Asia's emerging economies. In this section, a number of old and new arguments against floating are discussed. They by no means justify the pervasiveness of intervention in the foreign exchange market in East Asia. They are presented here to describe the alleged rationale behind interventionist exchange rate policies of East Asian economies.

- *Export-Led Development Strategy*

As will be argued in Chapter 23, there is every indication that East Asia's emerging economies including China will continue to adhere to an export-led growth strategy to catch up with the living standards of advanced economies. Free floating conflicts with this development strategy for two reasons: high volatility of the exchange rate and a lack of market supporting infrastructure. With the deregulation of capital account transactions, capital flows have increasingly dominated changes in the nominal exchange rate in many emerging market economies. In this new financial environment there is no reason to believe that a market-determined equilibrium real exchange (that may or may not satisfy the arbitrage relation) will also be the rate that could balance the current account or maintain export competitiveness. If stabilizing a real effective exchange rate is a policy objective as in many of East Asia's emerging economies, then this objective may not be consistent with free floating. This means that large swings in the nominal exchange rate could cause misalignment of the real exchange rate. The misalignment then poses a major policy concern to those economies pursuing an export-led development strategy.

Under flexible rates, exchange rates often fluctuate excessively as a result of unexpected changes in investors' sentiments, in particular in small economies with open capital markets.[1] As shown in Figures 16.1(*a*) and (*b*)

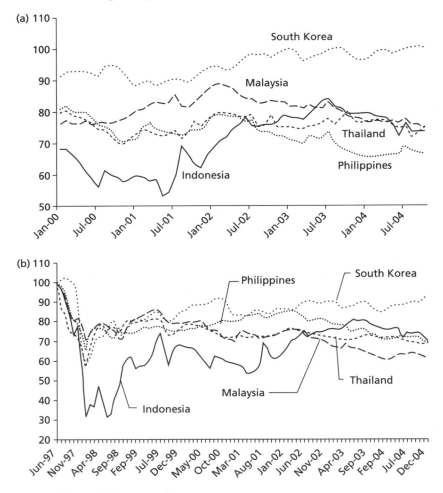

**Figure 16.1.** Real effective exchange rate

*Source*: (a) Asian Development Bank, Asia Regional Information Center (www.aric.adb.org). (b) International Monetary Fund, International Financial Statistics.

[1] See Mussa et al. (2000) for a higher degree of volatility of the exchange rate in the free floating system.

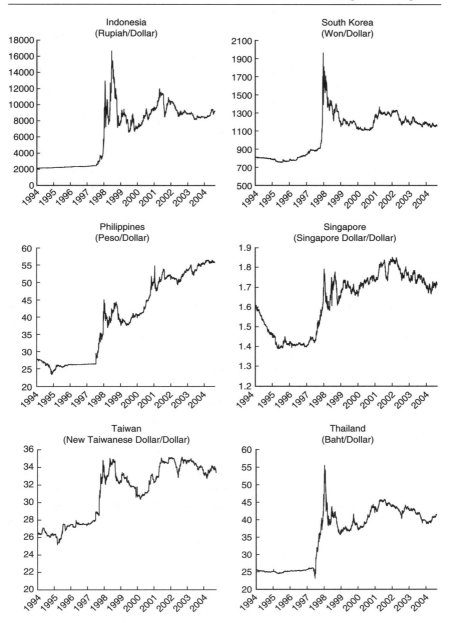

**Figure 16.2.** Daily exchange rate movements

*Source*: Bloomberg Terminal Ltd.

and 16.2 indices of both real as well as nominal exchange rates of East Asia's emerging economies have displayed considerable instability. After a relatively stable period thereafter, the real exchange rates collapsed when the crisis broke out in 1997. Since then, they have been fluctuating over a wide margin. These fluctuations are often unrelated to fundamentals, causing undesirable changes in real exchange rates. This volatility is the rationale behind insulating exchange rates from destabilizing speculation and is a component of the fear of floating.[2]

Changes in the exchange rates of the three major currencies—the US dollar, the euro, and the yen—could, and in fact do, augment volatility of both the nominal and real effective exchange rates of the East Asian currencies. Most of East Asia's emerging economies trade heavily with Japan and increasingly compete against Japanese exporters in third markets. Large swings in the yen–dollar exchange rate are then translated into large changes in their real effective exchange rates, causing unwarranted changes in their export competitiveness.

For example, when the yen depreciates against the dollar, the other East Asian economies experience an appreciation of their currencies in real effective terms so long as their dollar exchange rates remain unchanged. Unless their currencies depreciate vis-à-vis the dollar, they will be too strong, even though their fundamentals have not changed. The Japanese economy then expands as their exports become relatively more competitive, while other East Asian economies experience a slowdown in their growth, generating a divergence in the business cycles of Japan and the rest of East Asia. Policymakers of other East Asian economies will then come under pressure to restore their export competitiveness.

The volatility problem is compounded when foreign exchange markets are shallow, illiquid, and deficient in the market supporting infrastructure as they are in many East Asian emerging economies. At the initial stage of deregulation in the early 1990s, there was the concern that the high degree of volatility would be unbearable to small and medium sized firms when they had limited or no access to hedging. The number of participants in the foreign exchange market was small. Domestic banks were unable to serve

---

[2] Jeanne and Rose (1999) introduce noise trading in a model of exchange rate determination. Noise traders who decide whether or not to enter the currency markets endogenously determine the size of the volatility. In this model, free floating is associated with multiple equilibria with different levels of exchange rate volatility for the same level of fundamental volatility, because noise trading causes high exchange rate volatility. The presence of more trading is a free floating regime. This means that a credible commitment to reduce exchange rate stability could pin down the economy on an equilibrium characterized by low exchange rate volatility and low noise trading without sacrificing monetary independence.

as market makers because they had limited lines of foreign exchange credit from foreign banks and many of them were inexperienced in and lacking skilled staff capable of managing the risks involved in forward transactions. A small variety of short-term financial instruments in terms of maturities available in the domestic financial market limited the menu of forward contracts. Because of these institutional deficiencies, domestic banks had difficulty in squaring their foreign exchange position and hence were reluctant to offer forward contracts even when they were able to do so.

After almost a decade of reform, these institutional deficiencies still remain.[3] Currency futures and options are available in some emerging market economies, but the markets for these instruments are in their infancy— small and illiquid. Building a market infrastructure is likely to stretch over a long period. In the short run policymakers find justification to intervene in the currency market on the grounds of a lack of market infrastructure. The intervention then delays market infrastructure development.

- *Destabilizing expectations and Currency mismatches:*
  *Boom-Bust Cycle*

In a world of free capital mobility, free floating could exacerbate rather than temper the boom and bust cycle as capital flows tend to be procyclical. Because of this cyclical feature the system may not be able to guard against speculative disturbances. For example, a large increase in capital inflows attracted by the prospect of a boom in asset markets such as those of equities and land generate pressure on the currency to appreciate. But if foreign investors expect that the boom will be sustained, the initial appreciation may not deter or reverse the inflows. In fact, so long as this expectation persists, both domestic and foreign investors are likely to come to believe that asset prices will go up further.[4]

This expectation could in turn attract further foreign capital inflows. In the absence of sterilization, the inflows will then lead to monetary expansion, fulfilling the asset inflation expectation. If, on the other hand, the

---

[3] In South Korea, for example, only large industrial groups have been able to hedge their foreign exchange exposure through forward transactions. Small and medium sized firms are required to provide collateral for forward cover, making the cost of hedging much higher than that of large firms. Most small and medium sized firms also lack skilled staff capable of managing complex arrangements involved in hedging operations.

[4] For the sake of simplicity, it is assumed that the domestic bond market is underdeveloped and closed to foreign investors as it is in many emerging market economies.

inflows are sterilized, then domestic interest rates will increase, inducing further inflows. Asset price inflation keeps the currency strong, but the booming asset markets and the subsequent expansion in domestic demand may fail to generate expectations of depreciation as long as the speculative binge continues, resulting in further inflows, which in turn, feed on speculation in the asset market.[5]

The appreciation of the currency is bound to undermine the competitiveness of exports and to shift resources to the nontradeable sector; eventually export earnings fall, causing a deterioration in the current account. It may take some time for the appreciation to run its course. Only when the current account begins to show signs of a large deterioration would an expectation of currency depreciation set in. Once the current account deficit is perceived to exceed sustainable levels, market expectations may suddenly shift and foreign portfolio investors and lenders may pull their investments out all at once. Such an exodus of foreign investors could easily cause an overshooting of exchange rate depreciation and provoke a major financial crisis as it did in Thailand in 1997.[6]

A large depreciation could subsequently downgrade sovereign ratings and reduce accessibility of the emerging economy in question to international financial market (Goldfajn and Werlang 2000, Calvo and Reinhart 2000, and Hausmann et al. 1999). The depreciation could also cause a sharp deterioration of balance sheets of financial institutions and corporations exposed to a large amount of US dollar denominated debts (Calvo and Reinhart 2000; Eichengreen and Hausmann 1999; Goldfajn and Olivares 2001; and Mussa et al. 2000).

Although Hernandez and Montiel (2001) discount the fear of floating associated with currency mismatches in the East Asian context, the fear was serious enough to prioritize the protection of the currency over economic recovery in Thailand. In June 2001, the Thai authorities raised the short-term interest rate by 100 basis points when the economy was in a severe recession in order to prevent capital outflows and hence depreciation of the baht (Bhanupong 2003). At that time, the yen depreciated against the dollar so that the Thai authorities were prepared to let the baht appreciate in real terms. Although short-term foreign debt as a proportion of

---

[5] In a floating regime, there is a tendency that a change in the spot rate leads to an almost identical change in the forward rate (Svensson 1991). Williamson (2000) argues that this evidence implies a lack of market expectation that the exchange rate may return to an equilibrium level 'within any time horizon relevant to market participants.' Given this exchange rate behavior, the expected future exchange rate may simply appreciate as the spot rate appreciates.

[6] For a similar argument, see Furman and Stiglitz (1998).

long-term debt or foreign reserves was declining and so was the ratio of foreign debt to GDP, the Thai authorities would not take any risk of letting the balance sheets of financial institutions and corporations deteriorate.

- *Viability of Inflation Targeting with Floating*

The emerging consensus that free floating is decidedly less vulnerable to speculative attacks in a world of mobile capital has led the IMF and many experts to recommend variants of the Mundell-Fleming model with a Phillips curve and inflation targeting as a new macroeconomic policy framework for emerging market economies open to international capital flows.[7] Although the IMF has maintained its support for inflation targeting as a nominal anchor, East Asian policymakers have been reluctant to accept such a framework because their financial systems are not mature enough to operate it and even when they can they are not convinced that it will help ensure price stability with robust growth while avoiding large current account imbalances. Taken together with old and new arguments against free floating, this lack of confidence in the new macroeconomic system appears to have been critical in shifting East Asia's emerging economies to managed floating or other intermediate regimes.

In models of free floating and capital mobility with inflation targeting, such as the one developed by Svensson (2000), the current account appears to be immaterial and its imbalances do not pose any policy problems at least in the long run because they are adjusted through changes in the capital account and the exchange rate. For a given intertemporal budget constraint, for example, the amount of money a country can borrow on a net basis from international capital markets at any point in time can be approximated by its debt servicing capacity, which is the present value of its future current account surpluses.

For a given level of external debt, then, consider an adverse external shock to exports in this economy. This shock is likely to result in a lower level of income, a fall in the interest rate, a weaker currency, and a deficit on the current account (assumed to be in balance to begin with). In the new macroeconomic policy framework, this deficit does not pose any serious problem because it can be financed from international financial markets to the extent that this economy operates within its debt servicing capacity. If not, then this economy may have to let its currency depreciate in real terms to generate more future current account surpluses. In reality,

---

[7] See Svensson (1997 and 2000) and McCallum (1996).

however, most emerging market economies are subject to severe constraints on borrowing from international capital markets in major currencies, or more so their own.

The inadequacy and poor quality of information, non-transparency of government policies, and political instability often make it difficult to evaluate the long-term debt servicing capacity of emerging market economies. This difficulty is then translated into a borrowing constraint: emerging market economies cannot borrow as much as their debt servicing capacity allows. Therefore, maintaining the current account in balance or its deficit at a manageable level can be an important policy objective, as indeed it is in emerging market economies.

In the new macroeconomic policy framework, monetary policy is reserved for price stability, leaving fiscal policy for the attainment of other objectives. Faced with the slack in export earnings, this economy may choose to pursue expansionary fiscal policy to prevent a slow down in the economy, but it will aggravate the current account deficit problem further. If monetary policy is activated to deter further deterioration of the current account, then this economy runs into an unsustainable situation in which fiscal policy is expansionary whereas monetary policy is tight. This economy may in the end have to intervene in the currency market to engineer a depreciation of its currency. The new macroeconomic model is short of at least one policy instrument to achieve the objectives of growth, price stability, and current account balance.

Similar problems arise in the case of an exogenous increase in the foreign interest rate. This change induces an increase in capital outflows, which subsequently causes, other things being equal, a depreciation of the currency, build-up of inflationary pressure, a gain of export competitiveness, an output increase, and an incipient surplus on the current account (assumed to be balanced initially). Depending on the strength of the inflationary pressure caused by the currency depreciation, policy authorities may have to tighten money market conditions further to meet a predetermined inflation target. Tightening of monetary policy may prevent further weakening of the currency, but its effects on the current account are again ambiguous. If the initial capital outflow and the subsequent increases in output and interest rate create expectations of further depreciation of the currency, then the current account may record a surplus. Otherwise it will deteriorate. The new macroeconomic framework where inflation targeting is predicated on the assumption that the current account balance is not a policy concern may therefore be out of touch with the realities of many emerging market economies.

A higher degree of volatility in the nominal exchange rate also weakens the effectiveness of monetary policy in this new macroeconomic framework because it requires a higher risk premium for foreign investors to hold domestic currency denominated assets. The domestic interest rate that satisfies the parity condition will then be higher than in less flexible exchange rate regimes. The high premium will limit the flexibility of monetary policy in adjusting the interest rate consistent with inflation targeting; in particular, it may create a downward rigidity in the interest rate, making it difficult to ease monetary policy, even when a deflationary tendency sets in. In particular, this potential rigidity means a limited applicability of the Taylor rule in emerging market economies (McKinnon 2005).

The free floating with inflation targeting presents another problem in economies where pass-through is high and risk-premium shocks are rather frequent. In these economies, high pass-through and the lack of credibility manifested in frequent risk-premium shocks may require tighter control over the exchange rate (Calvo and Reinhart 2002).

Velasco and Larrain (2001) suggest that monetary policy could be employed to achieve objectives other than an inflation target. Indeed, if inflation is not a serious problem, they argue monetary policy could be directed to stabilizing the nominal exchange rate and even to exploit the trade-off between inflation and output. Goldstein (2002) also suggests that interest rate policy could be employed to smooth out changes in the exchange rate when meeting the inflation target does not pose a serious policy concern. Adding the current account balance to this list of objectives, policymakers of emerging market economies may be forced to shift from one target to another in conducting monetary policy, thereby losing the credibility of their policy actions.

## 16.2. Intermediate Regimes for East Asia

In view of the discussion in the preceding section that led to the rather ambivalent conclusions on the applicability of free floating to emerging market economies, questions arise as to whether East Asia's *de jure* floaters should move to regimes with less flexibility. Whatever its merits, East Asian economies would not find it practical or politically acceptable at this stage to move to a currency board. For one, they face an implementation problem of choosing a currency to peg. Although the US dollar and the yen are plausible candidates, neither appears to be acceptable to many East Asian economies. The fact that the currency board system is completely devoid of domestic lender of last resort also poses a serious problem to these countries. Intermediate arrangements such as crawling pegs with wider bands or the BBC (basket, band, and crawl) are other options, but they have their share of problems.

In reality, East Asian policymakers of the floating regimes do intervene in the foreign exchange market; they are, de facto, on an intermediate regime. According to Williamson (2000), the basic rationale for opting for an intermediate regime may be 'the fear that freely floating exchange rates are badly behaved, i.e. prone to losing touch with the fundamentals, as to become misaligned.' When nominal exchange rates fluctuate as widely as they have in many emerging market economies, Williamson (2000) points out that the real exchange rates could be misaligned. This means that the East Asian economies may not be able to maintain the competitiveness of their exports and hence to sustain the rapid growth they were able to achieve for more than a quarter century prior to the East Asian crisis.

Although it is speculated that the purpose of intervention in East Asian economies is primarily to keep the competitiveness of their exports, little information is available as to how and to what extent they intervene to influence the exchange rate movement. This lack of information on the modality of intervention creates considerable uncertainty in the foreign exchange market, which could, in turn, be a source of instability for the exchange rate. This section discusses the advantages and disadvantages of several intermediate regimes that include variations of the BBC, a floating regime with reserve intervention (Dooley, Dornbusch, and Park 2002), and managed floating plus (Goldstein 2002).

- *The BBC Regime*

In the post-1997 crisis period, Hernandez and Montiel (2001) argue that East Asian economies, in particular victims of the crisis, have been driven to generate current account surpluses to service their foreign debts as well as increase their holdings of reserves. At the same time, these countries were forced to float their exchange rates and to liberalize capital account transactions. These reforms have been inconsistent with policy objectives, in particular with accumulating current account surpluses, which has entailed intervention in the foreign exchange market.

Foreign exchange market intervention, though it may be justifiable, has been fraught with problems. As Williamson (2000) notes, East Asian policymakers have not made any clear reference to parity or an equilibrium exchange rate, or an intervention point in managing their exchange rate policy. As a result, the exchange rate policy has not provided an anchor for expectations on the exchange rate needed for stabilizing speculation. For a BBC system to serve as an effective mechanism for stabilizing the nominal exchange rate, market participants should be persuaded that the authorities are committed to the system. There is also the problem of managing the system when the exchange rate reaches the limits of the band. For example, when the exchange rate is driven to the depreciation limit, speculators begin to test the resolve of the authorities to maintain the band. In such a case, the BBC system often runs into the same problems as fixed exchange rate systems.

To mitigate these weaknesses, Williamson (2000) proposes three new intermediate regimes, which are less prone to crises by relaxing the obligation of intervention when the exchange rate moves out of a predetermined band. These new intermediate regimes include: (1) a reference rate system in which the authorities are not required to defend a parity or an equilibrium exchange rate, but are not allowed to push their currencies away from parity; (2) regime of a soft margin in which authorities target a moving or geometric average of current and past market exchange rates to remain within a predetermined band rather than targeting the market exchange rate to remain within a predetermined band at all times; and (3) a monitoring band system that requires a hands-off policy within a preannounced band, but allows intervention without obligation once the rate goes out of the band in order to bring it back in.

The three modified versions of the BBC may be more effective than old systems in reducing vulnerability to speculative attacks, to the extent that the band does not have to be defended. Nevertheless, they are not necessarily immune to the criticism that a reference rate or an equilibrium exchange rate cannot be easily defined or estimated largely because some of the economic fundamentals that presumably determine the exchange rate are not easily identifiable or cannot be estimated. Even when a set of fundamentals can be identified, in reality it may not be easy to observe changes in these variables as a whole that may dictate changes in the equilibrium exchange rate around which a soft margin is to be established. This problem may become more pronounced with the deregulation of capital account transactions, which may amplify the volatility of capital movements as it has in East Asia (see Chapter 17).

Another criticism of the modified BBCs is that they still may not be flexible enough to deal with large and unexpected shifts in capital movements and investor sentiments. A third problem with Williamson's modified BBCs is that since the modified versions remove the obligations of the authorities to defend the edge of the zones, their ability to attract stabilizing speculation becomes even more remote (Goldstein 2002). Finally, all three modified BBCs are not able to provide a clear nominal anchor for monetary policy. In these systems, the band serves as a weak nominal anchor for the exchange rate. Fischer (2001) questions whether such an anchor is preferable to inflation targeting. More important, all of the new BBC proposals for an operational intermediate regime have not been subject to a market test, and, hence, there is no way of knowing how serious these problems would be in a real setting.

- *Floating with Reserve intervention and Managed Floating Plus*

There are two new proposals for an intermediate regime that lie between pure floats and the BBC. The floating regime with reserve intervention developed by Dooley, Dornbusch, and Park (2002) has no exchange rate target or band: exchange rates are essentially determined by market forces, as in pure floating. It has an inflation target as a nominal anchor. The major difference between the floating with reserve intervention and pure floating is that the former allows monetary authorities to engage in sterilized intervention for smoothing-out operations. Policy authorities would intervene in the market if the nominal exchange rate fluctuated in either direction by more than a given percentage against a currency basket over a predetermined period. For the purpose of intervention, authorities would buy or sell foreign reserves within a predetermined band of reserve changes, for example, within a range of 25 percent on both sides of an appropriate level of reserves. If reserve losses or gains exceed the limit, then the authorities cease their smoothing-out operations with the assumption that the observed changes in the exchange rate are driven by changes in economic fundamentals, rather than noise trading or other speculative activities.

In the Dooley-Dornbusch-Park model, market intervention is carried out according to a set of rules. The rules include the following three components:

(1) Introduction of a flexible inflation targeting rule: A short-term interest rate would be used as an intermediate target to stabilize output in the short run and inflation in the long run.[8]

(2) Sterilized intervention: Volatility in daily nominal exchange rates in excess of, say, three percentage points against a basket of the dollar,

---

[8] Changes in the level of a central bank's total assets, therefore its monetary base, would allow the central bank to determine a short-term interest rate in financial markets.

euro, and yen is moderated through changes in the composition of the central bank's assets between domestic assets and foreign assets (denominated in foreign currencies). This rule allows the central bank to participate in the foreign exchange market without altering the monetary base. It could be extended to resist cumulative movements in excess of a given percentage in a predetermined period, say a week. The sterilized intervention rule would be symmetric for appreciation and depreciation as long as net reserves remain within a normal range. The authorities would not be obliged to intervene, however, if they considered large changes in the rate an appropriate reaction to changes in the economic fundamentals.

(3) Establishing a target level for net foreign assets (foreign exchange reserve net of foreign currency liabilities and derivative positions): Deviations in the level of reserves caused by operations in limiting exchange rate volatility would be eliminated over a six-month period according to a pre-announced rule. The target level of reserves should be large enough to initially forestall a bank run, but with accumulation of the experience in managing reserves, the level could be adjusted to balance the cost and benefit of maintaining a large stock of foreign assets.[9]

Altering the intervention rule would reverse deviations in the level of reserves generated in limiting exchange rate volatility. If reserves deviate by more than, for instance, 25 percent from their target level, the intervention rule would become asymmetric. If reserves fall (rise) by more than 25 percent, a larger subsequent daily depreciation (appreciation) of the currency would be permitted. If reserves deviate by more than 50 percent the rule would again be adjusted to 3 percent in the direction that moves away from their target level and 0.5 percent in the direction that moves reserves toward their target level.

The Dooley-Dornbusch-Park model requires the three rules for three reasons. First, one country's exchange rate policy is important to its trading partners. It is necessary, therefore, to effectively communicate what the policy is and how it will be carried out. Because governments will be active participants in the foreign exchange market, it is crucial that their intentions be clear both to private market participants and to their trading partners.

---

[9] It is expected that, in establishing its target, the government would balance the cost of maintaining a stock of liquid foreign assets against the benefit of being able to mitigate the effects of swings in private capital flows. In the early days of an interim regime, the desired stock of reserves might be quite large by historical standards.

Second, the success of a regime that accepts some level of nominal exchange rate volatility depends on the private sector's ability and willingness to provide liquidity to foreign exchange markets. Markets can deal with volatility if market participants are free to profit from trading strategies that exploit volatility. This eventuality is more likely if the government's intervention in the market is limited.

Finally, in the absence of a tightly controlled nominal exchange rate the authorities will need to explain their monetary policy objectives and performance in terms of some variable or set of variables other than the exchange rate: a flexible target for inflation has many advantages for emerging market economies.

Goldstein's managed floating plus (2002: 48) is quite similar to the managed floating with reserve intervention except that it has an additional component—'an aggressive set of measures to reduce currency mismatch.' Goldstein argues that unless measures are available to discourage currency mismatching, large exchange rate movements will not be ignored and hence exchange rate considerations will be dominated by inflation targeting.

Both proposals for managed floating are designed to minimize volatility of the pure floating system with inflation targeting by specifying the objective and modus operandi of market intervention. Goldstein's proposal uses interest rate policy as an intervention instrument whereas Dooley, Dornbusch, and Park (2002) would rely on foreign reserves. Goldstein (2002: 49) emphasizes the importance of preventing or limiting currency mismatch and, for this purpose, proposes a number of measures ranging from 'publication of data on indicators of currency mismatch, to regulatory provisions limiting banks' net open positions in foreign currency, to the development of better hedging mechanisms and deeper capital markets . . .'. However, a system of prudential regulation and supervision would normally include all these measures and, in this sense, the major difference between the two proposals rests on the method of intervention.

# 17

# Capital Account Liberalization

## 17.1. Capital Account Liberalization and Economic Recovery in East Asia

> Excessively rapid financial and capital market liberalization was probably the single most important cause of the crisis.
>
> (Stiglitz 2002: 89)

Of the four crisis countries, Malaysia, instead of seeking IMF rescue financing, decided to go its own way in dealing with the crisis by pegging its exchange rate to the US dollar and imposing various capital controls on both capital inflows and outflows. This move stood in sharp contrast to South Korea, for instance, which has followed the IMF program and substantially liberalized the capital account regime. The experiences of Malaysia and South Korea therefore provide an interesting case study of the effects of both capital controls and liberalization on recovery from the crisis in East Asia. This section analyzes the background and economic consequences of capital account liberalization in Indonesia, South Korea, and Thailand, as well as capital controls in Malaysia.

In measuring the degree of capital account liberalization in these countries before and after the crisis, Johnston et al. (1999), using a disaggregated classification of capital account transactions in the IMF Annual Report on Exchange Arrangements and Restrictions (AREAR), show that Indonesia had been well ahead of the other crisis countries in removing capital controls before the crisis.[1] In compliance with the IMF reform program after the crisis, South Korea broadened the scope of liberalization of capital movements it agreed to as a condition for joining the OECD. As noted

---

[1] Indonesia really had no choice regarding removal of capital controls very early on because of the ease with which money could be smuggled into and out of the country. Its borders were very porous, so capital controls were quite ineffective.

before, Malaysia reversed its liberalization policy to return to tighter control of its capital account regime. Since the crisis both Indonesia and Thailand have made some progress in opening their capital markets, but they still maintain a relatively large number of capital account restrictions compared to other emerging market economies, including South Korea.

Miniane (2004) follows an approach similar to that of Johnston et al., using the same data from the IMF's AREAR. Miniane's estimation, however, is based on 13 broad categories of capital account transactions, whereas Johnston et al. use more disaggregated data on 44 breakdowns. In contrast to the estimates of Johnston et al., Miniane's indices for two benchmark years, 1989 and 1999, show that over the ten-year period, the East Asian economies he covered made little progress in deregulating capital account transactions.

The two indicators developed by Johnston et al. and Miniane are likely to be biased by virtue of an equal weight assigned to all categories of capital account transactions without differentiating their relative importance. For example, deregulation of portfolio capital investment may lead to a higher degree of volatility of capital flows than the removal of restrictions on foreign direct investment. To mitigate this bias, many authors have used the ratio of total volume of capital flows to GDP as a long-run measure of capital account liberalization.[2] Baek and Song (2002) estimate the ratios for the 1985–9 and 1994–8 periods for ten East Asian economies. According to their estimates, increases in these ratios in all ten countries are striking. In Indonesia, the average ratio during 1994–8 was more than six times the average of the 1985–9 period. The Philippines saw a fourfold increase over the decade. In China, the ratio more than tripled, and more than doubled in other countries. Therefore, with the exception of Miniane, both the index of capital control by Johnston et al. and changes in the capital flows–GDP ratios provide evidence that East Asian economies have achieved some degree of capital account liberalization.

Kaminsky and Schmukler (2002) developed another index, which jointly evaluates the liberalization of the capital account, the stock market, and the domestic financial sector. It takes values between 1 and 3: fully liberalized (1), partially liberalized (2), and repressed (3). To measure the extent of financial liberalization, the authors track the evolution of the regulatory regime covering all three sectors over the 1973–99 period. The East Asian economies covered in their study include: Hong Kong, Indonesia, Malaysia, the Philippines, South Korea, Taiwan, and Thailand. As

---

[2] See Kraay (1998), Swank (1998), and Lane and Milesi-Ferretti (2001).

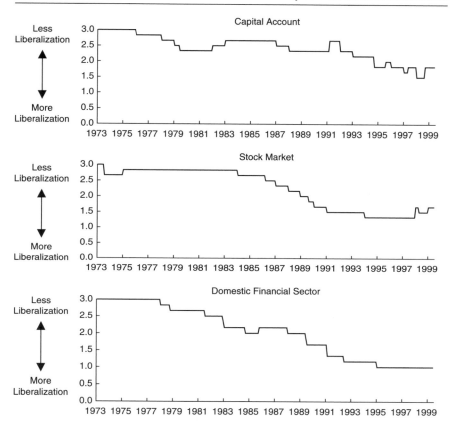

**Figure 17.1.** Indices of financial liberalization by sector

Note: 3 = high restrictions, 2 = partial liberalization, and 1 = full liberalization. East Asian emerging market economies include: Hong Kong, Indonesia, South Korea, Malaysia, Philippines, Taiwan, and Thailand.

*Source*: Kaminsky and Schmukler (2002).

shown in Figure 17.1, the Kaminsky and Schmukler index suggests that the East Asian economies were able to manage, on average, partial liberalization of capital account transactions during the sample period.

After a quick bouncing back from the crisis, all of East Asia, except China, suffered the burst of the IT bubble in 2001. The subsequent slowdown continued until 2004 when the resurgence in growth began throughout the region. The pace of recovery in East Asia, adjusted for the global downturn, has been much faster overall than other crisis episodes would predict. Although it is too early to make a definitive judgment, the experience of South Korea and Malaysia suggest that the degree of capital account liberalization has been immaterial to the recovery. Indeed, judging from changes in macroeconomic indicators such as GDP growth, CPI inflation, and current account balances, the performance of the Malaysian economy has been as impressive as that of South Korea (see Table 2.1).

It would indeed be presumptuous to argue that capital account liberalization for South Korea has produced substantial efficiency gains or stimulated investment to drive the ongoing recovery, simply because the second, and more extensive, phase of capital account liberalization started only in 2001. In fact, a recent study (Park 2001) shows that the removal of capital controls cannot be credited with the recovery and may not have even triggered the upturn. Instead, the easing of monetary and fiscal policy, export expansion, and most important of all, changes in market perceptions that the crisis was, after all, a temporary shock have buttressed the ongoing recovery.

In contrast to the Korean experience, imposition of capital controls was associated or at least did not interfere with impressive recovery in Malaysia. Park (2001) argues that in Malaysia, the government's decision on September 1, 1998, to impose capital controls and to peg the ringgit to the US dollar precipitated the economic turnaround that began in the fourth quarter of 1998. Contrary to expectations, Malaysia's imposition of capital controls disrupted neither the domestic nor regional financial markets. Dornbusch (2001), on the other hand, argues that at the time of the imposition of capital controls, Malaysia was no more vulnerable than other crisis countries to the financial crisis. In his view, it is incorrect to argue that capital controls contained a situation that otherwise would have been much worse. In fact, he points out that Malaysia had more favorable macroeconomic and financial conditions compared to other crisis countries. Moreover, the timing of controls coincided with the reversal of the yen's appreciation, the end of the crisis elsewhere in East Asia, and the Fed's rate cuts. Fischer (2001) makes a similar point: by the time Malaysia imposed capital controls, most of the turbulence of the East Asian crisis was over and regional exchange rates were already appreciating.

According to Jomo (2001) the positive effects of capital controls were exaggerated, because the bulk of foreign funds had already fled the country when capital controls were imposed, penalizing investors who had not left in the preceding fourteen months. He also agrees with Fischer (2001) and Dornbusch (2001) that the external environment became favorable to Malaysia when the controls were imposed. For these reasons, in Jomo's view the control regime was never tested in a very real sense. He speculates that the capital control imposition is likely to have slowed recovery and acted to contain inflows of foreign direct investment.

In a more rigorous study of Malaysian capital controls, Kaplan and Rodrik (2001) compare the economic performance of Malaysia after their imposition on September 1, 1998, with that of South Korea and Thailand when they were undergoing IMF programs, that is, after accepting IMF rescue financing and conditionality (November 21, 1997 for Korea and July 28, 1997 for Thailand). Using a time shifted and difference-in-difference approach, they estimate the effects of capital controls on financial markets and the economy as a whole. Their conclusion is that Malaysia suffered a smaller decline in the GDP growth rate, employment in manufacturing, and stock prices, and experienced a larger decrease in interest rates and lesser currency depreciation than did South Korea.

Haggard (2000) and Hood (2001) also reach a positive conclusion: Malaysian capital control measures were effective in revitalizing the stock market, lowering domestic interest rates, and building up foreign exchange reserves, which in turn sparked and sustained Malaysia's recovery. Equally important, they provided breathing space in which the planning and implementation of economic reform could be undertaken requiring substantial costs for restructuring ailing financial institutions and corporations. The Malaysian decision was not without cost, however: one of the major downsides was that Malaysian banks and corporations had to pay a higher risk premium on their borrowing from abroad (Hood 2001).

Given these pieces of contradictory evidence, it is difficult to determine whether capital controls or the application of an explicit IMF program have resulted in better economic performance in East Asia. This is largely due to the fact that the costs and benefits of capital controls unlike those of trade liberalization remain ambiguous, as we discuss in the next section.

## 17.2. Prospects for Capital Account Liberalization

There is a widely held belief that emerging market economies will in due course be disposed to liberalize the capital account and integrate into global capital markets because that is the course of development advanced countries have taken (Fischer 2001). In theory one can identify a number of channels through which global financial integration can promote economic growth in emerging market economies. In reality, however, there is no reliable empirical evidence supporting or rejecting the theory outright.[3] Although Fischer supports capital account liberalization as a matter of principle, he recognizes that the use of market-based inflow controls may be necessary to gain monetary policy independence and to increase the long-term share in capital inflows, while controls on capital outflows can be used to help maintain a fixed exchange rate system. In the long run, he believes that capital controls lose their effectiveness and efficiency and should therefore be phased out, perhaps gradually.

Among the East Asian crisis economies, less developed ASEAN economies and China have shown little enthusiasm for deregulating the capital account anytime soon. In fact, there are indications that some of those countries including Thailand, Indonesia, and South Korea, which have been on the liberalization track, may reinstate various capital controls as a means of stabilizing the nominal exchange rate. Why do these countries have so little confidence in the efficiency of an open capital account regime and place so little value on the benefits of integration into the global capital market? One simple answer may be that they believe that the costs of capital controls are greater than the benefits. More important is that there is no convincing empirical evidence showing that the effect of financial integration on growth is quantitatively significant. The remainder of this section discusses a number of factors that may explain, and possibly rationalize, the reluctance of East Asian economies to liberalize capital account transactions.

- *Sustainability of capital controls*

A number of studies have shown that capital controls, either on inflows or outflows, tend to lose their effectiveness and efficiency over time. Only short-run capital controls may be effective in strengthening monetary independence with pegged exchange rates and in influencing the composition of capital inflows. The celebrated case of the Chilean controls, according to Edwards (2000), lost much of their effectiveness after 1998.[4] If, indeed, the long-term effectiveness of capital controls is at best doubtful, then one can make a strong case for capital account liberalization: emerging market economies would be better off by removing capital controls

---

[3] Direct channels are: larger availability of financing for investment at a lower cost of capital; transfer of technological know-how; efficiency improvement; and growth of the domestic financial sector. Indirect channels are: specialization, better economic policies, and signaling. See Prasad et al. (2003).

[4] See also Valdes-Prieto and Soto (1996), Simone and Sorsa (1999), and Cardoso and Laurens (1998) on the ineffectiveness of Chilean capital controls.

gradually over time regardless of, and despite the costs of, liberalization in the short run.

In a review of recent studies on the Chilean capital controls, Williamson (2000: 29) shows that the literature devoted to the Chilean control has exaggerated its ineffectiveness and that 'capital controls can be a useful complement to macroeconomic policies designed to limit counterproductive movements in the exchange rate.' The controversy over the effectiveness of capital controls is not likely to be resolved anytime soon. Unless capital controls are proved to be ineffective in the long run beyond any reasonable doubt, and there is no such evidence. East Asian policymakers are unlikely to be persuaded to take further steps in deregulating capital account transactions.

- *Benefits of capital account liberalization*

Despite voluminous empirical literature on the effects of capital account liberalization, recent studies have failed to produce convincing evidence that the benefits of capital account liberalization are indeed greater than the costs. Rodrik (1998) fails to find evidence that capital account liberalization increases investment as a proportion of GDP in a cross-section study that includes 100 developing and advanced countries. Edwards (2001) and Arteta, Eichengreen, and Wyplosz (2001) also fail to find strong causal effects of capital account liberalization on economic growth in developing economies.

However, Bekaert, Harvey, and Lundblad (2001) present evidence that equity market liberalization raises annual real per capita GDP by 1 percent over a five-year period through an increase in both the investment/GDP ratio and factor productivity. As the authors admit, however, this increase is very high and after controlling for variables representing structural reforms, they still find that the statistical significance of the equity market opening remains valid. According to the findings of Galindo, Micco, and Ordoñez (2002), financial market opening could stimulate the growth of the sectors intensive in external financing as it fosters financial development (measured by credit to the private sector and market capitalization as percentage of GDP). They point out that the impact could be very small if financial liberalization and opening is not supported by financial institutional reform, including protection of creditor rights.

Reinhart and Tokatlidis (2002) use data of fifty countries (fourteen developed and thirty-six developing) over the 1970–98 period to examine changes in macroeconomic variables following financial deregulation and

155

market opening. Their findings indicate that financial liberalization leads to higher real interest rates, lower investment, but not lower growth, suggesting some efficiency gains. They also note that there is no significant causality between financial deregulation and savings.

A time series analysis by Chari and Henry (2002) does not provide any strong evidence on allocative improvement resulting from capital account liberalization: rather their results are more consistent with the 'animal spirit' view that international capital flows have little or no connection to real economic activity.

Does capital account liberalization contribute to financial deepening and efficiency? Except for OECD member countries, there is no empirical evidence supporting any causal relationship between financial development and capital account decontrol in emerging market economies (Kraay 1998). Klein and Olivei (1999) find that capital account liberalization contributes to financial development in a cross-section study of ninety-three developed and developing countries. However, when only twenty Latin American countries, which maintain a relatively free capital account, are excluded from the sample, they do not observe any positive effects of capital account liberalization on financial deepening. In East Asia, there is as yet no clear evidence that open capital accounts have been associated with financial deepening.

Using a database on a chronology of financial liberalization and opening (domestic market deregulation and capital account and stock market liberalization) of twenty-eight emerging market economies, Kaminsky and Schmukler (2002) show that financial liberalization could be painful in the short run as it triggers financial excesses, but in the long run it improves the efficiency of financial markets as it fuels institutional reform and dampens the boom-bust cycles in equity markets.

Capping all these empirical studies, Prasad et al. (2003) show that 'there is as yet no clear and robust empirical proof that the effect [of financial integration] is quantitatively significant' (p. ix). According to the authors, integration into the global financial system does not appear to help developing countries reduce macroeconomic volatility, and the beneficial effects of financial globalization are likely to be detected when developing countries have a certain amount of absorptive capacity (in terms of an institutional and macroeconomic framework) (ibid.). Bhagwati (1998) suggests that another possible reason for small or absent beneficial effects may be that free capital mobility can be immiserizing in the presence of trade distortions. The efficiency gains from free capital mobility should also be discounted to the extent that excessive short-term capital inflows and associated panics driven by herd behavior could increase the probability of a crisis. In the end, as Prasad et al. conclude, there may not be a clear roadmap for the optimal pace and sequencing of integration.

Could free capital mobility generate strong incentives to policymakers to adhere to a rational and responsible policy regime so that bad policies, such as maintaining an overvalued exchange rate for an extended period of time, can be avoided, in light of the Asian crisis? All four East Asian economies had achieved a relatively high degree of capital account liberalization before the crisis, as compared to many other emerging market economies, but there is no evidence suggesting that the policymakers of the four countries became more prudent in managing macroeconomic policies.

- *Globalization without global governance*

If there is any lesson to be learned from the 1997–8 Asian financial crisis, it is that the global financial system based on private transactions and the IMF as a crisis manager-lender is in need of a more effective governance system. Financial globalization would therefore garner broader public support and be sustainable if it were accompanied by the development of an effective system of global financial governance consisting of a global lender of last resort and global regulatory authorities. Since it is politically unrealistic to establish these global public goods, setting and enforcing various international standards for financial management, accounting disclosure, and even for fiscal and monetary policy has been put forward as a second best alternative.

From the perspective of emerging market economies, integration into global financial markets means a considerable loss of their policy autonomy, in particular monetary policy even in the floating exchange regime, as shown in the previous section. Global financial integration therefore underscores the need to coordinate or harmonize macroeconomic and other policies with those of developed countries (G-7 in particular). Although the advocates of financial globalization claim that the universal acceptance of common standards and codes will help stabilize international financial markets and reduce the frequency of financial crises, there is precious little evidence to support their argument. On the contrary, as Pistor (2000) notes, harmonization of standards may produce perverse results.

A group of advanced economies dominated by the G-7 has provided the driving force for a plan that will make other countries comply, and to authorize international financial institutions, such as the IMF, to enforce compliance, with various global financial standards and codes. Setting and enforcing a set of common standards is akin to providing a quasi-governance of international finance, as it is an attempt to develop a de facto global legal architecture for international financial markets through legal harmonization. If indeed this is the case, East Asian economies, which are largely left out of this standard setting process, may justifiably ask whether this group of countries promoting universal standards is also prepared to take into consideration economic and financial market underdevelopment specific to them and to provide public goods such as the services of lender of last resort and global financial supervision.

This question arises because there is no guarantee that those emerging market economies that comply with the common standards will become less vulnerable to financial crises in the future. If a financial crisis erupts and spreads to other countries, can developing economies expect that the group of countries providing the quasi-governance assist them with unconditional liquidity support to prevent them from falling victim to contagion? At this stage of development, the G-7 countries have not shown any indication that they would collectively provide such global public goods as evidenced by their loss of interest in reforming the international financial architecture.

As long as controversies on capital account liberalization are not properly addressed, China and less developed ASEAN member states with a controlled capital account regime would be better advised if they retain some control over the capital account until they have gained policy expertise in sustaining macroeconomic stability and established an effective and efficient financial regulatory system before moving to a regime of free capital mobility. Other countries, which have taken steps towards liberalizing the capital account, will be better off, if they take Bhagwati's advice that they should 'exercise caution instead of making a U-turn precipitously to capital controls' (1998: 18).

### • *Sequencing of liberalization: Is East Asia Ready?*

An accepted norm for sequencing liberalization in emerging market economies is that capital account liberalization should be carried out at the end of the reform process, that is, after completing trade liberalization, FDI liberalization, and domestic financial deregulation (McKinnon 1973, 1993). One of the lessons of the Asian crisis is that emerging market economies stand to gain little, and most likely suffer from financial instability, if liberalization of the capital account is prematurely undertaken when domestic financial markets are underdeveloped, soundness and safety of banks and other financial institutions are not assured, an effective system of prudential regulation of financial institutions is not established, and many trade restrictions remain.

Fischer (2001: 5) also points to a number of preconditions for capital controls (on outflows) saying that 'they would need to be removed gradually ... as the necessary infrastructure—in the form of strong and efficient domestic financial institutions and markets, a market-based monetary policy, an effective foreign exchange market, and the information base necessary for the markets to operate efficiently- is put in place.' Judging by this set of sequencing criteria, most East Asian economies, except for Singapore, Hong Kong, and Japan, may not have reached a stage of financial development where they could safely open their capital markets.

While the case for open trade is hardly disputed, the case for integrated international capital markets remains controversial. In theory, financial globalization leads to more efficient allocation of resources, diversification of opportunities, and equalization of risk-adjusted returns. The controversy on the desirability of open capital markets persists largely because there is no clear evidence that countries with open capital accounts grow faster or develop a deeper and more sophisticated financial system in contrast to significant empirical literature that documents the large costs of trade restrictions.

Despite conflicting evidence on the costs of capital controls, one can still make a strong case for integrated international financial markets, given that all developed countries have open capital accounts. The issue concerning capital account liberalization in emerging market economies is therefore not whether they should open their capital markets, but how they should go about doing it. In this regard, many important questions as to the sequencing of market opening and the preconditions for capital account liberalization remain unanswered.

# Part V

# Economic Integration in East Asia

# 18

# Trade Integration

## 18.1. Proliferation of Bilateral FTAs

There has been a concerted movement toward freer, if not free, trade in East Asia since the early 1990s. Berg and Krueger (2003) show that emerging economies in the region have achieved a great deal in reducing tariffs and lowering non-tariff barriers. In parallel with domestic trade liberalization, East Asian economies have mounted collective efforts for region-wide free trade. In 1993 the ASEAN states agreed to establish an ASEAN free trade area (AFTA). In 1995, APEC leaders proposed a plan for bringing about free trade in Asia and the Pacific by 2020 in what is known as the Bogo declaration.

At the East Asian leaders' summit in 1998, it was agreed to create an East Asia Vision Group (EAVG), and an East Asian Study Group (EASG) two years later with the mandate for the EAVG, which was composed of private sector experts, to develop a long-term vision for economic cooperation in East Asia. The EAVG proposed the creation of an East Asian FTA as part of its recommendations in 2001 (EAVG 2001). The EASG, consisting of government officials, subsequently gave its endorsement to the EAVG recommendation for the regional FTA. However, the proposal for an East Asian FTA has not seen the light. East Asian leaders have been reluctant to proceed with an East Asian FTA that is likely to be opposed by protectionist forces at home. There has also been an absence of leadership such a regional movement would require.

The activities of EAVG and EASG were followed up by the creation of the 'Network of East Asian Think-Tanks (NEAT)' in 2003. NEAT, which is supported by ASEAN+3, is to continue dialogue and deepen mutual understanding among the members. Meetings of NEAT were held in 2003 and 2004 to discuss issues related to forming an East Asian Community, of which an East Asia FTA is an important component.

Despite the slow progress in regional trade liberalization, regional efforts for free trade have contributed to a large increase in intra-regional trade in East Asia. In terms of imports, intra-regional trade (ASEAN+3 and Taiwan) accounted for 46 percent of the region's total trade in 2001, when the entire region was still recovering from the crisis, up from 36 percent from a decade earlier (see Table 18.1(*a*) and (*b*)). There is every indication that this trend will continue.

In recent years, however, the regional movement for free trade has lost its momentum. Since 1998, trade liberalization has disappeared from the APEC agenda with the breakdown of the Early Voluntary Sectoral Liberalization program and security issues have taken its place (Ravenhill 2004). The movement has given way to a major proliferation of bilateral free trade agreements (FTAs) (see Table 18.2).[1] ASEAN has been negotiating or discussing a number of bilateral FTAs with other Asian countries— China, Japan, and Korea—and with the US and India from outside of the region. On November 4, 2002, China and ASEAN agreed on a framework for creating a large free trade area that would have a total GDP of nearly $2 trillion. The two sides started negotiation in 2003 and a year later signed an agreement on an FTA for trade in goods. They are scheduled to move on to FTA negotiations concerning trade in services and investment in 2005. ASEAN has been negotiating an FTA with both Japan and Korea respectively. Several ASEAN members have sought to establish bilateral FTAs independently of ASEAN's FTA negotiations. Of the ASEAN states, Singapore has been the most aggressive, as it is prepared to talk to just about anyone willing to negotiate an FTA.

Japan has taken a two-track approach in conducting negotiations for bilateral FTAs with Asian countries. In November 2002, it concluded an economic partnership agreement with Singapore and also signed a joint declaration with ASEAN to negotiate a framework for a comprehensive economic partnership that includes a free trade agreement. Since then, Japan has approached individual members of ASEAN such as the Philippines and Thailand for a bilateral FTA. Japan and Korea have also been exploring the possibility of forming a bilateral free trade agreement.

---

[1] In the GATT/WTO, regional trade agreements (RTAs), which violate one of its basic principles of nondiscrimination, are permitted under GATT Article XXIV with several conditions, which include liberalization of substantially all the trade of the members, not increasing trade barriers on non-members, and completing the RTA process within ten years. For developing countries, more lenient conditions are applied under the enabling clause. An FTA is considered to be a shallow form of regional integration, because it only removes tariff and nontariff barriers among the members, while a customs union is a deeper integration, as it adopts common external tariffs on nonmembers, in addition to the removal of tariff and nontariff barriers on trade among the members.

**Table 18.1(a).** Trade Share in East Asian Countries (export)  (%)

| Export from | East Asia | | | China | | | Japan | | | Korea | | | Other NIEs | | | ASEAN4 | | |
|---|---|---|---|---|---|---|---|---|---|---|---|---|---|---|---|---|---|---|
| To | '80 | '90 | '01 | '80 | '90 | '01 | '80 | '90 | '01 | '80 | '90 | '01 | '80 | '90 | '01 | '80 | '90 | '01 |
| East Asia | **32.0** | **36.2** | **42.2** | **52.9** | **66.9** | **44.9** | **21.8** | **24.2** | **32.6** | **28.5** | **33.0** | **38.9** | **31.3** | **39.9** | **49.5** | **54.2** | **50.6** | **47.4** |
| China | 2.8 | 4.6 | 9.8 | 0.0 | 0.0 | 0.0 | 3.9 | 2.1 | 7.7 | 0.0 | 0.0 | 12.1 | 4.0 | 15.7 | 24.2 | 0.8 | 2.1 | 4.4 |
| Japan | 10.2 | 8.2 | 8.9 | 22.3 | 14.8 | 16.9 | 0.0 | 0.0 | 0.0 | 17.4 | 19.4 | 11.0 | 6.3 | 6.9 | 6.6 | 34.6 | 24.4 | 16.1 |
| Korea, Rep. | 2.7 | 3.8 | 4.0 | 0.0 | 0.7 | 4.7 | 4.1 | 6.1 | 6.3 | 0.0 | 0.0 | 0.01 | 1.3 | 2.3 | 2.6 | 1.7 | 3.9 | 3.7 |
| Other NIEs | 9.3 | 12.3 | 11.5 | 26.4 | 47.0 | 19.6 | 6.7 | 8.3 | 9.4 | 6.2 | 8.6 | 9.0 | 6.0 | 4.5 | 4.7 | 13.8 | 16.0 | 15.9 |
| ASEAN 4 | 7.0 | 7.1 | 8.1 | 4.3 | 2.9 | 3.8 | 7.0 | 7.7 | 9.3 | 5.0 | 5.0 | 6.8 | 13.7 | 10.6 | 11.5 | 3.2 | 4.2 | 7.2 |
| South Asia | 1.7 | 1.4 | 1.5 | 1.1 | 1.5 | 1.5 | 1.6 | 1.2 | 0.8 | 2.0 | 1.7 | 1.8 | 2.8 | 1.9 | 2.1 | 1.1 | 1.3 | 1.8 |
| Central Asia | 0.0 | 0.0 | 0.1 | 0.0 | 0.0 | 0.4 | 0.0 | 0.0 | 0.0 | 0.0 | 0.0 | 0.3 | 0.0 | 0.0 | 2.0 | 0.0 | 0.0 | 0.0 |
| CER | 2.8 | 2.2 | 2.0 | 1.4 | 0.8 | 1.5 | 3.1 | 2.8 | 2.2 | 1.5 | 1.7 | 1.6 | 4.3 | 2.2 | 2.0 | 1.8 | 1.8 | 2.5 |
| USA | 21.4 | 25.7 | 21.0 | 5.4 | 8.6 | 20.4 | 24.5 | 31.7 | 30.4 | 26.4 | 29.9 | 20.8 | 19.4 | 23.0 | 10.3 | 18.8 | 19.4 | 20.0 |
| EU | 14.6 | 17.7 | 14.9 | 13.1 | 10.1 | 15.4 | 14.0 | 20.4 | 16.0 | 15.5 | 15.4 | 13.1 | 17.9 | 17.2 | 14.0 | 13.6 | 16.7 | 15.0 |
| Others | 27.5 | 16.8 | 18.2 | 26.1 | 13.6 | 15.9 | 35.1 | 19.6 | 18.0 | 26.0 | 18.3 | 23.4 | 24.3 | 15.9 | 22.1 | 10.4 | 10.2 | 13.2 |
| World | 100 | 100 | 100 | 100 | 100 | 100 | 100 | 100 | 100 | 100 | 100 | 100 | 100 | 100 | 100 | 100 | 100 | 100 |

**Table 18.1(b).** Trade Share in East Asian Countries (import)  (%)

| Export from | East Asia | | | China | | | Japan | | | Korea | | | Other NIEs | | | ASEAN4 | | |
|---|---|---|---|---|---|---|---|---|---|---|---|---|---|---|---|---|---|---|
| To | '80 | '90 | '01 | '80 | '90 | '01 | '80 | '90 | '01 | '80 | '90 | '01 | '80 | '90 | '01 | '80 | '90 | '01 |
| East Asia | **30.4** | **38.7** | **45.8** | **33.3** | **49.0** | **32.3** | **20.7** | **23.4** | **36.2** | **33.4** | **34.4** | **39.9** | **47.9** | **57.1** | **62.8** | **41.1** | **46.2** | **50.8** |
| China | 3.9 | 7.8 | 15.0 | 0.0 | 0.0 | 0.0 | 3.1 | 5.1 | 16.6 | 0.1 | 0.0 | 9.4 | 10.8 | 22.6 | 29.9 | 2.8 | 2.6 | 5.6 |
| Japan | 11.2 | 12.8 | 9.0 | 27.0 | 14.7 | 13.7 | 0.0 | 0.0 | 0.0 | 26.3 | 26.6 | 18.9 | 20.4 | 17.8 | 12.2 | 24.3 | 25.6 | 19.8 |
| Korea, Rep. | 1.8 | 3.4 | 5.4 | 0.0 | 0.5 | 8.5 | 2.2 | 5.0 | 4.9 | 0.0 | 0.0 | 0.0 | 2.3 | 3.8 | 4.1 | 2.0 | 3.4 | 5.1 |
| Other NIEs | 3.1 | 6.4 | 5.1 | 4.0 | 29.6 | 9.8 | 1.5 | 2.4 | 2.0 | 1.2 | 2.2 | 3.0 | 4.3 | 3.6 | 3.8 | 8.3 | 10.6 | 10.9 |
| ASEAN 4 | 10.4 | 8.2 | 11.2 | 2.4 | 4.2 | 2.4 | 14.0 | 10.9 | 12.7 | 5.9 | 5.6 | 8.6 | 10.2 | 9.2 | 12.8 | 3.8 | 4.1 | 9.4 |
| South Asia | 0.9 | 1.1 | 1.4 | 1.0 | 1.7 | 0.6 | 0.9 | 1.0 | 0.8 | 0.3 | 0.7 | 1.1 | 1.2 | 1.0 | 1.5 | 0.7 | 1.5 | 1.6 |
| Central Asia | 0.0 | 0.0 | 0.1 | 0.0 | 0.0 | 0.6 | 0.0 | 0.0 | 0.0 | 0.0 | 0.0 | 0.1 | 0.0 | 0.0 | 0.0 | 0.0 | 0.0 | 0.0 |
| CER | 4.7 | 4.1 | 3.4 | 6.4 | 2.9 | 3.6 | 5.6 | 6.0 | 4.7 | 3.4 | 4.4 | 4.4 | 2.3 | 1.6 | 1.4 | 4.3 | 3.8 | 3.1 |
| USA | 17.0 | 17.8 | 14.5 | 20.0 | 12.7 | 15.4 | 17.4 | 22.5 | 18.3 | 21.9 | 24.3 | 15.9 | 13.0 | 11.5 | 10.3 | 16.1 | 13.9 | 12.9 |
| EU | 8.8 | 14.9 | 12.9 | 14.7 | 17.6 | 20.9 | 5.9 | 16.1 | 12.8 | 7.2 | 13.0 | 10.6 | 11.7 | 11.8 | 10.5 | 13.5 | 16.4 | 11.7 |
| Others | 38.3 | 23.4 | 22.0 | 24.6 | 16.2 | 24.8 | 49.5 | 31.0 | 27.3 | 33.6 | 23.4 | 28.0 | 23.9 | 17.1 | 13.5 | 24.2 | 18.3 | 19.9 |
| World | 100 | 100 | 100 | 100 | 100 | 100 | 100 | 100 | 100 | 100 | 100 | 100 | 100 | 100 | 100 | 100 | 100 | 100 |

*Note:* Other NIEs (Singapore, Hong Kong), ASEAN4 (Indonesia, Malaysia, Philippines, Thailand), South Asia (India, Sri Lanka, Bangladesh, Pakistan), Central Asia (Kazakhstan, Uzbekistan), CER (Australia, New Zealand).
*Source:* International Monetary Fund, *Direction of Trade Statistics Yearbook*, various years.

**Table 18.2.** Free Trade Agreements in East Asia

| | Year | participants and status |
|---|---|---|
| *FTA in force* | | |
| ASEAN Free Trade Area (AFTA) | 1992 | 10 ASEAN members |
| Australia–New Zealand Closer Economic Relations Trade Agreement (CER) | 1983 | Australia, New Zealand |
| Singapore–New Zealand FTA | 2001 | Effective in January |
| Japan–Singapore Economic Partnership Agreement (JSEPA) | 2002 | Effective in November |
| Singapore–EFTA (European Free Trade Association) FTA | 2002 | Signed in June and effective in January 2003 |
| South Korea–Chile FTA | 2003 | Signed in February |
| *Agreements being negotiated, studied, or considered* | | |
| East Asia Free Trade Area (EAFTA) | 2000 | |
| China–Japan–South Korea FTA | 2000 | |
| ASEAN–China Free Trade Area (ACFTA) | 2001 | |
| Japan–ASEAN Closer Economic Partnership | 2002 | |
| ASEAN-India Regional Trade and Investment Agreement | 2002 | |
| Taiwan–Panama | 2002 | |
| *Bilateral FTA under consideration* | | |
| ASEAN-US | | |
| China | | Hong Kong SAR, Australia, New Zealand |
| Japan | | Malaysia, Mexico, Philippines, South Korea, Thailand |
| South Korea | | Japan, Mexico, Thailand, ASEAN |
| Singapore | | Australia, Canada, Mexico, United States, New Zealand, Bahrain, Egypt, India, Sri Lanka, Panama |
| Thailand | | Australia, India, Japan |

*Source*: Park et al. (2005) and various other sources.

Not to be outdone by Japan, China has been equally active in courting other Asian countries for bilateral FTAs. At a Northeast Asian summit meeting at the ASEAN+3 talks in November 2003, in addition to the China–ASEAN FTA, China proposed a study on a three-way free trade agreement involving China, Japan, and South Korea. It has also indicated its interest in a China-South Korea FTA. China's eagerness for forging free trade ties with ASEAN, where Japan has invested heavily for the past four decades, may turn the region into an economic battleground between the two countries.

If China and Japan succeed in concluding their negotiations with neighbouring East Asian economies for bilateral FTAs, they may lead to hub and spoke trade arrangements in which as major economic powers, they will emerge as hubs (Baldwin 2003). Although China and Japan may be natural hubs, ASEAN has been at the center of the movement to bilateral FTAs in East Asia. Indeed, ASEAN has been a popular partner for bilateral FTAs: not only Northeast Asian counties, but also the US, India, and other counties in different continents have courted the association.

Since the ASEAN–China FTA will be the most significant, it will serve as a basic framework for similar agreements for other countries. ASEAN knows very well that it could easily be marginalized as a spoke in either China or Japan's network of bilateral FTAs. In order to avoid this marginalization and to gain access to other export markets, ASEAN and other Asian countries appear set to join other FTAs or establishing an alliance with other partners so that they could prevent both China and Japan from taking advantage of their economic leverage in regional trade.

It should be noted that many of the FTAs discussed in this study cover not only liberalization of trade but also various types of economic cooperation. As such, some of the FTAs established in East Asia are termed as Economic Partnership Agreement (Japan–Singapore EPA), or Closer Economic Partnership Arrangement (China–Hong Kong CEPA). These new types of FTAs typically include facilitation of foreign trade, liberalization and facilitation of foreign direct investment (FDI), and economic and technical cooperation, in addition to trade liberalization. It may be worth noting that the basic philosophy of these new types of FTAs is similar to that of Asia Pacific Economic Cooperation (APEC) forum, whose three pillars are (1) liberalization and (2) facilitation of foreign trade and foreign investment, and (3) economic and technical cooperation.

## 18.2. Factors behind the Proliferation of FTAs in East Asia

There are several factors that have led to the proliferation of FTAs in East Asia; some of them are common to many economies, while others are specific to individual ones. One factor has been the rapid expansion of FTAs in other parts of the world, in particular in North America and Western Europe. Faced with the possibility of losing their market access or being discriminated against in their exports many East Asian economies have sought to improve their negotiating positions by forming FTAs with their regional partners and other countries outside of the region.

Another has been the slow progress in multilateral trade liberalization under the WTO. Despite the efforts over many years, trade liberalization under the WTO has become an agonizingly slow process. The increase in the number of WTO members with different agendas on the pace and the extent of trade liberalization has made it increasingly difficult to reach consensus on the start of a new round. The new Doha round has failed to initiate substantive negotiations. It was only July 2004 when the modality of the negotiations was more or less agreed. Frustrated with the stalemate in trade liberalization on a global scale, many countries have chosen FTAs with like-minded countries to open their trade regimes. For instance, knowing that multilateral or regional trade negotiations can be a protracted process, some East Asian economies, such as Korea, may wish to enter into bilateral FTAs to signal their commitment to trade liberalization or not to lose their access to export markets. ASEAN states appear to be attracted to bilateral FTAs with China and Japan due to the large export markets offered by the two countries.

A third factor is that the GATT/WTO rules cannot adequately deal with newly emerging international economic activities such as FDI, trade in services, and mobility of labor. FTAs may allow going deeper beyond border measures to set up rules governing domestic markets such as competition policy, which the GATT/WTO cannot provide. Some East Asian economies, notably Japan, have sought to take advantage of external pressure FTAs can generate to speed up and broaden the scope of domestic reform. In some quarters of East Asia, it is sometimes suggested that FTAs could provide a new impetus for reform that has been losing momentum in recent years.

A fourth factor is the belief that FTAs could serve as channels of cooperation and mutual assistance. As noted earlier, some existing and prospective FTAs in East Asia include not only trade liberalization, but liberalization and facilitation in FDI and economic and technical assistance. These features of FTAs could lay the foundation for financial and other cooperation and policy coordination in general. Finally, there is the intensifying rivalry between China and Japan for a dominant leadership role in East Asia that has escalated competition for a larger FTA hub.

## 18.3. Negotiated Liberalization or Protectionism?

It is too early to judge how discriminatory the existing and proposed East Asian FTAs will be in regard to market access and rules of origin and whether they will facilitate or stand in the way of regional trade integration, because the number of concluded FTAs is small and details of other FTAs under discussion are not yet known (Park et al. 2005). Depending on how one interprets the objectives of East Asian FTAs, one can be either an optimist or pessimist on the prospect of multilateral trade liberalization in the region. This section begins with a pessimistic scenario and ends with an optimistic outlook.

There is indeed no shortage of arguments supporting bilateral FTAs. They could be complementary to, and to the extent that they can be concluded quickly they can become building blocks for global trade liberalization under the WTO. Bilateral FTAs have other advantages in that they could provide rules in various areas such as FDI and labor mobility that are not covered by the WTO.

While these advantages may be real, pessimists would argue that the proliferation of bilateral FTAs might not necessarily lead to region-wide trade liberalization. A survey on simulation studies on FTAs show that the bilateral movement is likely to produce an outcome inferior to a large FTA such as an East Asian FTA or a China-Japan-Korea FTA, because East Asian bilateral FTAs could, among other things, divert more trade from low-cost to high-cost producers. If indeed, both China and Japan succeed in creating hub-and-spoke networks of bilateral FTAs, then Baldwin (2004) cautions that these networks could marginalize the spoke countries both economically and politically while giving leverage to the hub economies. In order to avoid this marginalization, smaller East Asian emerging economies will attempt to negotiate as many FTAs as possible with one another and with partners from elsewhere. A further proliferation of bilateral FTAs could then make East Asia less attractive to foreign direct investment, a problem Baldwin calls the noodle bowl problem.

If China and Japan are motivated to negotiate bilateral FTAs with other East Asian economies in order to protect and strengthen their political and strategic interests in East Asia, then the proliferation of bilateral FTAs would not necessarily speed up either regional or global trade liberalization and integration. This is because these politically motivated bilateral FTAs could turn into strategic alliances rather than economic unions.

Indeed, there is concern that some of the bilateral FTAs concluded, negotiated, or under consideration in East Asia are examples of negotiated protectionism rather than negotiated liberalization, because they tend to leave out politically sensitive sectors such as agriculture by making a rather self-serving interpretation of GATT Article XXIV.8, which stipulates that the preferential agreement eliminates duties and restrictions on not all but substantially all trade between the participants (Ravenhill 2004).

Developing economies in East Asia can also take advantage of their exemption to Article XXIV.

As the countries engaged in negotiating bilateral FTAs in East Asia resort to many provisions for rules of origin to give selective protection to domestic industries, they will strengthen domestic protectionist forces while weakening the domestic pro-liberalization coalition. At the same time, different rules of origin and coverage of imports for liberalization in different bilateral FTAs could create a bewildering spaghetti bowl of complex and incompatible agreements, thereby inhibiting broadening of the geographical scope of integration (Ravenhill 2004). If this happens, then consolidating different bilateral FTAs for region-wide trade liberalization will not be easy because of the difficulty of standardizing different FTAs into one agreement. This means that it is highly unlikely that an East Asian FTA will emerge by itself as a result of amalgamation of bilateral FTAs (Cheong 2002). Given the intensifying rivalry between China and Japan for regional leadership, the two countries may make it more difficult to create an East Asian FTA.

In the end the pros and cons of bilateral FTAs will have to be judged on the basis of their contribution to regional and global trade liberalization. So far there is little evidence that dispels Ravenhill's concern that the new wave of bilateral FTAs in East Asia will be supportive of region-wide free trade. As Ravenhill puts it, 'the move to bilateralism in the Asia Pacific appears to have come at the expense of transregional APEC grouping' as evidenced by the fact that none of them makes any mention of possible extension to other parties. Ravenhill also observes that East Asian governments preoccupied with bilateral FTA negotiations often do not find the time or resources to engage in regional and multilateral free trade negotiations.

Many East Asian trade officials and experts would argue that the pessimistic scenario is not firmly grounded in facts nor in the FTA strategies of the ASEAN+3 members. All East Asian economies depend on trade for growth and industrialization and are aware that an economically integrated East Asia will offer large markets for their exports and imports and new investment opportunities that will help sustain rapid growth. East Asian policymakers cannot afford degeneration of FTAs into a convoluted noodle bowl. In light of the commitment of East Asian leaders to region-wide free trade, these separate FTA developments would be amalgamated into an East Asian FTA (EAFTA).

If East Asian bilateral FTAs are to serve as building blocks for regional and multilateral trade liberalization, two issues deserve special attention in negotiating an East Asian FTA. One is the definition of the rules of origin

(ROO). Individual FTAs conducted by East Asian economies have each negotiated different ROO. This poses an obstacle to the establishment of an EAFTA, as a uniform set of rules of origin must be adopted. A liberal definition of the ROO is preferable in order to achieve a freer trading environment and at present, ASEAN's 40 percent (cumulative) value added rule appears to be the most desirable option.

Another issue is coverage of the EAFTA. Considering diverse economic backgrounds including the level of economic development of East Asian economies, it is important to cover not only trade and liberalization and facilitation in FDI, but also to include a variety of technical and economic cooperation programs such as human resource development and technology transfer. Programs for cooperation are needed to improve the quality of human resources and technological capability of East Asia's developing economies, so that their gap vis-à-vis the region's developed countries could be reduced. Closing the gap will help promote social and political stability in the region as well as regional trade integration.

All East Asian economies will face opposition to FTAs at home, in particularly in noncompetitive sectors. To deal with any opposition, East Asian economies should provide temporary safeguards in the form of income support and/or education/training, so that adversely affected workers could be transferred to other productive jobs. In the end, it is strong political leadership with a future vision that will make possible the formation of an East Asian FTA possible.

# 19

# Financial Integration

## 19.1. The Chiang Mai Initiative

The 1997 Asian financial crisis has set in motion two interrelated financial developments in East Asia. Most East Asian economies, including those affected by the crisis, have increased the pace and scope of domestic financial reform to liberalize and open their financial markets and also to improve soundness, corporate governance, and risk management at financial institutions. The other development is the regional movement for financial cooperation and integration that has culminated in the Chiang Mai Initiative (CMI) and Asian Bond Market Development Initiative (ABMI).

When the financial crisis that broke out in Thailand became contagious spreading to other East Asian economies in the second half of 1997, Japan proposed the creation of an Asian monetary fund (AMF) as a framework for financial cooperation and policy coordination in the region, particularly for creating lending facilities, in addition to those of the IMF, against future financial crises in East Asia. Although the proposal was well received throughout the region, the idea was shelved at the objection of the US, EU, and IMF.

The AMF idea was revived again when the finance ministers of ASEAN, China, Japan, and South Korea (ASEAN+3) agreed on May 6, 2000 in Chiang Mai, Thailand, to establish a system of bilateral currency swap arrangements among the eight members of ASEAN+3 in what is known as the Chiang Mai Initiative. The eight countries participating in the CMI—the original ASEAN 5 plus China, Japan, and South Korea—have also institutionalized regular meetings of finance ministers (AFMM+3) and deputy ministers (AFDM+3) for policy dialogue and coordination as well as the annual summit for ASEAN+3.[1] As a sequel to the CMI for

---

[1] Financial market participants have ignored the CMI as a defense mechanism against future crises because the amount of liquidity any member can draw from the system is small and worse yet, it is uncertain whether it can activate the swap borrowing. Despite these criticisms

regional financial integration, ASEAN+3 also launched the Asian Bond Market Initiative (ABMI)—for the development of regional bond markets in Asia. Six working groups have been established to construct regional financial infrastructure and to devise plans for the coordination of market practices and policies of individual Asian countries.

A regional financial arrangement (RFM) for economic cooperation and policy coordination in general comprises: (i) a mechanism of short-term liquidity support for participating members experiencing balance of payments deficits such as the CMI; (ii) a surveillance mechanism for monitoring economic and policy developments in member countries and for imposing policy conditionality on those countries receiving financial support; and (iii) a regional collective exchange rate system to stabilize bilateral exchange rates of member countries. Having established a liquidity support system, the ASEAN+3 states are working on a plan to create a surveillance system for the CMI network. There has so far been no serious discussion on developing a collective exchange rate system for the region as a whole. The ABMI will be complementary to the CMI as it is a plan to integrate the bond markets of individual countries in East Asia.

The structure of financial cooperation conceived by the architects of the CMI covers only the basic principles and operational procedures for bilateral swap transactions. To serve as a full-fledged regional financial mechanism comparable to the European Monetary System, for example, further organizational and operational details on surveillance and exchange rate policy coordination will have to be worked out. Although the leaders of the ASEAN+3 states profess their firm commitment to developing the CMI network into a regional lending scheme or the AMF, questions have been raised whether ASEAN+3 can and should emulate Europe's experience with monetary and financial integration in a world economy that has seen a fast pace of financial globalization. In order to move regional financial integration forward, individual countries in East Asia will have first to open their financial markets. Market opening will then be integrating their markets into both regional and global financial markets at the same time unless they discriminate against nonregional market participants.

The architects of the CMI have primarily been interested in creating a regional cooperative system that can be activated immediately to provide liquidity support to any member country that comes under a speculative

and the market's disregard, ASEAN+3 has managed to close ranks to expand the scope of policy dialogue and to move to the second stage of integration.

attack or suffers from serious financial turbulence that triggers a large capital outflow so that the occurrence and contagion of a financial crisis can be prevented. However, there is no evidence that regional financial arrangements, whatever forms they may take, are effective in warding off financial crises. There is also the lingering doubt whether ASEAN+3 could avoid moral hazard in managing the CMI because the participating countries may face political and other constraints in imposing tight conditionality on other members borrowing from the swap arrangement. Although these arguments raise legitimate questions, they do not mean that the creation of a regional financial arrangement in East Asia is not justified. Depending on how it is structured and managed, it could facilitate multilateral trade and financial liberalization, thereby contributing to global financial stability (Bergsten and Park 2002). This chapter analyzes recent developments in and prospects for regional cooperation for financial integration in East Asia through the consolidation of the CMI and promotion of the ABMI.

- *Structure of Recent Developments in the CMI*

The CMI consists of two regional financial arrangements. One is the expanded ASEAN swap system and the other is the network of bilateral swaps and repurchase agreements among the eight members of ASEAN+3. In 1977, the original five ASEAN member states agreed to establish an ASEAN swap arrangement (ASA). In May 2000 when the CMI was inaugurated, the ASA was expanded to include the other five members, and the total amount of the facility was raised to US$ 1 billion from the initial amount of US$ 200 million.

The CMI network of bilateral swap arrangements (BSA) among the eight members of ASEAN+3 provides for liquidity assistance in the form of swaps of US dollars with the domestic currencies of participating countries. The maximum amount that can be drawn under each of the BSAs is to be determined by the contracting parties. The bilateral swap agreement allows an automatic disbursement of up to 10 percent of the maximum amount drawn. A country drawing more than the 10 percent from the facility is placed under an IMF program for macroeconomic and structural adjustments.[2] Because of this linkage, the network of BSAs is complementary to IMF lending facilities.

---

[2] Thus far regional financial cooperation and integration has been complementary to the global financial system, whereas the bilateral trade approach may be in direct competition with the multilateral (WTO) system.

**Table 19.1.** Progress on the Chiang Mai Initiative (as of May 30, 2004)

| BSA[a] | Currencies | Conclusion Dates | Size ($)[b] billion |
|---|---|---|---|
| Japan–Korea | $/won (one way) | 4 July 2001 | 7 |
| Japan–Thailand[c] | $/baht (one way) | 30 July 2001 | 3 |
| Japan–Philippines | $/peso (one way) | 27 August 2001 | 3 |
| Japan–Malaysia | $/ringgit (one way) | 5 October 2001 | 3.5 |
| Japan–PRC | Yen/renminbi (two way) | 28 March 2002 | 3 |
| Japan–Indonesia | $/rupiah (one way) | 17 February 2003 | 3 |
| Korea–PRC | Won/renminbi (two way) | 24 June 2002 | 2 |
| Korea–Thailand | $/local (two way) | 25 June 2002 | 1 |
| Korea–Malaysia | $/local(two way) | 26 July 2002 | 1 |
| Korea–Philippines | $/local (two way) | 9 August 2002 | 1 |
| PRC–Thailand | $/baht (one way) | 6 December 2001 | 2 |
| PRC–Malaysia | $/ringgit (one way) | 9 October 2002 | 2 |
| PRC–Philippine | $/peso (one way) | 29 August 2003 | 1 |
| Japan–Singapore | $/sing $ (one way) | 10 November 2003 | 1 |
| PRC–Indonesia | Rupiah/renminbi (one way) | 30 December 2003 | 1 |
| Korea–Indonesia | $/local (two way) | 3 December 2003 | 1 |

[a] BSA: Bilateral Swap Arrangement.
[b] The US dollar amounts include the amounts committed under the new Miyazawa Initiative: $5 billion for South Korea and $2.5 billion for Malaysia.
[c] The first contract has expired. The two countries are now negotiating a two-way BSA.

*Source*: Yung Chul Park and Yunjong Wang (2004).

The participating countries are able to draw from their respective BSAs for a period of ninety days. The first drawing may be renewed seven times. The interest rate applicable to the drawing is the Libor plus a premium of 150 basis points for the first drawing and the first renewal. Thereafter, the premium rises by an additional 50 basis points for every two renewals, but it is not to exceed 300 basis points.

The BSAs include one-way and two-way swaps (see Table 19.1). Since China and Japan are not expected to request for liquidity assistance to the five ASEAN members, their contracts with these Southeast Asian economies are one-way BSAs. Since only the ASEAN five can draw from these swaps, the contracts represent the lending programs of both China and Japan. So far, the eight members of ASEAN+3 have concluded the sixteen BSAs that amount to US$ 36.5 billion in total. Japan concluded seven agreements, and both China and South Korea concluded five respectively (see Table 19.1). South Korea, which is the largest beneficiary of the CMI, can draw on a maximum of $12 billion from the system including the Miyazawa initiative. In the eyes of global financial market participants, however, the availability of liquidity to South Korea and other members may not be large enough to be of any significance for preventing future crises.

Although the CMI is comparable to the liquidity support arrangements of the European Monetary system before monetary unification in 1999, in comparison with Europe, it had a different motivation from the beginning. The European facilities were created with the purpose of limiting bilateral exchange rate fluctuations among regional currencies. The CMI started with high capital mobility and flexible exchange rates, although some members of ASEAN+3 have maintained a fixed exchange rate or moved to managed floating regime. So far, the ASEAN+3 countries have not presumed any manifest interest in exchange rate coordination. In its absence, incentives for mutual surveillance will be limited because a member country facing a speculative currency attack may be free to float its exchange rate vis-à-vis those of other neighboring countries (Wang and Woo 2004).

As long as the CMI is simply a supplementary source of financial resources to the IMF, the size of the swap does not have to be large enough to meet potential liquidity needs. Although the CMI can be managed without its own conditionality at this point, it does need to establish its own surveillance mechanism to avoid breach of the swap contract. Up to 10 percent of each BSA swap can be disbursed only with the consent of the swap providing country, but the BSA system does not provide any provisions when a swap borrowing country is in default on its repayment. Swap providing countries therefore need to formulate their own assessments of capacity as well as credibility of swap requesting countries to honor their contracts.

A number of participating countries proposed to delink the BSA network from IMF conditionality and to a gradual increase of an automatic 10 percent drawing. Most participating countries agree in principle that the CMI network needs to be supported by an independent monitoring and surveillance system that monitors economic developments in the region, serves as an institutional framework for policy dialogue and coordination among members, and imposes structural and policy reform on the countries drawing from the BSAs. However, the ASEAN+3 countries at the current stage do not seem well prepared for establishing a policy coordination mechanism as part of the surveillance process although collective efforts are being made in this regard.[3]

[3] For instance, the ASEAN surveillance process is built on the basis of consensus and informality in keeping with the tradition of non-interference (Manzano 2001). East Asia in contrast to Europe lacks the tradition of integrationist thinking and the web of interlocking agreements that encourage monetary and financial cooperation (Eichengreen and Bayoumi 1999). Eichengreen and Bayoumi (1999) stress that East Asia does not meet the necessary intellectual preconditions for regional integration. For this reason, they conclude that it is unrealistic to speak of pooling national sovereignties. While there is no doubt that considerable work must be done in promoting policy coordination in the region, it is wrong to infer that it cannot be done in East Asia.

At the annual meeting of the ADB in April 2004, finance ministers of ASEAN+3 agreed to undertake a further review of the CMI to explore ways in which the scope of the CMI operations can be further expanded and consolidated. The working group presented a report on some of the major issues related to the enlargement and consolidation of the CMI to the finance ministers' meeting at the annual ADB meeting in Istanbul in May 2005 (ASEAN+3 2005). One issue was the enlargement of CMI's liquidity support.

The amount of liquidity any country could draw from the CMI at present is small. In order to develop the CMI into a more credible and effective liquidity support system, the ASEAN + 3 finance ministers approved at the Istanbul meeting a proposal that would double the size of existing individual bilateral swaps with the provision that the actual increase would be decided by bilateral negotiations.

The second issue is to increase the automatic drawing limit. As noted earlier, the swap requesting country can draw up to 10 percent of the contract amount without subjecting itself to IMF conditionality on policy adjustments. Some members of the CMI have argued that the limit should be raised to 20 or 30 percent. At the 2005 Istanbul meeting, the limit was raised to 20 percent.

The third issue is multilateralization of the BSAs. Under the current CMI arrangement, any country wishing to obtain short-term liquidity must discuss the activation with all swap providing countries individually. Therefore, there is no guarantee that BSAs will be activated since some of the swap providing countries may exercise their opting-out right. If a large number of members refuse to provide swaps and different swap providers demand different terms and conditions, then the CMI may cease to be an efficient liquidity support system. The discussion of the swap activation with a multiple of contractual parties may take time and hence may deprive the swap requesting country of the ability to mount an effective and prompt defense against a speculative attack. In order to avoid this bias inherent in the system, the creation of a secretariat or committee was proposed, which will determine the joint activation of all contracts of swap-requesting countries, so that swap disbursements can be made in a concerted and timely manner.

CMI members also realize that joint activation or multilateralization of the BSAs together with the increase in the drawing limit of more than 20 percent would not be possible unless a more effective surveillance system is established. As pointed out earlier, creating a surveillance mechanism for the CMI has been a controversial issue, and the ASEAN+3 working group has not been able to develop a system acceptable to all members. ASEAN+3 policymakers have not been able to agree on the role, structure, and location of the proposed secretariat and are not likely do so in the near future. If CMI members were to agree on the multilateralization and creation of a regional surveillance unit, then their agreement would amount to establishing an institution similar to a regional monetary fund. The ASEAN+3 members may find it premature to set up such an institution, but they do need an institution that can manage and set terms and conditions of bilateral swap transactions and conduct informal meetings for policy dialogues and coordination among the members.

Finally, in recent years foreign exchange policy issues have dominated policy debates and dialogues within ASEAN+3. With the growing need to stabilize bilateral exchange rates among the ASEAN+3 states, proposals have been made to strengthen the CMI network so that it could serve as an institutional base for monetary integration in East Asia in the future. A formal discussion of monetary integration has been put on hold as this was not brought up at the meeting of finance ministers in 2005.

## 19.2. The Asian Bond Market Initiative (ABMI)

• *Structure and Objectives*

Since the 1997–98 East Asian crisis, many countries in the region have given priority over domestic financial reform to developing domestic capital markets in order to compliment the bank-based financial systems of the region. Underdevelopment of domestic bond markets and the absence of efficient regional bond markets are often pointed out as having exacerbated capital outflows in East Asia during the crisis and the associated loss of output and employment. Since the crisis the absence of regional bond markets is claimed to be one of the major causes of the massive increase in the region's overseas portfolio investment (see Table 19.2).

While there is a clear need to develop domestic bond markets in many East Asian economies, smaller countries may find that their economic size does not allow supporting efficient domestic capital markets that are broad and deep in terms of the variety of financial instruments, issuers, and investors. Even to larger economies, the costs of constructing financial and other institutional infrastructure are so high that they may discourage financial restructuring that could develop a more balanced financial

**Table 19.2.** Net Overseas Portfolio Investments of East Asian Economies[a] (USD, billions)

| | Net portfolio investments of private sector (A) | | | Net portfolio investments of public sector[b] (B) | | | Total (A + B) | | |
|---|---|---|---|---|---|---|---|---|---|
| | 1998 | 2002 | 2003 | 1998 | 2002 | 2003 | 1998 | 2002 | 2003 |
| China | 3.7 | 10.3 | −11.4 | 6.2 | 75.2 | 117.0 | 9.9 | 85.5 | 105.6 |
| Hong Kong | −22.1 | 38.8 | 30.5 | −6.8 | −2.4 | 1.0 | −28.9 | 36.4 | 31.5 |
| Indonesia | 1.9 | −1.2 | −2.3 | 2.1 | 4.0 | 3.7 | 4.0 | 2.8 | 1.4 |
| South Korea | 1.2 | 0.1 | −10.7 | 31.0 | 11.8 | 25.8 | 32.2 | 11.9 | 15.1 |
| Malaysia | n.a. | 1.4 | −1.1 | 10.0 | 3.7 | 10.3 | 10.0 | 5.1 | 9.2 |
| Philippines | 0.9 | −1.9 | 0.7 | 1.9 | −0.4 | 0.1 | 2.8 | −2.3 | 0.8 |
| Singapore | 9.4 | 12.6 | 10.9 | 3.0 | 1.3 | 6.8 | 12.4 | 13.9 | 17.7 |
| Thailand | −0.4 | 1.6 | 0.6 | 1.4 | 4.2 | 0.1 | 1.0 | 5.8 | 0.7 |
| TOTAL | **−5.4** | **61.7** | **17.2** | **48.8** | **97.4** | **164.8** | **43.4** | **159.1** | **182** |
| *Memo item* | | | | | | | | | |
| Japan | 39.2 | 106.0 | 98.7 | −6.2 | 46.1 | 189.4 | 33.0 | 152.1 | 288.1 |
| Taiwan | 2.4 | 9.1 | 5.9 | 4.8 | 33.7 | 37.1 | 7.2 | 42.8 | 43.0 |

[a] This Table was prepared by Julia Leung. See Park et al. (2004).
[b] Reflected by increase in reserves.
*Source*: International Financial Statistics, IMF.

system with vibrant bond markets. To overcome the efficiency and cost problems of domestic capital markets, repeated calls have been made for East Asian economies to join forces to develop larger and more efficient regional capital markets.

At the informal AFDM+3 meeting in Tokyo in November 2002, South Korea proposed a feasibility study to create new and improve existing Asian bond markets under the ASEAN+3 framework. This proposal received broad support among the thirteen members, and a month later, Japan introduced a comprehensive plan for the development of regional bond markets in Asia, and the Asian Bond Market Initiative (ABMI) was born. Subsequently, six working groups were established to conduct detailed studies on the construction of market infrastructure and creating new debt instruments including bonds denominated in local currencies.

While ASEAN+3 has been primarily engaged in constructing regional infrastructure for Asian bond markets and harmonizing various financial standards, regulatory systems, and tax treatments throughout the region, another regional institution has taken the initiative in creating Asian bond funds to generate demand for Asian bonds. Eleven central banks in East Asia and the Pacific belonging to EMEAP (Executive Meetings of East Asia and Pacific Central Banks) launched the Asian Bond Fund (ABF) I and II.[4] ABF I

---

[4] They are South Korea, China, Japan, Hong Kong, Singapore, Thailand, Malaysia, the Philippines, Indonesia, Australia, and New Zealand.

invests only in dollar denominated Asian sovereign bonds whereas ABF II is structured to invest in local currency denominated Asian bonds.

The establishment of ABF I was announced in June 2003. All eleven EMEAP central banks invested in ABF I at its launch, which had a capitalization of about one billion US dollars. The fund is now fully invested in US dollar-denominated bonds issued by sovereign and quasi-sovereign issuers in eight EMEAP economies (China, Hong Kong, Indonesia, South Korea, the Philippines, Malaysia, Singapore, and Thailand).

Building on the momentum of developing ABF I, EMEAP has proceeded to develop ABF II, which consists of two components: a Pan-Asian Bond Index Fund (PAIF) and a Fund of Bond Funds (FoBF).[5] The ABF II funds are intended to be passively managed against a set of transparent and predetermined benchmark indices, covering local currency bonds issued by sovereign and quasi-sovereign issuers in EMEAP economies.

In view of its small size, market participants believe that ABF I may have had little effect on the market for East Asian sovereign US dollar bonds. If anything, the Fund may have crowded out private investors. The creation of Asian Bond Fund II has been more controversial as there is no shortage of demand for high quality Asian bonds denominated in Asian currencies. Managers of the FoBF will certainly not touch any Asian local currency bonds below investment grade in which private and institutional investors would not invest in. ABF II may then end up competing for a limited supply of high quality Asian bonds, in particular when their spreads are as tight as they are now.

There are also two other concerns about the management of ABF II. One is that since ABF II is likely to invest in East Asian sovereign bonds denominated in local currencies, it may serve as a mutual scheme for financing fiscal deficits among the countries belonging to EMEAP. In such a case, the investment policy of ABF II cannot solely be dictated by profit motives alone, even though a private institution manages the Fund. The second concern is the possible signaling problem. If ABF II is of considerable size, then it is also possible that its investment operations could affect the

---

[5] The PAIF is a single bond index fund investing in local currency-denominated bonds in EMEAP economies. It will act as an investment fund and new asset class for regional and international investors who wish to have well-diversified exposure to bond markets in Asia.

The FoBF is a two-tier structure with a parent fund investing in a number of country sub-funds comprising local currency denominated bonds issued in respective EMEAP economies. While the parent fund is confined to EMEAP investment, country sub-funds are intended to provide local investors with low-cost and index-driven investment vehicles and at the same time give regional and international investors the flexibility to invest in the Asian bond markets of their choice. See Park et al. (2004).

foreign exchange and interest rate policies of the EMEAP member countries whose bonds are purchased or sold by the Fund. Even if the amount of a sale or purchase is relatively small, the Fund's operations may send the wrong signals to the financial markets against the wishes of EMEAP central banks. This signaling problem is likely to remain even if a private institution manages the Fund insofar as EMEAP central banks have a controlling stake. Despite these concerns, EMEAP member central banks could contribute more to the development of Asian bond markets, if they were to use the leverage from ABF II to persuade East Asian economies to build and strengthen the regional financial infrastructure and to remove restrictions that limit the supply of high grade Asian corporate and sovereign bonds in local currency.

- *Rationale and Need*

While policymakers from ASEAN+3 have shown keen interest in advancing ABMI, they have failed to answer several fundamental questions on the need and rationale for the creation of Asian bond markets. This failure may not help produce a realistic development plan that many countries can support and may even foreshadow the ABMI's collapse. One such question is why existing regional capital markets have not been able to serve as alternative sources of financing to local or global bond markets. In particular, Tokyo was, and perhaps still is, a logical place to host a regional center for bond trading, but it has yet to develop a regional bond market that can compete against the euro or Yankee bond market.

Another question that remains unanswered is the structure of the proposed Asian bond markets; that is, whether they are going to be distinct from domestic bond markets, on the one hand, and global bond markets, on the other. Even the concept of Asian bond markets has not been fully articulated and hence has been confusing. Presumably, a regional bond market is a market where bonds issued by corporations and governments in any particularly country are traded throughout the region. Several countries could develop their national markets to list all these bonds. A number of national markets could be linked through the liberalization of cross-border trading. If financial globalization proceeds as fast as it has in the past, domestic as well as regional markets will eventually have to be integrated into global bond markets. This being the case, one could argue East Asian economies may be better off by integrating their domestic bond markets with global markets rather than investing in the creation of regional bond markets. To many smaller East Asian economies, global integration may be neither practical nor feasible. But would these countries find it easier to integrate with the proposed regional bond markets, which may or may not be building blocks for a truly integrated global financial system?

A third question is related to the prospects of financial reform in East Asia. There is general consensus that developing deep and liquid regional bond markets should begin with removing the bewildering array of controls of domestic capital markets and of cross-border investment. ABMI proponents have not emphasized enough that financial market deregulation is the most important prerequisite to the development of Asian bond markets.

These questions suggest that the objectives of the initiative have not been articulated in drawing up the structure and characteristics of the proposed Asian bond markets. One of the most often heard objectives is that robust Asian bond markets will keep, at least in part, Asian savings in Asia, instead of sending them to other countries, in particular the United States, to finance their current account deficits. Another is that deep and liquid Asian bond markets will help East Asian economies defend themselves more effectively against future crises as they will be able to raise more long-term funds in their own currencies in regional bond markets, thereby avoiding the currency mismatch problem. A third is that the ABMI will exert peer pressure on and at the same time generate incentives to Asian countries to continue with their financial reform so that they can take advantage of regional bond markets from which they can secure long-term financing and where they can place their investments.

Of these objectives, the second appears to be the least important, because there is no theory or evidence that suggests that competitive regional bond markets can reduce susceptibility to financial crises. As for the first objective it is difficult to argue that holding most official reserves in East Asia in terms of short-term securities of developed economies is both a consequence and, to a lesser degree, a cause of the underdevelopment of the Asian bond markets.

It is also incorrect to argue that East Asian economies as a whole invest less than they save because of the absence or the inefficiency of existing regional or domestic bond markets. Before the 1997 crisis, when they had smaller and less liquid regional bond markets, East Asian economies invested much more than they have since the crisis. If East Asian economies unloaded a substantial portion of their holdings of US dollar reserves to acquire local Asian currency bonds, such an operation would certainly strengthen East Asian currencies vis-à-vis the US dollar. When the effects of currency appreciation are taken into account, it is not clear whether a greater availability of long-term financing through Asian bond markets would stimulate more capital investment than before.

In view of the preceding analysis, the most important objective of the ABMI is to build regional bond markets that are complementary to global bond markets for more efficient allocation of resources in and diversification of bank-based financial systems of the region. And the most realistic road map for the development of Asian bond markets is to begin with deregulating and opening domestic financial markets so that more investment grade local currency bonds can be issued, domestic investors are allowed to invest in foreign bonds, and foreign borrowers to issue bonds denominated in different currencies in East Asia's national bond markets. This market liberalization and opening would naturally form integrated Asian bond markets as it facilitates cross-border investment in bonds in Asia. In this evolutionary process, those countries with a well-developed financial infrastructure and few financial restrictions will then emerge as regional trading centers for Asian bonds.

Market liberalization and opening will not, however, be sufficient to develop regional bond markets unless regional financial infrastructure that includes a regional system of clearing and settlement, regional credit guarantee institutions, hedging facilities, and regional credit rating agencies is also constructed. In addition to the infrastructure construction, East Asian economies should also be able to harmonize their legal and regulatory systems, domestic clearing and settlement systems, market practices, and withholding taxes on bond coupon payments. However, in this regard, the prospects for close cooperation among ASEAN+3 members are not promising at this stage. Many of the smaller member countries have been indifferent to the promotion of the ABMI; to these countries, the benefits from efficient regional bond markets are rather abstract. And it is not clear which country or group of countries has the moral authority, influence, and money to lead region-wide financial reform and the construction of regional financial infrastructure in East Asia.

In developing strategies for regional capital markets, East Asian economies could take either a market-led or government-led approach. A government-led approach requires active participation on the part of East Asian governments not only in building financial and other institutional infrastructures, but also in producing a wide range of capital market instruments tailored to the preferences of investors through, for example, schemes to guarantee the principle and interest payments on private bonds, securitizing bank loans, and credit enhancement.

The market-led or evolutionary approach relies more on competition among countries vying for hosting a regional trading center for Asian bonds. In view of the lack of leadership, a high cost of constructing the financial infrastructure and differences in interests among ASEAN+3 members, the market-oriented approach may be a preferable strategy. It is preferable because the thirteen countries may find it difficult to agree on any of the strategies for Asian bond market development proposed by Thailand, Hong Kong, Japan, and South Korea. Even if they can reach agreement, the chosen strategy may not see daylight as long as some of the ASEAN+3 states are locked in competition for transforming their domestic capital markets into regional financial centers. This inter-country rivalry is one reason—perhaps the most important one—why a market-oriented approach would be more realistic than one that is government-led. If a market-oriented strategy were pursued, those national bond markets that survive global competition for financial intermediation would emerge as dominant regional bond markets. In this approach, the primary responsibility of East Asian governments is to develop financial, legal, and regulatory infrastructure at the regional level to ensure the efficiency and stability of regional capital markets.

# 20

# Prospects for Economic Cooperation and Integration in East Asia

## 20.1. Structural Constraints

In reading an endless series of press releases by East Asian governments, ASEAN+3 and journalistic accounts of bilateral FTAs under negotiation or discussion and the CMI and ABMI, many observers may conclude that the region is at a historical turning point in economic integration. Up close and delving into the latest developments in regional trade and financial integration, however, it will not take much time to conclude that East Asia is not Europe and far away in constructing basic economic and political foundations for economic integration. For the next several years, the ASEAN+3 states will be preoccupied with negotiating bilateral FTAs with one another and with other countries from different regions. This fervor of bilateralism will overshadow and defer any further discussion of or new initiatives for region-wide trade liberalization: even if they come to conclude a number of bilateral FTAs, they may not make much headway in achieving region-wide free trade insofar as there is a possibility that the East Asian bilateralism could erect new trade barriers.

Having amassed huge amounts of foreign exchange reserves and knowing that they can exploit the vast new Chinese export market, ASEAN+3 has lost a great deal of interest in augmenting and consolidating the CMI network. At the same time, the proliferation of bilateral FTAs has distracted ASEAN+3 leaders from financial cooperation and policy coordination, although there is a clear need for coordination at the regional level for exchange rate policy.

Despite these developments, the leaders of ASEAN+3 realize the importance of cooperation and policy dialogue among themselves on many issues such as the growing transpacific imbalance that may require a region-wide collective response. If they want to keep ABMI alive, ASEAN+3 policymakers will have to find ways in which cross-border investments can be deregulated. They will also find that policy dialogue is essential in educating East Asian bureaucracies and leaders about each other, and to come to grips with some of the practical problems of regional economic cooperation. This is inevitably both a long-run process, given the relatively low levels of knowledge and trust, and essentially a political process, using economic issues as a mechanism for enhancing dialogue. The democratization process in many of the ASEAN+3 member states is likely to sustain and facilitate both policy dialogue and cooperation. For these reasons, it is expected that East Asian policymakers will continue to search for a more realistic modality of cooperation for the promotion of the CMI, ABMI, and FTAs.

One of the impediments to economic integration in East Asia is, unlike in Europe, the region's lack of historical experience in regional economic and political cooperation. Despite the economic benefits financial and monetary integration bring to the region, regional efforts at establishing closer economic ties will be frustrated, if each country is unwilling to cooperate in the political arena. Although the ASEAN+3 members have so far shown remarkable solidarity in working together for the development of the CMI and ABMI, it remains to be seen whether China, Japan, and other members of ASEAN+3 could overcome their disputes on and differences in regional issues to sustain the integrationist movement.

Another institutional and political constraint on regional economic integration is the failure of the ASEAN+3 countries to coordinate their respective FTA negotiations with the CMI and ABMI. In contrast to the bilateral approach to trade negotiations, the ASEAN+3 has established a multilateral framework for financial market integration. The two regional financial initiatives are motivated, and have received region-wide support, for the promotion of financial stability and integration in East Asia. The ASEAN+3 fora are organized around finance ministers and central bank governors and their deputies. Trade officials do not participate in any of the ASEAN+3 agenda.

There is no plan for expanding the ASEAN+3 framework to include trade ministries for the coordination of trade policies. There is therefore an unfortunate dichotomy between negotiations for trade and financial integration in the ASEAN+3 group. The discussion on financial integration and cooperation has been carried on within the confines of ASEAN+3, whereas that on trade policy including FTA negotiations has transcended regional contiguity. This dichotomy, together with the growing enthusiasm for bilateralism in trade, may then run into conflict with the ASEAN+3 plan for region-wide financial liberalization and integration. This is because different countries participating in regional financial integration may demand in FTA negotiations not only different timetables of financial liberalization, but also different conditions and exemptions for participating in financial cooperation.

A third institutional constraint is related to the need to coordinate the activities of the CMI with other regional arrangements such as the APEC regional forums. At some point in the future, leaders of ASEAN+3 may have to decide on the mode of cooperation and division of labor in promoting regional growth and stability between these institutions and the ASEAN+3. Many of the thirteen ASEAN+3 countries have been engaged in policy review and dialogues through APEC sub-arrangements. There is the question of whether the thirteen countries of ASEAN+3 constitute an optimal currency area and whether they make up an appropriate grouping for trade integration.

The single most important obstacle to regional economic integration is the absence of leadership that could balance different interests of different countries in East Asia. The European experience shows that regional integration cannot progress very far without leadership that can keep participating countries as a coherent group dedicated to achieving a set of common objectives. China and Japan, which could provide the needed leadership, have not been able to agree on many regional issues.

China and Japan have different interests in and, therefore, different strategies for economic integration in East Asia. China has shown its loss of interest in regional integration as it has assumed a greater global role in recent years as a de facto member of the G-7. On regional economic issues, as far as China is concerned, its bilateral FTA with ASEAN may be vital to consolidating its strategic interests. Any economic gains the China–ASEAN FTA offers are of secondary importance. From the perspectives of Chinese policymakers, integration with ASEAN, South Asian, and central Asian countries carries more significance both economically and geopolitically than, or takes precedence over, financial cooperation or free trade with either Japan or South Korea. While China is a military superpower, it is still a developing economy with a huge gap in terms of technological and industrial sophistication vis-à-vis Japan. Although China has been growing rapidly, it has a long way to go to catch up with Japan. These differences in the economic and military status of the two countries suggest that China and Japan may, even if they manage to reconcile their troubled past, find it difficult to work together for regional integration in East Asia.

China has borders with Russia and many of the South Asian and central Asian countries in addition to several ASEAN members. It is natural, therefore, for China to seek expansion and deepening of its trade and financial relations with these countries. In fact, for this reason, in November of 2001, it joined the Bangkok agreement on a free trade area that includes the South Asian countries. China has also taken a leading role in establishing the Shanghai cooperation organization, a cooperative arrangement also including Russia, Kazakhstan, Kyrgyzstan, Tajikistan and Uzbekistan.

In contrast, Japan has not been able to articulate its strategic interests in East Asia. In particular, the geographical contiguity of East Asia from the Japanese perspective has not been altogether clear. For example, Japan suggested the formation of ASEAN+5, but the two countries to be added to ASEAN+3 have not been clear. At one point, the five countries were China, Japan, South Korea, Australia, and New Zealand. At another, Australia and New Zealand were replaced by Taiwan and Hong Kong. There is also the suspicion that Japan is not interested in free trade or financial integration per se in East Asia but preoccupied with countering China's penetration of ASEAN. Many analysts believe that Japan's active involvement in regional economic integration is therefore motivated by its desire to maintain its traditional position.[1]

On top of this suspicion, Japan is perceived to be insensitive to and unwilling to resolve its wartime legacy and disputes on historical and territorial claims. Japan has also been gripped by a decade-long recession and unable to restructure its economy, in particular its financial sector, making many East Asian economies apprehensive about supporting any regional initiative for financial integration promoted by Japan. These structural problems have combined with the lack of its strategy for East Asian development to undermine Japan's ability to bring East Asian economies together for regional cooperation and integration.

## 20.2. Trade Integration

What, then, are the likely courses trade integration will take in East Asia? How would regional trade integration proceed in East Asia? Answers to these questions will largely depend on future developments in China's trade relations with the rest of East Asia. China has become the largest trading partner to all East Asian economies including Japan. Given the vast

---

[1] See Wall (2002).

market China presents for exports and direct investment, it is quite possible that despite the differences in their strategies, both China and Japan could come to realize that region-wide trade liberalization and integration would be in their interests in the long run. If Japan believes it inevitable that economic integration in East Asia will be centered on China, and China realizes that Japan will continue to be the major source of capital and technology, then the two countries could cooperate for deeper trade integration in the region. However, this is a very unlikely scenario.

Another focuses on the possibility of China assuming a more central leadership role in regional integration and thereby forming an FTA hub. Knowing that ASEAN members will be more attracted to their FTA negotiations with China than Japan, China may decide to use its market leverage to negotiate deeper financial and trade integration with ASEAN. How viable would a China–ASEAN FTA be as a regional economic arrangement? China is not a full-fledged market economy and a communist society. It is also questionable whether ASEAN's interest would be served when it establishes a free trade area with a super military power that has an underdeveloped and closed financial system as a dominant partner. In order to diffuse China's dominance, ASEAN will attempt to establish as many bilateral FTAs with other countries as it can.

What options would be available to Japan and South Korea if China were to choose to pursue both trade and financial integration with ASEAN and become an FTA hub? This question leads to third and fourth scenarios. Japan is proposing a Korea–Japan FTA and similar agreements to ASEAN and its individual members. This strategy, if successfully carried out, will divide ASEAN+3 into two subgroups, making both China and Japan FTA hubs. A fourth scenario is the one in which Japan (and possibly Korea) searches for FTA partners beyond ASEAN+3 into other continents to include Australia, New Zealand, and countries from South Asia. This global reach for FTA negotiations could increase Japan's leverage in dealing with China.

The most realistic scenario is that ASEAN+3 members will continue to negotiate FTAs with as many interested partners as they can find. However, China appears to be less than enthusiastic about taking a leadership role in promoting trade integration in East Asia, because as a large and rapidly growing economy, China can capture the benefits of multilateralism through unilateral trade liberalization. This together with the fact that all East Asian economies depend on China's growing markets for their exports suggests that China may not find many incentives to engage in a multitude of FTAs except with ASEAN.

In the midst of confusion and uncertainty, paradoxically ASEAN may emerge as an FTA with China, Japan, and South Korea as spokes. ASEAN may also prevail in imposing its rules of origin in negotiating its bilateral FTA with the three north-eastern countries. Will this development move ASEAN+3 a step closer to creating an East Asian FTA? Not likely. The completion of the three FTAs will not make it any easier for the spoke countries to agree to free trade among themselves.

There is always hope, however. As shown by Lee et al. (2004), the benefits in terms of trade creation accruing from the proliferation and overlap of bilateral FTAs will decline. At the same time, the costs arising from different rules of origin and excluded sectors in different bilateral FTAs will increase. This development could discourage a further increase in bilateral FTAs or make East Asian economies realize the need for coordinating their trade polices, thereby producing incentives for laying the groundwork for regional trade integration in East Asia. Against this expectation, there has been an unmistakable shift in East Asia away from ASEAN+3 to a broader group of countries for trade integration. The movement may paradoxically defeat the very objective it has set out to achieve, which is regional economic integration centering on ASEAN+3. This development may or may not be bad depending on the outcomes of the proliferation of FTAs. What is clear, however, is that, given the possibility that the proliferation will undermine multilateral trade liberalization efforts, the global community will have to come up with a new multilateral approach that could ensure a smooth amalgamation of existing RTAs into a single global trading system.

## 20.3. Financial Integration

The CMI liquidity system has never been tested and will not be in the near future. This makes it difficult to assess its effectiveness as a regional arrangement for defense against future financial crises. However, it should be noted that the contribution of the CMI is not so much the availability of liquidity it can provide, as its nature as a milestone in policy dialogue and coordination in East Asia. Recognizing its deficiencies, as noted earlier, ASEAN+3 has taken steps to explore the ways in which the effectiveness of the CMI, including its multilateralization, can be enhanced.

ASEAN+3 policymakers are also aware of the fact that unless the cooperative efforts at the ABMI are carried out in conjunction with domestic financial reform in individual member countries, which will open their capital markets, efficient regional bond markets would not come into existence in Asia. Capital market development in East Asia has been hampered by many institutional weaknesses and regulatory controls. Among other things, the lack of professional expertise in the securities business, inadequacy of the financial and legal infrastructures including regulatory systems, low standards of accounting and auditing, and opacity of corporate governance have been the major culprits. Unfortunately, however, ASEAN+3 is not expected to address the urgency of the domestic reform, as members cannot intervene in the domestic affairs of other members. ASEAN+3's inability to organize a collective program for domestic financial reform will in the end frustrate the efforts of ASEAN+3 at creating robust Asian bond markets.

At present, the degree of capital control varies a great deal from country to country in Asia and prospects for further capital account liberalization are not promising. If the ASEAN+3 members succeed in consolidating the CMI network into an effective liquidity support system, however, they will be able to obtain more public support for region-wide capital account liberalization. Supporters of the ABMI are also beginning to find out how difficult it is to construct a regional financial infrastructure. For these reasons, there is no guarantee that regional efforts, even if they can be organized, could succeed in fostering regional capital markets that are competitive vis-à-vis global capital markets in North America and Europe.

Even if Asian bond markets are created, multinational commercial and investment banks and multinational institutional investors will play a major role in Asian bond market underwriting and secondary market transactions. Furthermore, globalization of financial markets and advances in financial technology that allow financial firms in international financial centers to reach investors and borrowers in remote corners of the world raise questions as to whether regional capital markets can compete against global market. It is also true, however, that given the economic dynamism of East Asia and its enormous pool of savings, the region could accommodate large and efficient regional capital markets.

Trade and investment liberalization have been the driving forces behind much of the increase in intra-regional trade in East Asia. This increase has in turn served to synchronize business cycles across East Asian economies, thereby producing economic conditions favourable for financial integration and the creation of a currency union in the region.

Against these trade and macroeconomic developments, financial deregulation and market opening have drawn East Asia away from regional to financial integration. As Eichengreen and Park (2004) show, East Asian economies share similar structural characteristics in common, pursue a similar development strategy, and display synchronized business cycles. To the extent that they are subject to symmetrical shocks, then, the risk diversification for consumption smoothing may induce them to integrate with those non-regional economies with different structural characteristics and cyclical patterns rather than regional ones, because credit and market risks of non-regional financial assets are likely to be less correlated with those of domestic assets. If indeed different regions are subject to idiosyncratic shocks to regional outputs, then a substantial portion of the risk related to stabilizing consumption can be shared through portfolio diversification across different regions.

Through global financial integration, countries can stabilize their consumption spending by lending to and borrowing from international financial markets with large pools of various financial instruments. Using a model of consumption risk sharing, Jeon et al. (2005) estimate the degree of global consumption risk sharing and find that their sample East Asian countries are moving to global rather than regional financial integration.[2]

Financial market deregulation and opening throughout East Asia, if sustained to liberalize cross-border investment, will lead many countries to establish closer linkages with international financial markets than with markets of other neighbouring countries in the region. In contrast, the financial markets of European countries were much more integrated with one another in the 1970s and 1980s than the markets of East Asian economies are at present. This difference suggests that unlike trade liberalization, financial market liberalization and opening may not contribute to economic integration in East Asia as much as it would under different circumstances (Eichengreen and Park 2003). What should then be the ultimate objectives of the CMI? Is the CMI going to be fostered as a regional liquidity support program or as a building block for a full-fledged regional

---

[2] Against risk diversification, there may be regional bias in portfolio investment. As McCauley, Fung, and Gadanecz (2002) show, Asian investors prefer holding Asian bonds and stocks to those issued by non-Asian entities largely because they have more and better information about the risk-return profiles of regional assets than about non-regional ones. There are few empirical studies that shed light on the relative effects of the risk diversification and regional bias. At present, the available evidence is not large and reliable enough to judge the possible direction of integration following region-wide financial liberalization and market opening.

The well-known home bias in asset holdings suggests that the benefit of risk diversification would not be as large as the theory would predict. Despite ongoing financial liberalization over more than two decades, the increase in international diversification in assets, particularly in bonds across countries, has been relatively small. McKinnon (2003) points to the principal-agent problem as the main cause of limited global portfolio diversification.

monetary system in East Asia? If bilateral swap arrangements of the CMI are activated collectively and supported by an independent surveillance system, they then constitute a de facto regional monetary fund. The CMI could then serve as a foundation for financial and monetary cooperation following in the footsteps of European monetary integration. At this stage of development, many countries in East Asia are not prepared to make the CMI a forerunner of the AMF.

What, then, are the likely courses of financial integration in East Asia? One scenario is that because of a congruence of interests both China and Japan could soften their positions so as to compromise on an institutional setting and expansion of the CMI. For instance, China may accept Japan's demand for its de facto control over monitoring and surveillance in return for Japan's pledge for a substantial increase in financial assistance in the form of one-way swaps and ODA to ASEAN members. China could agree to this scheme if it is confident about concluding a free trade agreement with ASEAN members in the near future. China may feel that its free trade pact with ASEAN could keep Japan's influence in ASEAN affairs within bounds, even if Japan is a major provider of finance to the region. However, this scenario is not realistic whatever its long-run advantages may be, given the intensifying rivalry between the two countries.

Another scenario focuses on the possibility that China decides to negotiate both financial and trade integration with ASEAN at the same time. In this case, the original CMI will become ASEAN+1. To the extent that financial integration will contribute to forming a free trade area with ASEAN, China may indeed seriously consider this option. However, without Japan, ASEAN+1 will not be a viable arrangement for a regional financing scheme simply because China at this stage is hardly in a position to commit itself to financing the balance of payments deficits of all ASEAN member states. It is also questionable whether ASEAN would be willing to join any regional financial arrangement in which a country like China with an underdeveloped and closed financial system and a looming banking crisis is going to be the dominant member.

If China chooses to pursue financial and monetary integration with ASEAN as a long-run objective. Japan will counter China's strategy by demanding the enlargement of CMI membership to include Australia and New Zealand and possibly other countries from South Asia. This is the third scenario favored by Japan. However, many members of ASEAN+3 believe that forming a critical CMI mass should precede any discussion of enlargement. Since enlargement is not likely substantially to increase the availability of short-term financing, the third scenario is not going to be taken seriously by ASEAN.

The most realistic scenario is that as in trade liberalization, countries participating in the CMI will continue to mull over the modalities of policy dialogue, the types of surveillance systems, and augmentation of swap amounts without making any substantial progress, largely because China and Japan will likely be unable to resolve their differences in developing the CMI. However, a possible breakthrough may come over the next several years during which ASEAN+3 succeed in multilateralizing the CMI network. Once multilateralization is agreed upon, East Asia will enter a new era of regionalism as it will be easier to take the next step of creating an Asian Arrangement to borrow, a forerunner of a regional monetary fund while simultaneously concluding a number of bilateral FTAs.

# 21

# Reserve Accumulation in East Asia and Transpacific Trade Imbalance*

The foreign currency reserves held by a group of ten East Asian economies[1] have risen enormously since the 1997–98 crisis. As of May 2005, the total reserves of these economies stood at $2.4 trillion, up from 1.0 trillion five years earlier. All of these countries have been running sizeable amounts of surpluses on their current accounts, the bulk of which have been sterilized and added to their reserves (see Table 21.1). Forty-six percent of East Asia's trade surpluses has come from the region's trade with the US in 2003, and not surprisingly have been converted into its holdings of short-term US treasury securities (see Table 21.2).

## 21.1. Causes and Potential Consequences of the Transpacific Imbalance

Although the US current account deficit rose to 6 percent of its GDP in 2004, according to *The Economist* (2003), Alan Greenspan does not believe that America's current account deficit poses any dangers. Dooley, Folkerts-Landau, and Garber (2003) agree: in their new Bretton Woods system the imbalance does not present any systemic risks to the global financial system as it can be carried for a long time as long as East Asian economies are fixated on an export-led growth strategy. Bernanke (2005) argues that the global imbalance is not made in the US. A global savings glut forces the US to live beyond its means. Balancing the federal budget, according to

---

* This chapter draws on chapter 4 of Geneva Reports on the World Economy 7 (2005).
[1] They are: China, Japan, South Korea, Taiwan, Hong Kong, Indonesia, Malaysia, the Philippines, Singapore, and Thailand. For analytic purposes, these ten countries may be divided into Japan, China, and other emerging market economies of East Asia.

**Table 21.1.** International Reserves of East Asia, 1999–2005 (USD, billions)

|              | 1999      | 2000    | 2001    | 2002    | 2003    | 2004    | 2005*   |
|--------------|-----------|---------|---------|---------|---------|---------|---------|
| Japan        | 287.0     | 354.9   | 395.2   | 461.3   | 663.3   | 833.9   | 829.9   |
|              | (31.8)**  | (34.9)  | (35.1)  | (34.3)  | (37.2)  | (36.4)  | (35.2)  |
| **Subtotal** | **287.0** | **354.9** | **395.2** | **461.3** | **663.3** | **833.9** | **829.9** |
|              | 96.3      | 107.5   | 111.2   | 111.9   | 118.4   | 123.5   | 122.4   |
| Hong Kong    | (10.7)    | (10.6)  | (9.9)   | (8.3)   | (6.6)   | (5.4)   | (5.2)   |
|              | 74.0      | 96.1    | 102.8   | 121.4   | 155.3   | 199.0   | 206.0   |
| Korea, South | (8.2)     | (9.5)   | (9.1)   | (9.0)   | (8.7)   | (8.7)   | (8.7)   |
|              | 76.9      | 80.1    | 75.4    | 82.1    | 95.7    | 112.2   | 116.0   |
| Singapore    | (8.5)     | (7.9)   | (6.7)   | (6.1)   | (5.4)   | (4.9)   | (4.9)   |
|              | 106.2     | 106.7   | 122.2   | 161.7   | 206.6   | 242.0   | 253.2   |
| Taiwan       | (11.8)    | (10.5)  | (10.9)  | (12.0)  | (11.6)  | (10.6)  | (10.7)  |
| **Subtotal** | **353.4** | **390.6** | **411.6** | **477.1** | **576.0** | **676.7** | **697.6** |
|              | 26.5      | 28.5    | 27.3    | 31.0    | 35.0    | 35.0    | 33.3    |
| Indonesia    | (2.9)     | (2.8)   | (2.4)   | (2.3)   | (2.0)   | (1.5)   | (1.4)   |
|              | 30.6      | 29.5    | 30.5    | 34.2    | 44.5    | 66.4    | 74.1    |
| Malaysia     | (3.4)     | (2.9)   | (2.7)   | (2.5)   | (2.5)   | (2.9)   | (3.1)   |
|              | 13.2      | 13.1    | 13.4    | 13.1    | 13.5    | 12.9    | 14.8    |
| Philippines  | (1.5)     | (1.3)   | (1.2)   | (1.0)   | (0.8)   | (0.6)   | (0.6)   |
|              | 34.1      | 32.0    | 32.4    | 38.1    | 41.1    | 48.7    | 47.1    |
| Thailand     | (3.8)     | (3.1)   | (2.9)   | (2.8)   | (2.3)   | (2.1)   | (2.0)   |
|              | 157.8     | 168.3   | 215.7   | 291.2   | 408.2   | 614.5   | 659.1   |
| China        | (17.5)    | (16.6)  | (19.2)  | (21.6)  | (22.9)  | (26.9)  | (28.0)  |
| **Subtotal** | **262.2** | **271.4** | **319.3** | **407.7** | **542.2** | **777.5** | **828.4** |
| **Total**    | **902.6** | **1,016.9** | **1,126.1** | **1,346.1** | **1,781.5** | **2,288.1** | **2,355.9** |

*Source*: IMF, International Financial Statistics and *The Economist* (2005), July 16–22 and June 11–17.
*Note*: * at the end of May.
      ** Percentage of the total.

**Table 21.2.** US bilateral trade with East Asian economies, 1997–2004 (USD, billions)

| Country      | 1997      | 1998      | 1999      | 2000      | 2001      | 2002      | 2003      | 2004      |
|--------------|-----------|-----------|-----------|-----------|-----------|-----------|-----------|-----------|
| Japan        | −56.1     | −64       | −73.4     | −81.6     | −69.0     | −70.0     | −66.0     | −75.6     |
| Hong Kong    | 4.8       | 2.4       | 2.1       | 3.1       | 4.4       | 3.3       | 4.7       | 6.5       |
| Korea, South | 1.9       | −7.5      | −8.2      | −12.5     | −13.0     | −13.0     | −13.2     | −19.8     |
| Singapore    | −2.4      | −2.7      | −1.9      | −1.4      | 2.7       | 1.4       | 1.4       | 4.2       |
| Taiwan       | −12.3     | −15       | −16.1     | −16.1     | −15.3     | −13.8     | −14.2     | −12.9     |
| Indonesia    | −4.7      | −7.0      | −7.5      | −8.0      | −7.6      | −7.1      | −7.0      | −8.1      |
| Malaysia     | −7.2      | −10.0     | −12.4     | −14.6     | −13.0     | −13.7     | −14.5     | −17.3     |
| Philippines  | −3.0      | −5.2      | −5.1      | −5.1      | −3.7      | −3.7      | −2.1      | −2.0      |
| Thailand     | −5.3      | −8.2      | −9.3      | −9.8      | −8.7      | −9.9      | −9.3      | −11.2     |
| China        | −49.7     | −56.9     | −68.7     | −83.8     | −83.1     | −103.1    | −124.1    | −161.9    |
| **Total**    | **−133.9** | **−174.1** | **−200.5** | **−229.7** | **−206.3** | **−229.5** | **−244.3** | **−298.1** |
|              | *(74.2)   | *(75.8)   | *(61.0)   | *(52.7)   | *(50.1)   | *(49.0)   | *(45.9)   | *(45.8)   |

*Source*: US Census Bureau.
*Note*: * Percentage of East Asia in total US trade balance.

Bernanke's estimation, will reduce the US current account deficit by less than one percentage point of GDP over the medium term.

On the other hand, Obstfeld and Rogoff (2004) are not as sanguine as these optimists, saying that the dollar could fall by as much as 20 to 40 percent, unless the US manages to bring the federal deficit under control and to raise the private savings rate. Roubini and Setser (2005) believe that the existing imbalance, which is likely to grow further, will provoke a major financial crisis before the end of 2006. Obstfeld and Rogoff do not, however, believe that this massive decline in the dollar would be catastrophic for Europe and Japan. This chapter shows that it could be for East Asia with the possible exception of Japan and China.

What will happen to the imbalance if it is left unattended? Is there any market mechanism that will resolve the imbalance in an orderly manner without destabilizing the global financial system? This section discusses a number of plausible patterns of adjustment of the imbalance, which depend on policy changes that the US and East Asia may or may not make.

Such a discussion would demand a careful examination of the causes and potential consequences of the imbalance that in some quarters is viewed as posing a risk of throwing the global economy into financial turmoil and a recession. The recent debates on the imbalance have focused on three different views on the causes of the global imbalance: one is that East Asians do not consume enough; another points to America's growing budgetary deficit and a low private savings rate; and the third view accuses East Asian economies of manipulating their exchange rates.

- *A Global Savings Glut: Emergence of Bretton Woods II*

Bernanke (2005) believes that there is a global savings glut created largely by emerging economies. The developing world has moved from an aggregate current account surplus of $87 billion in 1996 to a surplus of $205 billion by 2003. Unless emerging and developing countries invest more, they will have to transfer their excessive savings to borrowers in advanced countries who borrow to finance their investment or consumption. Since the EU has been running a trade surplus, it is the US that has been forced to absorb these savings. According to Bernanke, there is little the US can do to resolve its current account deficit, as long as the rest of the world saves more than it invests. Bernanke thus provides another reason for the emergence of the new Bretton Woods system of Dooley, Folkerts-Landau, and Garber.

Does East Asia's high propensity to save create a deficiency of global demand for goods and services? It does *ex ante*, but Bernanke could have asked why the emerging and developing economies have been unable to use their savings to finance their own investment instead of asking why they have been saving so much.

East Asia as a whole has been a net supplier of saving to the rest of the world for a long time and more so since the 1997–98 Asian financial crisis. How could this net-saving position of the region be a problem, unless the region-wide high savings rate is the result of forced saving or policy measures such as restrictions on imports of consumer goods or lending for consumption? There is indeed little evidence of forced saving with the possible exception of the National Provident Fund of Singapore, or the incentive structure that artificially generates excessive saving that is not fully used to finance domestic investment.

A more rational interpretation of the high savings rate of the region is that it is the outcome of intertemporal spending decisions of households—decisions that also reflect their self-insurance motive. East Asia's fear of exposing itself to financial crises in the future lingers on. Their holdings of large reserves serve therefore as war chests to be used to fend off any speculative attack or to meet other unexpected large capital outflows. And a lack of opportunities of profitable investment has produced a large current account surplus.

Viewed from the saving and investment balance, the excess of savings over investment—the current account surplus or net foreign investment—will not necessarily be a policy problem if the savings are invested in foreign investment projects with higher rates of return than those in East Asia. However, the bulk of East Asia's savings has not been allocated in an efficient manner, as it has been channeled to the US for financing its consumption. Many view this to be less desirable on the grounds of global welfare compared to an allocation that would send East Asia's savings to other parts of the world or keep it in the developing world for their own investment financing.

Emerging and developing economies from other regions cannot easily tap into the pool of East Asia's savings, largely because international capital markets have not developed either efficient mechanisms or instruments that can help mediate between East Asia's savers and investors from other emerging and developing economies. Only a small number of corporate and institutional borrowers from these economies can raise funds on international capital markets: most of them simply cannot issue bonds denominated either in domestic or foreign currencies in international financial markets because of their low credit ratings.

The experience of these economies also suggest that financial market deregulation and opening does not necessarily improve their effective access to global financial markets. On the contrary, capital account liberalization could increase the amplitude of cycles in swings in domestic financial markets, leading to a larger holding of foreign reserves.

Although it may sound paradoxical, the Washington Consensus reforms that contributed to liberalizing and opening domestic financial markets and to smaller government with a reduced scope of intervention appear to have weakened investment demand throughout East Asia. Banks and other financial institutions have become much more reluctant to finance long-term and risky investment projects out of concern for the quality of their asset portfolios. Governments have also refrained from expanding their own investment or supporting private investment in social infrastructure, education, research and development, rural development, public health, and the environment.

Even the Asian Development Bank has curtailed its financing of infrastructure to a minimum in the region. Financial institutions, corporations, and governments themselves have all been preoccupied with strengthening their financial positions to insulate themselves against external shocks and speculations. If indeed there is a glut of savings in the global economy, this may reflect the failures of international financial markets that advanced countries have not sought to rectify.

- *East Asia's Exchange Rate Manipulation and Export-led Development Strategy*

A number of US-based economists including Bergsten have accused East Asian economies of rigging their exchange rates to keep their currencies undervalued to subsidize exports. In their view, this foreign exchange market intervention is one of the causes of East Asia's ballooning trade surplus that has been sterilized to augment their reserves. Would a real appreciation of East Asian currencies then set in motion an adjustment that will ultimately restore global balance?

At the outset it should be noted that East Asia's export-led growth strategy itself is not responsible for the reserve accumulation. Many East Asian economies ran large current account deficits before when they were promoting exports more aggressively. This experience suggests that it is too simplistic to argue that the export-led strategy is the principal cause of the growing imbalance unless it can be shown that there is a mechanism through which the strategy has led to the increase in the savings–investment gap in East Asia. As shown in Figures 21.1 and 21.2, most East Asian currencies in

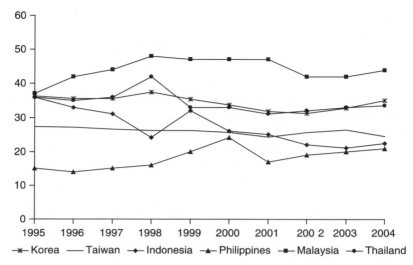

**Figure 21.1.** Investment share in GDP (%)

*Source:* IMF, *International Financial Statistics*, various issues, World Bank, *World Development Indicators*, 1997–2004; World Bank *World Development Report*, 1995–6; and country sources.

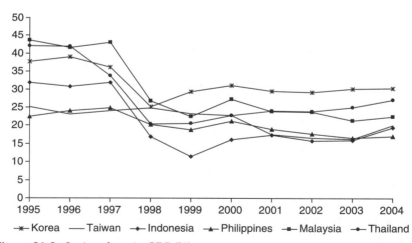

**Figure 21.2.** Saving share in GDP (%)

*Source:* IMF, *International Financial Statistics*, various issues, World Bank, *World Development Indicators*, 1997–2004; World Bank *World Development Report*, 1995–6; and country sources.

real trade-weighted terms have appreciated since the 1997–98 crisis, and this has not prevented export growth in the region. Finally, no one has presented any convincing evidence that East Asia's alleged currency manipulation can explain its growing savings gap.

During the 1970s and 1980s, sustained export expansion invariably created a favorable environment for business investment and powered an upturn in the economy, which then led to a large increase in imports of capital and intermediate goods and to the deterioration in the current account in East Asia. For a number of reasons this chain of reactions triggered by an expansion in exports appears to have broken down in many of East Asia's emerging market economies, resulting in a large and persistent current account surplus in the region.

One possible explanation for this breakdown is that the East Asian economies, particularly those hit by the crisis, have yet to complete the paring down of excess capital stock built in the run-up to the 1997–98 crisis. From the point of view of East Asia's policymakers, the 1997 crisis together with the IMF-imposed structural reform left them with a large excess stock of capital to be disposed of overtime. This stock adjustment together with the bursting of the IT bubble in 2001 has dramatically curtailed domestic investment demand. Between 1995 and 2003, investment as a proportion of GDP fell in all East Asian economies while their savings rates have remained relatively stable (see Figures 21.1 and 21.2). In Indonesia, the investment–GDP ratio in 2003 was less than half of what it was in 1995. Malaysia saw its ratio plummet to 24.4 percent in 2003 from a high of 43 percent in 1997. South Korea and Thailand experienced a similar setback amounting to decreases of 11 and 20 percentage points of their ratios respectively over the same period.

- *US Fiscal Deficit*

The international financial and monetary system at present finances the enormous US current account deficit and the associated fiscal deficit. To Roubini and Setser (2005) this financing is 'the defining feature' of the current system. That is, the US budgetary deficit and the dependence of the rest of the world on an expansion of US domestic demand are the causes of the global imbalance. And as Roubini and Setser see it, the US fiscal deficit is likely to remain large—more than 3.5 percent of GDP—in coming years if the tax cuts of the current US administration become permanent. They do not believe the World's central banks are prepared to continue to finance the growing US current account deficits indefinitely: the new

Bretton Woods system of Dooley, Folkerts-Landau, and Garber may last at most for another two years.

In response to Roubini and Setser's pessimistic forecast, Greenspan, Dooley, Folkerts-Landau, Garber, and Bernanke would argue that a reduction in federal deficit spending risks setting off a global economic slowdown as it contracts both the US current account deficit and global aggregate demand, unless the reduction is offset by a corresponding demand increase elsewhere. Although it may be right in saying that the US adjustment could create a deficiency in global aggregate demand, it does not follow that running a budgetary deficit in the US is either unavoidable or a desirable policy choice. The implication of the global imbalance is that the dependence on the US fiscal deficit is unhealthy and that the international community should look for areas—regions, markets, and industries—where institutional and policy reforms could support more balanced growth of global aggregate demand between regions and between consumption and investment.

## 21.2. Policy Adjustments in East Asia: Monetary and Fiscal Policy

The preceding section highlighted the importance of reviving domestic demand, particularly in fixed investments, to curb a further expansion of foreign exchange reserves in East Asia. More expansionary monetary and fiscal policy is called for and if needed, currency appreciation should not be resisted if East Asia wants to participate in a policy strategy, coordinated with the US and the EU in order to diffuse the growing tension over the resolution of the transpacific imbalance. In view of the severe recession and financial turmoil that a disorderly resolution of global imbalances could provoke, East Asia has every reason to participate actively in any policy adjustments on which the three regions can agree. Although East Asia's policymakers realize the need for making macroeconomic policy changes for their own sake, they are finding that monetary policy is ineffective and that a host of structural constraints are limiting the sphere of influence of other policy intervention.

• *Monetary Policy*

Many East Asian emerging economies have introduced or have been in the process of adopting inflation targeting as a nominal anchor in their macroeconomic policy management since the 1997–98 crisis. In reality, however, they have not strictly tied monetary policy with the targeting as they have moved to an intermediate exchange rate regime with capital controls (partial at least), and stable prices have created room for monetary expansion.

In fact, most of these countries with or without inflation targeting guided interest rates to historically low levels in recent years. Except for Indonesia and the Philippines, domestic interest rates in other East Asian economies are as low as those in advanced countries, including the euro area. However, this easy monetary policy has done very little in reviving investment demand, reminding one of the old adage that you can take a horse to water, but cannot make it drink. The near zero interest rate and its muted effect on domestic spending in Japan do not appear to encourage further easing of monetary policy throughout East Asia.

As part of their stabilization policy to cool off overheating of the economy, China has been trying to rein in the rapid growth of credit with dubious results. Although China's aggregate supply of goods and services still appears to be highly price elastic, the rapid growth averaging almost 9 percent per annum in recent years has put a strain on its supply capacity. In 2004, the supply of broad money grew by 9.7 percent after a 20 percent increase in the preceding year. Despite the tightening of credit growth, there is still excess liquidity in the system, which is likely to continue to fuel real estate speculation and kindle consumer price inflation as well.

In the absence of currency market intervention, the asset market boom will lead to a real appreciation of the currency as it induces more speculative capital inflows. It will also spur domestic investment, particularly construction investment, but the asset market bubble is bound to burst. East Asia's policymakers are not prepared to go through another boom-bust cycle as they did in the run-up to the crisis in 1997. The painful experience of the crisis will therefore continue to serve as a reminder that these economies should tread carefully in further easing monetary policy.

- *Fiscal Policy*

Fiscal prudence is an Asian value that has been held in high regard and with the IMF on watch, East Asian economies have generally considered fiscal expansion as a means of stimulating domestic demand only with reluctance. In many nascent democracies in the region fiscal policy suffers from rigidity of implementation and a long lag, since it often has to go through a notoriously slow and complicated political process of obtaining consensus on tax cuts and determining the size and distribution of government expenditure between projects, sectors, and regions. Fiscal policy can therefore be procyclical if the lag is long and persistent. East Asian policymakers are also determined not to replicate Japan's experience with a pump-priming policy that has resulted mostly in constructing highways and public buildings that are deserted, and other idle infrastructure with a massive increase in national debt.

Whatever one can say about the desirability of restoring the current account balance, it would be difficult to pressure China to cut taxes and increase government spending knowing the risks of growing inflationary pressure and the inefficiency of China's tax and budgetary management system. The central government cannot easily control fiscal expenditures or organize and implement a government spending program without securing the cooperation of provincial governments. The share of central government expenditures in GDP is relatively small and more importantly no one seems accurately to know the true level of China's national debt. If nonperforming loans of state-owned banks and other financial institutions are included, the level of the debt would be enormous, and would be unsustainable. Along with a tightening of monetary policy, Chinese authorities have taken administrative control to curb spending of the local as well as central government to engineer a soft landing of an economy threatened with acceleration of price inflation and real estate speculation. The medium-term fiscal objective of the Chinese government is to keep the nominal budgetary deficit constant. Few would disagree with this objective.

As for Japan, a right macroeconomic policy mix would hardly include more spending for investment in infrastructure and other public projects when the country is faced with the difficult task of managing a national debt which is approaching 150 percent of GDP. And expansionary fiscal policy has done very little in turning around the economy from its decade-long stagnation. It is beyond the scope of this chapter to discuss the prospects of the Japanese economy, but it is clear that fiscal policy is one policy instrument Japan will no longer rely on to revive its economy.

The exclusion of the two major players leaves the ASEAN states, Taiwan, and South Korea as plausible candidates that could accommodate an expansionary fiscal policy in East Asia. Among the ASEAN states, Indonesia and the Philippines are in no position to contemplate any further increase in government spending or cut taxes. The Indonesian government is committed to further fiscal consolidation to reduce the vulnerability arising from the high level of public debt. Its objective is to achieve a broad budgetary balance by 2006–07 consistent with lowering public debt to below 50 percent of GDP. The Indonesian government has also been engaged in fiscal reform that envisages more efficient tax administration and improvement in budget preparation and execution. The size of the public debt in the Philippines exceeds 100 percent of GDP, which is high and unsustainable. The new administration has committed itself to balancing the budget by 2009 through tax increases and streamlining fiscal expenditures.

Thailand and Malaysia have been able to bring down budgetary deficits to a manageable level, and as such they do not have either budgetary deficit or national debt problems that rule out an expansionary fiscal policy. Malaysia has in fact turned to fiscal policy to revive its sagging economy. Although Thailand has room for additional fiscal stimulus, its authorities have been reluctant to run a budgetary deficit. Its goal has shifted to maintaining a neutral stance in fiscal policy as the economy has begun to recover through the expansion of exports.

South Korea, Singapore, and Taiwan are all known for their fiscal conservatism. They could certainly take on a more expansionary stance of fiscal policy. Of these countries, South Korea has moved ahead with an expenditure switching policy that combines an increase in government spending with exchange rate appreciation. The two other economies have not been as active as South Korea as export earnings have generally supported relatively high rates of growth.

Suppose, however, that all three countries are persuaded to implement an expansionary fiscal policy. To what extent would their policy change contribute to slowing the increase in East Asia's aggregate trade surplus? As a group, Singapore, South Korea, and Taiwan account for 24.3 percent of East Asia's total foreign reserves at the end of May 2005. During the 2000–2004 period, their combined current account surplus amounted to $268.8 billion, or 21 percent of East Asia's total (see Table 21.3). Although these countries will benefit from fiscal stimulus, these figures suggest that the expansionary policy will hardly be sufficient to reverse the growing trend in the transpacific imbalance even if it has an impact on all of the three economies.

There is also a structural characteristic rather unique to East Asia that raises the question as to the effectiveness of fiscal expansion in East Asia's emerging economies as a means of reducing the transpacific imbalance: expansion of domestic demand in ASEAN, Taiwan, and South Korea may not necessarily increase their imports from or decrease their exports to the US. For instance, according to a simulation study based on a multi-country intertemporal general equilibrium model (Lee, McKibbin, and Park 2004) a fiscal expansion in East Asian economies excluding Japan amounting to

**Table 21.3.** Current Account Surpluses (US dollars, billions)

|             | 2000  | 2001  | 2002  | 2003  | 2004  | Total    | Share |
|-------------|-------|-------|-------|-------|-------|----------|-------|
| Japan       | 119.7 | 87.8  | 112.4 | 136.2 | 172.1 | 628.2    | 48.8  |
| Hong Kong   | 7.1   | 9.9   | 12.6  | 16.7  | 16.0  | 62.4     | 4.9   |
| Korea, South| 12.3  | 8.0   | 5.4   | 12.3  | 27.6  | 65.7     | 5.1   |
| Singapore   | 13.2  | 16.1  | 18.9  | 28.2  | 26.1  | 102.5    | 8.0   |
| Taiwan      | 8.9   | 18.2  | 25.6  | 29.3  | 18.7  | 100.6    | 7.8   |
| Indonesia   | 8.0   | 6.9   | 8.1   | 7.5   | 3.1   | 33.7     | 2.6   |
| Malaysia    | 8.5   | 7.3   | 7.2   | 13.4  | 14.9  | 51.3     | 4.0   |
| Philippines | 6.3   | 1.3   | 4.4   | 3.3   | 2.0   | 17.3     | 1.3   |
| Thailand    | 9.3   | 6.2   | 7.0   | 8.0   | 7.3   | 37.8     | 3.0   |
| China       | 20.5  | 17.4  | 35.4  | 45.9  | 68.7  | 187.9    | 14.6  |
| **Total**   | 213.7 | 179.2 | 237.1 | 300.8 | 356.5 | 1,287.30 | 100   |

*Source*: IMF, International Financial Statistics and CEIC Data Company Ltd. (www.ceic.com).

2 percent of GDP causes current account balances to worsen by between 0.2 and 1.1 percent of GDP in the first year. The corresponding improvement in the current account of the US is a much smaller share of its own GDP because the combined size of the expanding countries is small relative to the US. Another interesting result of this exercise is that the same fiscal expansion in Japan tends to increase Japan's trade surplus, which amounts to 0.11 percent of GDP. This result is not surprising in view of the fact that Japan is the major import market for other East Asian economies.

## 21.3. Adjustment of Exchange Rate Policy in East Asia

Changes in both the nominal and trade-weighted real exchange rates of East Asia's emerging market economies leave little doubt that the authorities of these countries have been intervening in foreign exchange markets (see Figures 3(*a*) and 3(*b*) and 4). Park and Wyplosz (2004) discuss a number of objectives for their intervention. Maintaining their export competitiveness is certainly one of them.

The ten East Asian economies that include the original ASEAN 5, China, Japan, South Korea, Hong Kong, and Taiwan have piled up large amounts of reserves, which are excessive by any standard; the fear of another round of financial crisis has receded, and more importantly the expectation of currency appreciation has attracted more capital inflows into the region, thereby exacerbating the imbalance and complicating the management of exchange rate policy. Under these circumstances, one would expect that these economies would be inclined to intervene less frequently in the foreign exchange market than before so that the market could steer their dollar exchange rates closer to a long-run equilibrium level. In fact most East Asian economies with an intermediate regime have seen their nominal exchange rates appreciate vis-à-vis the dollar in recent periods. Over a three-month period beginning last October, for example, the South Korean won has appreciated 15 percent. Many market analysts, not to mention US Treasury officials and Fred Bergsten and his associates, believe that East Asian currencies may have to appreciate much more before they can have any discernible effect on their trade surpluses.

Currency appreciation could send a signal to the market that the East Asian country in question is serious about making a needed macroeconomic adjustment and shifting resources to the nontradeable sector over time. In particular, China has been under pressure to revalue further or to increase flexibility of the renminbi, but the country is unlikely to succumb to the external pressure. Other East Asian economies except for Japan have shown little indication they will move to free floating anytime soon. Their unwillingness reflects their dilemma of having to rely on exports for growth, but also a collective action problem faced by East Asian economies in coordinating their exchange rate policy.

• *Policy Impasse: Collective Action Problem*

East Asian economies with an intermediate exchange rate regime would be reluctant to allow their currencies to appreciate as long as local trading partners and competitors do not, because doing so would lead to a loss of their share of export markets both in and out of the region. In particular, if China insists on a rigid managed float, other East Asian economies may not be able to afford to let their currencies strengthen vis-à-vis the Chinese renminbi as China has emerged as their export competitor in regional as well as global markets. A 2004 IMF report on Indonesia reflects this gridlock when it says that in 2003, Indonesia's currency level was not seriously misaligned as it was broadly in line with other regional currencies from a competitiveness point of view.[2]

Whatever the objective of China's foreign exchange rate policy, would it not be in the interest of other East Asian countries to pursue a more independent exchange rate policy, which could strengthen their currencies relative to the dollar? Apparently to many East Asian economies, it is not. If the dollar falls, as is widely expected, and China maintains its fixed parity

---

[2] The same report advocates maintaining a floating exchange regime, however.

vis-à-vis the dollar, then other East Asian economies with an intermediate currency regime fear that their currencies will appreciate much more than otherwise as they will be forced to absorb to a disproportionate extent, the effect of an weakening in the dollar. That is, when the dollar is expected to depreciate, as it is now, more speculative capital will find its way into these economies because they may not be as able and determined as China in defending their exchange rates.

East Asia's policymakers admit that there is a need for a collective exchange rate policy and even raise the possibility of creating a regional monetary union in the future. They have established institutional arrangements such as the ASEAN+3 meetings of finance ministers or their deputies, which could serve as fora for coordination of exchange rate policy among the ASEAN+3 states. However, if past experience with policy coordination among ASEAN+3 is any guide, member countries will not be able easily to agree on an issue as complicated as the coordination of exchange rate policy.

One problem is that Japan and China, the two major countries, which can and should provide leadership for any collective policy actions and cooperation, have not seen eye to eye on many regional issues, largely because of their rivalry for greater economic and political influence in East Asia. Another problem is more fundamental in that the economies belonging to ASEAN+3 may not necessarily constitute an optimum currency area: given the structural diversity and differences in the level of development, as they are likely to be exposed to external shocks too asymmetric to accommodate a uniform monetary policy. Even if China and Japan were able to work together, they would not be able to persuade other ASEAN+3 countries to join any collective exchange rate system such as a common basket pegg or an Asian version of the EMS that has been floated around as a possible regime ASEAN+3 could adopt.

In the absence of any collective policy coordinating arrangement, external pressure for appreciation on East Asian economies whether it comes from the IMF or the US Treasury, will meet strong resistance unless the pressure can bear on the original ASEAN+5, Hong Kong, and South Korea to agree to bilateral exchange rate adjustments among themselves—who should appreciate and by how much. This is because they are locked in competition for a larger share of regional and third markets for their exports.

This potential disagreement is further complicated by the ambiguous position of Japan on East Asia's exchange rate policy coordination. Since the yen is a major free floating currency comparable to the US dollar and euro, Japan has taken the position that it cannot join any East Asian collective exchange rate arrangement for the foreseeable future. The exclusion of Japan creates another hurdle for exchange rate policy coordination in East Asia.

When East Asian economies are divided into China, Japan, and the group consisting of other East Asian emerging market and developing economies, Japan has been running a surplus in its trade with all other East Asian economies including China. The group of emerging market and developing economies on the other hand has been running a surplus with China, but a large deficit with Japan.

Because of these different profiles of the bilateral imbalances, the group of East Asian emerging market and developing economies may be able to accept a simultaneous appreciation of their currencies and the renminbi against the dollar, but they will also demand an appreciation of the yen at the same time. But there is no guarantee that the yen will appreciate as much as other East Asian currencies vis-à-vis the US dollar unless Japanese authorities intervene. If the yen is not expected to appreciate, other East Asian economies will be cautious of any collective exchange rate appreciation, out of fear that the appreciation of their currencies vis-à-vis the yen will deepen their persistent structural trade deficits with Japan. To economists, bilateral trade imbalances may not matter, but to East Asia's politicians and policymakers, they matter a lot, especially when bilateral exchange rate changes are negotiated against the backdrop of their growing trade deficits with Japan.

- *What will an Across-the-Board Appreciation of East Asian Currencies Do?*

To date, the demand for currency appreciation in East Asia has been directed primarily at China and the region's other emerging economies although Japan accounts for almost half of ASEAN+3's total reserves. US Treasury officials and Washington-based exchange rate policy hawks are leaving Japan out of their demand for appreciation in part because the yen is floating but mostly because a large yen appreciation could be too disruptive to the global financial system, not to mention the lack of association between the yen's real appreciation and Japan's current account.

Suppose, for the sake of argument, the group of the original ASEAN 5, China, and South Korea manage to clear the hurdles to adjust their bilateral exchange rates to bring about an overall appreciation of currencies of the group vis-à-vis the dollar. How much of a group-wide exchange rate adjustment would then be needed to balance its aggregate current account? This is an empirical question, and not surprisingly there are many contending views.

The sources of contention are two interrelated empirical issues: the magnitudes of price elasticities of both imports and exports of these seven economies and the costs and benefits of the group's unilateral real appreciation. Bergsten (2005) urges China to revalue its currency by 25 percent and other Asian countries by half as much. This currency adjustment would take $50–60 billion off the annual US current account deficit. If China and other Asian countries do not permit such a revaluation, he calls for a multilateral name and shame campaign against them for the manipulation of their exchange rates.

Cline (2005) echoes a similar view by suggesting that these currency manipulators should face trade penalties unless they let market forces bid up their exchange rates against the dollar. In making this demand, however, Cline contradicts the results of the simulation of his own general equilibrium model, which shows that an exogenous depreciation of the dollar generates very little external adjustment and that fiscal contraction is needed as a central part of the US external adjustment process.

In terms of a real sector model that includes both tradeables and nontradeables, Obstfeld and Rogoff (2004) estimate the amount of depreciation of the US trade-weighted real exchange rate that will occur when relative demand shocks to tradeables and nontradeables close the US current account gap. Their results suggest that depending on the rigidity of nominal prices and the degree of exchange rate pass-through, the dollar may have to depreciate anywhere from 20 to 40 percent.

The simulation of a concerted revaluation of East Asian exchange rates by 10 percent in a multi-country intertemporal general equilibrium model (Lee et al. 2004) show that it does not make any significant impact on the trade balances of East Asian economies. The trade impacts of this policy for global imbalances are small with minor impacts on the current accounts of the revalued East Asian economies as well as other countries.

The reasons are clear. The revaluation makes export less competitive on world markets during the period that domestic prices have not adjusted to the effective tightening of monetary policy. The revaluation also reduces domestic demand. Thus, the effect of the decrease in East Asian economies' import demand offset the effect of stronger currency exports. Whether a country is positively or negatively affected depends on the size and nature of trade with the East Asian economies and the impact of changes in East Asian economies' demand on other countries. The demand and relative price (or competitiveness) effects tend to cancel in their impact on the trade balances of most countries. The estimation result shows that the East Asian currency revaluation will have no effect on the US current account balance.

McKibbin and Stoeckel (2004) also explore the implication of a 10 percent appreciation of the Chinese exchange rate. The main result is similar. Chinese revaluation has significant impacts on the Chinese economy by decreasing GDP growth by 0.41 percent relative to the baseline in the first year, but the effects disappear over time. The Chinese current account balance worsens by close to 0.5 percent of GDP but with minor impacts on the trade positions of other economies including the United States.

A 1999 study of the export demand equations of fifty-three advanced and developing countries (Senhadji and Montenegro 1999) show that on average East Asian economies have higher price elasticities of exports than both industrial and developing countries. Short- and long-run price elasticities for the four Asian countries are:

|             | Short-run | Long-run |
|-------------|-----------|----------|
| China       | −0.63     | −3.13    |
| Japan       | −0.17     | −1.27    |
| Korea       | −0.52     | −2.17    |
| Philippines | −0.51     | −1.24    |
| USA         | −0.17     | −0.78    |

*Source*: Senhadi and Montenegro (1999.)

Another study (Bayoumi 1996) produces substantially different estimates (see Table 21.4). In fact, differences in the magnitudes of these elasticities are so large that it is difficult to gauge the effect of real appreciation on trade balances in the sample East Asian economies. In the short run, however, price elasticities of both exports and imports are small, suggesting that the J-curve effect could be substantial.

From an East Asian perspective it is difficult to determine whether and, if they are undervalued, how much East Asian currencies are in real terms because there are no widely accepted conceptual and operational definitions of an equilibrium real exchange rate. For the sake of argument, assume that East Asian economies including China go through with a substantial real appreciation of their currencies. What would be the effect of this currency adjustment in the medium term? If both exports and imports are reasonably

**Table 21.4.** Long-run trade elasticities for East Asian economies

| | Exports | | Imports | |
|---|---|---|---|---|
| | Output | Real exchange rate | Output | Real exchange rate |
| Hong Kong | 4.11 | −0.07 | 1.92 | 1.01 |
| Indonesia | 1.27 | −0.32 | 1.66 | 0.68 |
| Japan | 2.10 | −0.69 | 0.79 | 0.55 |
| South Korea | 3.12 | −0.52 | 1.36 | 0.61 |
| Malaysia | 1.86 | −0.53 | 1.47 | 0.01 |
| Philippines | 1.34 | 0.10 | 1.65 | −0.75 |
| Singapore | 1.77 | −0.21 | 1.05 | 0.00 |
| Taiwan | 3.28 | −0.70 | 1.23 | 0.66 |
| Thailand | 2.73 | −0.99 | 1.03 | 0.75 |
| United States | 1.47 | −0.85 | 2.46 | 0.26 |
| Panel of all countries | 1.96 | −0.80 | 1.46 | 0.28 |

*Source*: This table is reproduced from Bayoumi (1996) based on annual data for 1974–93.

sensitive to changes in relative prices, in theory a real appreciation is likely to reduce the current account surplus in the long run.[3]

As a first approximation, a long-run equilibrium exchange rate may be defined as one that ensures current account balance (ignoring the financial sector) although this definition is subject to a number of qualifications. How much of a real appreciation would East Asian economies then have to bring to balance the current account and over how long a period? Given the surpluses that range anywhere from 2 to 10 percent of GDP, the required amount of real appreciation to balance the current account would be substantial.

When the J-curve effect is large, a real appreciation could in fact augment the initial current account surplus. If the increase is against what the market expects, it could set off a destabilizing dynamic as it forms expectations of further appreciation, which further induces capital inflows into the region. This destabilizing expectation could stretch the current account adjustment over a long period as it did in Japan. A large appreciation is bound to cause a sharp deceleration of output growth and could even threaten a recession as it chips away exports and the associated domestic demand. The real appreciation will slow down the economy so much that it could even produce a larger current account surplus than

[3] A standard textbook explanation is that when the Marshall-Lerner condition holds, a decrease in real income caused by the appreciation reduces saving more than investment. A fall in the interest rate that is brought about by a decrease in the trade surplus encourages investment. Lower prices of imported capital and intermediate goods could also stimulate investment.

before over the medium term as the economic contraction induced by the appreciation further depresses investment as well as import demand.

This perverse effect would be more pronounced in export-oriented economies. If the real appreciation holds back growth in East Asian economies, this together with the J-curve effect could mount pressure for additional real appreciation of East Asian currencies until it produces the results expected by the market. As these currencies increase further in value relative to the US dollar, the J-curve effect will continue to be at work, further delaying the current account adjustment. This is what the Japanese experienced in the 1990s.

If East Asia's surplus position remains unchanged despite the strengthening of East Asian currencies and the weakening of the dollar, the weaker dollar may or may not improve the US current account. If it does not, the dollar's depreciation will put more pressure on the appreciation of the euro and other flexible currencies.

In order to prevent a slowdown in East Asian economies and possibly in the global economy as well, inducing global financial turmoil, a real appreciation of East Asian currencies or depreciation of the dollar will have to be combined with East Asia's expansionary monetary or fiscal policy. Otherwise, the depreciation of the dollar, depending on how large it is, could also trigger serious financial turbulence as it will increase US long-term interest rates and cause a collapse in equity and housing prices in the US. This asset price adjustment will put the brakes on the US economy. Together with East Asia's slowdown, this could then lead to a severe global economic contraction (Roubini and Setser 2005).

In contrast to the experiences of other economies in East Asia, much of the increase in China's foreign exchange reserve in recent periods has come from the sterilization of the surplus on the capital account. Almost half of the increase in reserves in China was accounted for by net non-FDI capital inflows, which was attracted by a combination of interest rate differentials and the expectation of an appreciation of the renminbi in 2003. The current account ran a surplus of $68.7 billion, whereas the capital and financial account is expected to register a surplus of $110 billion in 2004.[4]

One might speculate that the investment boom and the signs of real estate speculation in major cities together with a current account surplus would give Chinese authorities more confidence in enlarging the band in which the renminbi fluctuates. A wider band could engineer a smooth

---

[4] China's reserves rose by $206 billion in 2004. According to preliminary data, about 96 billion or 46 percent of the increase was accounted for by speculative inflows.

appreciation of the currency. Unless they tighten capital controls further, nothing short of currency appreciation will stem the increase in capital inflows.

While acknowledging the need to increase flexibility of the renminbi–dollar exchange rate, Chinese policymakers shifted to a managed float against a basket of currencies with an initial revaluation of 2.1 percent against the dollar. It is unclear how this new system will work as of July 21, 2005. A larger move may be necessary to restrain capital inflows, but such a policy change has not been seriously contemplated because of its negative impact on employment and growth and on the banking sector saddled with large amounts of nonperforming loans. It may be true that there is little persuasive evidence that the renminbi is substantially undervalued from a competitiveness point of view. However, if the Chinese authorities continue to delay the currency adjustment, then it will induce further capital inflows with consequences more serious than the loss of employment and output.

## 21.4. Intra-regional Policy Adjustments and Coordination in East Asia

Although it is somewhat too early to judge, there is an optimistic outlook that as the current upswing in East Asia's business cycle continues the transpacific imbalance may resolve itself into a transitory adjustment problem between East Asia on the one hand and the US and the EU on the other. This does not mean that East Asia can and should wait until the imbalance itself and the ongoing debate on what the region should do dissipates. There is little disagreement that East Asian economies need to develop more competitive domestic markets and strong domestic demand for the region's financial stability and growth. Any decrease in East Asia's trade surplus that follows should be regarded as a by-product.

### • Japan Should Take the Lead

One of the implications of the discussion in section 21.2 is that as long as Japan remains unable to revive domestic demand and China is laboring for a soft landing of its economy, other smaller East Asian economies individually or collectively could do little to curb a further increase in the transpacific imbalance, simply because the number of the economies that could reflate domestic demand is small and their combined economic size is also small. Unless Japan is prepared to absorb more goods and services not only from the US but also from other East Asian economies, the external pressure on the rest of East Asia to expand domestic demand will not be well received. If Japan makes headway in pulling the economy out of its decade-long slow growth, other East Asian countries will be better disposed to cooperating with Japan and the US to make necessary policy changes.

One could argue that China and other surplus emerging economies in East Asia could be pressured to run deficits on their current accounts to liberalize private capital outflows so that they can deplete at least some of their reserve holdings. It is not clear whether such a policy prescription is realistic or desirable in view of the fact that there is as yet no accepted norm for an optimum holding of reserves for self-insurance and access of most East Asian economies to international financial markets cannot be assured in a crisis situation.

If indeed it is critical that East Asia as a whole embraces a more domestic demand-based growth strategy to curtail the existing (and prevent a future) transpacific imbalance, Japan is the country that should take the lead. Unless Japan breaks out of its economic doldrums, one cannot have much hope for restoring the balance between the two sides of the Pacific with only policy changes in the rest of East Asia. All efforts to resuscitate Japanese domestic demand have so far failed, although recently the prospect for an early recovery of the Japanese economy appears to be more encouraging. Other East Asian economies could make up for the lack of domestic demand in Japan, but only to a limited extent. This is East Asia's dilemma.

- *China Holds the Key*

On exchange rate policy, unless China is prepared to increase the flexibility of the new intermediate regime, no other country will be able to provide the policy leadership needed to bring about an across-the-broad appreciation or greater flexibility, if not free floating, of East Asian currencies. Chinese leadership is vital because China is the largest export market and at the center of East Asia's regional trade integration. China's remarkable growth and entry into the global trading system have produced market forces that are creating a triangular trade relationship involving China, the US, and Japan plus East Asia's emerging market economies.

In this relationship, Japan and East Asia's emerging market economies export capital goods and intermediate inputs to China. China in turn uses these goods and inputs to produce a wide variety of manufactured goods that are exported to the US, EU, and other regions. At present, it would not be too much of an exaggeration to say that the region that comprises ASEAN+3 is becoming 'a large conveyor belt, carrying components, sub-assemblies and capital equipment to factories in China' (Guy De Jonquieres, *Financial Times*, 2/18/05). If trade integration in East Asia is aligned along the vertical axis with China at the end of the production line, China naturally holds the key to exchange rate adjustment in East Asia.

- *Consolidation of Bilateral FTAs and the CMI*

Another regional development in East Asia that has important implications for the management of the imbalance has been the proliferation of FTAs. While skeptics abound as to the advantages of bilateral FTAs over multilateral trade liberalization, there is widespread agreement that the completed and proposed FTAs will serve as building blocks for regional trade integration in East Asia and global integration in the future.

Regional trade integration may lessen East Asia's export dependence on US and EU the markets to the extent that it increases the share of intra-industry regional trade. It may result in a significant trade diversion away from the US. This trade diversion will not necessarily contain the expansion of the imbalance, but it may spare East Asia the accusation of rigging exchange rates and conducting unfair trade practices and as such may defuse the growing tensions between the two sides of the Pacific. A continuing increase in intra-regional trade is expected to create new investment opportunities throughout the region including China through further trade liberalization. These new opportunities may also help keep more of East Asia's savings in the region.

But then there is a caveat. Trade integration among mostly export-oriented economies with China as the center of gravity of vertical integration may create a huge export-oriented region, which will push out more exports than before to the rest of the world. Again this is no more than conjecture, but one that deserves careful analysis.

China and other East Asian emerging and developing economies would be inclined to hold much less in foreign reserves for self-insurance, if they have access to market and official sources of liquidity support in addition to the IMF. The Chiang Mai Initiative established a regional currency swap arrangement to serve as a regional liquidity assistance system. If participating countries gain confidence in the system as a source of liquidity in addition to the IMF, East Asia's precautionary reserve demand may fall. In this regard, ASEAN+3's decision to expand and consolidate the CMI into a de facto regional lending arrangement is a welcome development.

The initiative for creating regional bond markets in Asia by the ASEAN+3 will also help East Asian economies accelerate regional financial integration. Creating liquid and deep regional bond markets where East Asian firms can issue local currency denominated bonds will then increase the availability of long-term financing, which can facilitate investment and thereby narrow the region's saving and investment gap as well as financing short-term liquidity for balance of payment deficit financing.

## 21.5. Inter-regional Policy Coordination

There is little doubt that the resolution of the transpacific imbalance requires both an East Asian and a US policy adjustment. As Obstfeld and Rogoff (2004) observe, 'Even very large autonomous exchange rate movements will not go forward closing a current account gap . . . of the U.S. The lion's share of the adjustment (of the imbalance) has to come from saving and productivity shocks that help equilibrate global net saving levels, and that imply dollar change as a by-product.'

• *Simultaneous Macroeconomic Policy Adjustments*

If outside observers believe that East Asia's emerging economies, including that of China, will continue to run up surpluses on their current accounts and use these surpluses to buy up US securities, they are ignoring the ominous macroeconomic adjustment already in view that will eventually stem the growth of East Asia's surplus. If American and European policymakers believe that unilateral policy changes in East Asia will stop the swelling of the transpacific imbalance in the short run, they are also ill advised.

Likewise, East Asian policymakers would be ill advised to believe that it is the US which is primarily responsible and should therefore take steps to cut its fiscal deficit to resolve the imbalance. It is true that a smaller US current deficit may result in a drop in real interest rates in both East Asia and Europe and this could produce expansionary effects. But as pointed out earlier, the lower cost of capital is not likely to resuscitate East Asia's weak investment demand. Given this possibility, one may argue that the best policy choice is simultaneous macroeconomic policy adjustments in all three regions: tightening of fiscal policy in the US, continued expansionary monetary policy in Europe, and loose fiscal policy together with currency appreciation in East Asia.

- *Articulation of Demand for Policy Changes in East Asia*

In insisting on East Asia's currency realignment, proponents have often failed to clarify their demands. Are they asking for nonintervention in the foreign exchange market? Or are they demanding discrete exchange rate adjustments by East Asian *de jure* floaters as well as those with a fixed exchange rate system? Are they also demanding capital account liberalization at the same time? The US, the EU, and multilateral financial institutions have vacillated between liberal reform on the one hand and short-run policy adjustments such as a unilateral revaluation of the currencies of East Asia's emerging economies on the other. This has weakened their voice in the reform debate.

There is no single exchange rate regime appropriate to all East Asia's emerging market and developing economies. There is no clear evidence that capital account liberalization will help sustain macroeconomic stability or growth in the short run. The outright demand for a unilateral revaluation of currencies in East Asia's emerging economies by international financial institutions and the G-7 is simply not persuasive and contradicts their long-standing demand for Washington Consensus reforms in East Asia. If the US and multilateral financial institutions believe that East Asian economies including Japan are in need of stimulating their domestic consumption and investment, then their suggestions for policy changes should be more specific in terms of policies and institutional reform needed in individual East Asian economies instead of asking for uniform changes throughout East Asia. Most of all, to be effective the demand for policy changes in East Asia will have to be accompanied by concomitant policy adjustments in both the US and EU.

If the G-7 countries were serious about encouraging institutional reform and policy changes in East Asia, it would also be important that they first decide whether and how they are going to adjust to East Asia's export-led growth strategy and the movement toward trade and financial integration in the region. Since the export push per se is not the cause of the imbalance, and knowing that to most East Asian economies it is the most realistic strategy for catching up with the West, the G-7 and international financial institutions should accept it as a *fait accompli*. A more realistic and appropriate response of the West would begin with its support for East Asia's efforts at economic integration as an intermediate step toward eventual integration with the global system.

## • A New Plaza Accord

If the ongoing expansion can be sustained, then East Asia's demand for imports from outside the region will increase, reducing its overall current account surplus. However, any narrowing of East Asia's surplus will not necessarily lead to a similar reduction in the US current account deficit so long as the US saving–investment gap remains unchanged. Instead a decrease in East Asia's surplus is likely to be matched by an almost equal increase in the combined surplus of other regions vis-à-vis the US. The resolution of the transpacific imbalance therefore requires policy coordination not only among the East Asian economies but also between East Asia on the one hand and the US and EU on the other.

The US may not make any policy adjustments on the assumptions that the imbalance is not likely to pose any serious threat to stability of its financial market or the global financial system and that it is not made in America. This benign neglect, however, may weaken the dollar further and put pressure on the euro to appreciate more than otherwise. In view of this need for policy coordination, the US, EU, and ASEAN+3 could consider establishing a framework of policy coordination in which participating countries devise interregional policy adjustments focusing on a scheme of domestic demand expansion and exchange rate appreciation in East Asia that will be matched by supporting policy changes in both the US and EU and structural reform in all three regions for the prevention of a recurrence of the imbalance. The world economy needs a new Plaza Accord, but for different objectives and different players.

## • Resurrecting Reform of the International Financial System

The large accumulation of reserves in East Asia, much of which is held for self-insurance, underscores the need for reform of the international financial system that will increase the availability of short-term liquidity financing for those economies experiencing temporary balance of payment difficulties, establishing global regulatory authorities and a mechanism that sets and enforces global financial codes and standards. As a long-run solution to the imbalance, the G-7 should therefore resurrect the reform of the international financial architecture they have set aside since 2001. The reform will allay the fear of many smaller East Asian economies that they are innately vulnerable to external shocks and that international financial markets will refuse their short-term liquidity assistance when they are faced with unexpected and large capital outflows. If a new international financial architecture were to be constructed, together with financial reform in the region it could then speed up East Asia's integration into the global financial system.

Fearing that the required reform will not be forthcoming, emerging economies including those in East Asia have taken the prevention of future financial crises into their own hands. Having accumulated large amounts of reserves, East Asian emerging economies feel secure about their financial positions and naturally have become complacent about continuing with their much needed structural reforms.

Part VI

# Whither Economic Liberalization and Integration in East Asia?

# 22

# In Search of a New East Asian Paradigm for Development

## 22.1. What is Left of the Pre-crisis East Asian Development Paradigm?

Since the 1997–98 crisis, the scope, pace, and effectiveness of liberal reform have varied from country to country in East Asia. Some countries such as South Korea have made considerable progress, whereas others have moved at a snail's pace and even suffered a setback. Nevertheless, democratization and market liberalization and opening have left an indelible mark on their economic systems as these changes have made dysfunctional or outdated some of the main components of the East Asian development model and as a consequence set the stage for major economic reform for market deregulation and opening even before the crisis. Many interventionist policies such as the export push, which was key to East Asia's success, had to be phased out, though they were not, long before the crisis, as the WTO rules left little room for subsidizing industries and exports. The consultative polity as a governance mechanism has become irrelevant to new democratic regimes. Political democratization and the emergence of civic society have also brought to the fore a large number of new economic and social issues that were largely ignored in the old regime such as the need for creating new institutions for social risk management and industrial relations.

The highly touted East Asian bureaucracy, insulated from political intervention and able to pilot export promotion, manage industrial policy, and facilitate private–public and private sector coordination, is no longer in control. East Asian bureaucracy may still be relatively more effective and less susceptible to political pressure compared to bureaucracies in other parts of the developing world, but its role in making and implementing economic policies has been circumscribed by the emergence of an independent legislative body, nongovernmental organizations, and the rise of labor unions. Many large family-owned industrial groups, which provided internal capital and labor markets, have been broken up, weakened, and collapsed under the sheer weight of their inefficiencies. They have also been subject to many new rules and regulations of corporate governance and are no longer in as congenial political and policy environments as they were before under the authoritarian governments.

What is then left of the pre-crisis East Asian development model? The East Asian growth engine is no longer roaring, but some of the economic fundamentals, which are the key features of the model, remain intact and could provide a base from which East Asian economies could attempt another take-off to regain their pre-crisis dynamism. These fundamentals are the traditional emphasis on education, the work ethic, high rates of savings, and entrepreneurship that keeps the returns on capital high through effective interactions between accumulation of capital and assimilation of foreign technology.

These main features may well serve the post-crisis development of East Asia, although as a whole, the old model is in need of major structural repair.[1] In fact, except for the basic building blocks of economic fundamentals, many institutions governing the financial system, corporate sector, and the labor market will have to be created a new or restructured. This need for reform is not surprising in view of the fact that the model as it is delineated by the World Bank miracle study (1993) had evolved as a development paradigm for nondemocratic or authoritarian regimes during an era characterized by tightly controlled and closed markets, as well as protectionist trade practices.[2]

## 22.2. Economic Restructuring: Is Emerging East Asia Halfway there?

By the early 1990s, some five or six years before the 1997–98 crisis, East Asia's emerging economies had already been engaged in an extensive reform of the Washington Consensus, deregulating and opening markets including the financial sector. Although it was not then clearly articulated, there was the expectation that this reform would over time steer these economies to an Anglo-American model of capitalism. And the 1997–98 Asian crisis provided

---

[1] Park (2002).    [2] World Bank (1993).

the rationale as well as a strong impetus for structural transformation as the crisis-hit countries went on to accept the Washington Consensus reforms as part of their commitment to IMF conditionality.

After seven years of liberal reform, even a casual observation would suggest that East Asia's emerging economies still have a long way to go before assimilating the Anglo-American political and economic systems: they are not yet halfway there as far as convergence is concerned. Is convergence occurring so slowly that it is not visible? Why is it so slow, if indeed the reforms are being carried out? Will they be able to sustain the reform or revert back to the old interventionist regime? It may be premature to make any judgment, but some of the political and economic developments in recent years suggest that most of the emerging economies in the region will not entirely repudiate the pre-crisis paradigm. Nor would they blindly follow the Washington Consensus policy regime. Instead, they are likely to reform the old system to make it better suited for and more flexible to adjust to the new realities of the region and the rest of the world rather than grafting the Anglo-American model on their economies.

This is the conclusion that can be drawn from a number of internal and external developments that have slowed or impeded the reform process and hence diverted the East Asian economies away from the liberal reform trajectory. One such development has been the rapid recovery itself. In imposing policy conditionality, the IMF and other international financial institutions steadfastly maintained that the Washington Consensus was critical to the recovery and reducing structural vulnerabilities of future crises. But even before the reform began, the crisis countries were able to engineer a recovery that was faster than similar crisis episodes in the past would have predicted. Understandably, with the strong and quick recovery, policymakers of the crisis-hit countries have become complacent about their reform drive and domestic support for the envisioned structural transformation has weakened. More importantly, it has raised the possibility that a resolution of the crisis might not have demanded such a heavy dose of liberal reform.

While complacency in reform has set in, neither private nor international financial institutions have been able or willing to monitor and enforce the reforms. The IMF and other international financial institutions have not had any mandate or justification for enforcing implementation of the reforms once their rescue loans to the crisis countries were repaid, more so with the growing evidence that the policy responses of the IMF in managing the crisis were inappropriate. The IMF's policy blunders and mismanagement have undermined its authority to demand that these countries continue with reforms. At the same time, there has been little improvement in private sector monitoring through regional and global ratings agencies on compliance of the crisis economies with the reforms. Major international commercial banks, Western investment banks, institutional investors, and ubiquitous market analysts have conveniently ignored East Asia's structural ills and have been preoccupied with short-term macroeconomic figures instead once the region regained its growth momentum.

Another reason for the slow progress of reforms has been the growing doubt as to the merits of some of the specific reforms which the effects have not been fully understood, and it is not known whether the reforms would safeguard East Asia's emerging economies from a future crisis. For example, the benefits of capital account liberalization remain controversial with conflicting empirical evidence. There is no clear consensus on an appropriate exchange rate regime for emerging and developing countries. Understandably, few countries in East Asia except for Japan have been willing to let their exchange rates move freely in response to changes in the foreign exchange market. Most of East Asia's emerging economies intervene in the foreign exchange market to achieve various policy objectives such as stabilizing the nominal exchange rate or a real effective exchange rate to maintain their export competitiveness. This intervention has in turn rendered it necessary to retain some control over capital account transactions. Unsure of whether the liberal reforms would be sufficient to prevent future crises, East Asia's emerging economies, including China, have been accumulating huge amounts of reserves more. Having succeeded in amassing reserves than they apparently need, they feel more secure than before and naturally have become lax in their reform efforts.

To many of East Asia's policymakers, these misgivings about the benefits of liberal reforms have been reinforced by the poor record of economic liberalization in delivering on its promises: in the eyes of East Asia's policymakers, it is not clear whether economic liberalization has had any visible effects on growth, stability, and distribution. The most telling story is that except for China, all East Asian economies have suffered a deceleration in growth after two years of rapid recovery from the 1997–98 crisis. The direct cause of the slowdown has been a substantial contraction of investment demand in the aftermath of the bursting of the IT bubble. However, investment demand, which dropped sharply after the crisis, has yet to recover, dragging down the economy. As a proportion of GDP, business fixed investment plummeted from a high of 42 percent in 1996 to about 21 percent in 2003 in Indonesia. The declines in other countries have not been as sharp as in Indonesia, but the overall drop in the ratio throughout East Asia has been unprecedented in the region's history. This investment cutback has clouded future prospects for rapid growth as it undermined the strength of economic fundamentals. Poverty remains unabated and corruption is rampant at least in some parts of East Asia. Available pieces of evidence, though fragmented, indicate that distribution of income and wealth has deteriorated since the crisis.

A third development that has stood in the way of the reform has been political democratization. It has brought into the decision-making process a large number of new players such as labor unions, farmers, and a growing number of civic organizations with varied reform agendas. They have challenged the economic as well as social rationale of liberal reforms and erected many roadblocks toward economic restructuring. Agriculture, small and medium sized firms, and many other service industries, which have borne the brunt of the cost of liberalization, have mounted strong opposition to market opening. While opposition has been growing many of East Asia's nascent democratic governments without a ruling majority have not been able to organize public support for reforms.

Demoralization in many East Asian economies has spawned proliferation of political parties. This political disarray has prevented competing political elites from organizing stable electoral majorities and created unstable political regimes of cohabitation in many East Asian economies. Nor have they developed efficient, transparent, and equitable public institutions needed for political stability. In many cases the political elites that control the democratic process are often one and the same who were behind the authoritarian regimes of the past. Partly for these reasons, and mostly for the corruption and inability to deliver on promises of economic well-being, political parties and politicians have not succeeded in earning public trust.

In this unstable political environment, the regimes in power have often sought to mobilize support within organized labor, low and middle income groups, and nontradeable sectors. And given the diversity as well as potential conflicts of interests among these groups, it is not surprising that they have not found common ground where they can agree to a consistent set of policies acceptable to all.

Not surprisingly, some of East Asia's emerging economies have veered to populist policies on the distribution of wealth and income. As the influence of labor unions and other civic organizations increases in a nation's economic policymaking, and when this influence is combined with slow growth, the move toward a populist policy regime is likely to become more visible than before in countries like Indonesia and the Philippines. For its part, freed from suppression and restrictions on union activities, organized labor in many East Asian emerging economies has not hesitated to resort to militant tactics to assert what they consider a rightful place for their members in society. Since political parties could hardly ignore labor's demand, it has been for all practical purposes impossible to remove rigidities in the labor market. In many countries, market-oriented labor reforms have in fact come to a halt.

A fourth development is that contrary to initial expectations, market deregulation and opening have not reduced the scope of the role of government, not certainly as much as was anticipated. Direct control over and many other indirect interventions in the market have been lifted, and a variety of new democratic and market supporting institutions including a new regulatory system have come into existence. But these new institutions in many countries have yet to take root and are hardly able to perform their functions. In this institutional void, the governments of East Asia's emerging economies have found room and the rationale for persisting with their interventionist policies.

For example, financial markets were deregulated, but a regulatory system has not been put in place or has not been effective in enforcing the prudential regulation of asset, risk management and governance of financial institutions. Governments have then stepped in to impose direct control to supposedly ensure an orderly conduct of financial markets and institutions. In privatizing state-owned financial institutions and enterprises, it is the government that identifies, values, and transfers asset and ownership rights. Although government bureaucracies are the targets of reform themselves, they also plan and execute structural and institutional reforms of not only the financial and corporate, but also the public sector of which they are part. In the aftermath of the 1997–8 crisis, establishing a social safety net to protect the elderly, unemployed, and other segments of society adversely affected by economic liberalization surfaced as a major economic and social issue. Many social welfare programs were introduced to deal with the issue, and their administration created new agencies and added new units to the existing bureaucracy.

While economic liberalization has not necessarily reduced the scope of state activities, together with political democratization it has decreased or constrained the ability and capacity of governments to plan and implement policies and to enforce laws (Fukuyama 2004). This divergence frustrates both the general public and policymakers alike as it often makes outcomes unpredictable, and in general, lessens the effectiveness of macroeconomic and other welfare policies. Losing control over policy would make governments look inept and weak. In order to assert that they are in control, governments often succumb to the temptation of returning to the old regime. This study turns to this question in the next chapter.

# 23

# A Long Road to Anglo-Americanization

## 23.1. Trade Liberalization or Export Push?

What then are the prospects for liberal reforms in East Asia? In searching for a new development paradigm, there is little doubt that East Asia's emerging economies will opt for a model that can speed up narrowing their gap in per capita income vis-à-vis developed economies. In this regard, East Asia's emerging economies do not appear to have much confidence in Anglo-American reform as an effective strategy of achieving their aspirations. A case in point is trade liberalization. There is growing evidence that the openness of an economy, which is defined as 'the degree to which nationals and foreigners can transact without costs that are not imposed on transactions among domestic citizens,' promotes growth (Berg and Krueger 2003: 5). Openness increases the productivity of firms and industries as it improves allocative efficiency and brings about a diffusion of technology (from advanced to developing economies). These advantages suggest that developing countries can grow faster and hence narrow the income gap vis-à-vis developed economies through trade liberalization. And Sachs and Warner (1995) show empirically that this is the case.

Since the early 1980s, East Asia's emerging economies have managed to lower tariff rates and remove some nontariff barriers. Before the crisis liberalizing the trade regime did not undermine their growth potential. Should this experience then not give them more confidence in eschewing the export push in favor of further trade liberalization as a development strategy? All the indications in the region are that they are not likely to do so; instead they will be as firmly attached to an export-oriented strategy as they have been in the past for a number of reasons. First of all, the absolute convergence through trade liberalization is hardly conclusive: there are many empirical studies showing that the convergence is weak or nonexistent.[1] As shown in Chapter 2, the strategy proved to be highly successful in sustaining rapid growth before the crisis; it has also been instrumental in pulling East Asia out of the 1997–98 crisis. Why then should they rock the boat? Whatever the policy implications of those recent studies questioning the causality between exporting and productivity improvement for long-run growth may be, the proven record of an export-led strategy will not make many converts out of East Asian policymakers.

If the export push is a preferred strategy, it could mean the perpetuation of market intervention in many East Asian emerging market economies including China. Barred from direct subsidization of exports by WTO rules, many of East Asia's emerging economies have increasingly resorted to undervaluating their currencies as a means of maintaining their competitive edge in exports. More advanced East Asian economies, which have become global players in some of their export markets, realize that such an exchange rate policy is not acceptable to and could provoke retaliation by their trade partners. Notwithstanding this realization, they continue to intervene in the foreign exchange market, and their policy inevitably entails the control of capital account transactions.

If past experience is any guide, an export-led development strategy will also call for tighter control of the behavior of large firms and financial institutions as this strategy tends to create monopolistic or oligopolistic market structures in many industries. Most economies in East Asia, particularly smaller ones, can support only a small number of large world-class producers—in some cases one or two—in each of the industries promoted for exports, as in iron and steel, shipbuilding, automobile, and semiconductor and other electronics industries. In global markets those large firms are small players, but they hold dominant positions in their home markets. Even when the trade regime is open, the pricing and supply behavior of the large producers may have to be regulated as some of them are operating in noncompetitive global markets. And East Asia's trade regime can hardly be classified as one that is free of tariff and other nontariff trade barriers.

To complicate further the industrial concentration, there has been similar concentration in financial industries, in particular in banking. Development in the information and communication technology has enabled banks to exploit the increasing returns strategy, which has resulted in a few large banks through mergers and acquisitions. Concentration of economic power in the hands of a limited number of large firms and financial institutions is not tolerated on equity and efficiency grounds and

---

[1] For *these* empirical studies, see Berg and Krueger (2003).

creates pressure for the government to control their market activities as was the case in the past.

The high propensity to intervene in the market will be bolstered by the mandarin bureaucratic tradition in which East Asia's governments tend to be more paternalistic than elsewhere. Bureaucratic elitism and paternalism in East Asia are often translated into aggressive market intervention on the part of the government in managing economic policy. East Asia's governments intervene in the market to give incentives to exporters, and they intervene again to mitigate the adverse effects created by export promotion.

## 23.2. China's Economic Ascent and Economic Liberalization in East Asia

The failure of the WTO regime to advance global trade liberalization and the dwindling interest of advanced countries in constructing a new international financial architecture has raised questions on the extent and speed of integration into the global economic system that are realistic as well as desirable for East Asia. Such integration is predicated on the assumption that the global community would be able to construct global standards and practices, establish a global last lender of last resort, a global regulatory system, and harmonize policies and institutions of different countries. Since 2001, the G-7 countries have done little in the way of constructing a new international financial architecture, one that could help safeguard East Asian economies from future financial crises. As the reform of the supply side of international capital markets is delayed or ignored, East Asian policymakers have become more skeptical than before as to whether the domestic economic restructuring and reform advocated by the IMF and other international financial institutions will be enough to protect them from future financial crises. In the absence of any global safety net, they have built up a large war chest of foreign reserves they may need to ward off future financial crises. This strategy of holding large amounts of foreign exchange reserves has been in part responsible for East Asia's fixation on its export-led development strategy.

The proliferation of bilateral FTAs could also complicate the leadership issue for regional financial integration. One possibility is that if China succeeds in forming an FTA with ASEAN, it may use its leverage to determine the scope and speed of financial liberalization and integration in East Asia. Since China and ASEAN, except for Singapore, have underdeveloped financial systems, their interest in and strategy for regional financial integration may collide with that of other countries in the region. If this were to happen, the proliferation of bilateral FTAs could slow and even bring to an end financial cooperation and integration in East Asia.

As pointed out in Chapters 18 and 19, reservations on economic global integration have propelled East Asia's move toward economic integration in the region. However, to the extent that regional economic cooperation and integration are centered around China and possibly Japan—the two major economic powers in East Asia—they will deter Anglo-Americanization in the region erecting a shield against the pressure to reform from the West. In fact, the growing political and economic clout of China in the region has adverse implications for economic liberalization and political development in East Asia for a number of reasons.

China has underdeveloped financial market, legal and regulatory systems, has a long way to go before establishing the rule of law, and is still a communist state. Improving living standards, an emerging civil society, increased levels of education, an expanding middle class, and extensive ties with the outside world all favor political democratization in China. However, full-fledged democratization appears to be a long way off largely because China will find it difficult to develop a new political paradigm that will guide the nation along an evolutionary process of political transformation. Without knowing a course of reform to follow, political reform in China will at best be gradual and partial, and China will tread the road to democracy in a very cautious manner.

If Indochina and North Korea strengthen their ties with China, they will not come under any pressure for political and economic liberalization. China has not hesitated to exercise its economic power to advance its political objectives as it has in dealing with the Taiwan issue. In other countries, the ascent of China as an economic power means that if they want to live with China, they will have to accommodate China's non-democratic political and state-controlled economic systems. Japan and other East Asian economies may not be able to influence China's political modernization and economic liberalization. Instead, they may increasingly find it necessary to turn a blind eye to or worse, compromise with China's non-democratic political and state-controlled economic systems. This compromise could dissipate any peer pressure and incentives for liberal economic reform that exists at present in East Asia. It could further weaken the domestic support for reform if regional economic integration around China as a hub moves forward.

If China continues its breakneck pace of growth, South Korea, Taiwan, and the ASEAN states regardless of their trade policies will be lured to, depend more and more on, and there is a high probability that they eventually will be integrated into, the Chinese economy. Will integrating with China help other East Asian economies grow faster than before and hence speed up convergence to an average level of per capita income of developed countries? Over the medium term there is little doubt that trade integration with China will help other East Asian economies stay on a rapid growth path, as the growing Chinese market will allow East Asia's developing economies to replicate the export-led strategy of South Korea and Taiwan in the 1960s and 1970s in which exports to China will increase the rate of labor participation through migration of workers from rural to urban areas. This will also bring about a higher rate of female worker participation and give a new lease of life to many industries that will otherwise be phased out in East Asia's emerging economies and Japan.

A rapidly growing China will therefore allow emerging East Asia to stay on longer than otherwise with a pattern of growth that depends on factor growth rather than technology improvement. In the long run, however, since China is not technologically more advanced and does not have comparative advantage in knowledge-intensive industries, integration with China may not necessarily help these emerging economies either to improve their allocative efficiency or to acquire and assimilate advanced technology. Suppose China's economic growth falls off, as it is inconceivable to imagine that China can sustain its near double-digit growth for many more years. This means that the contribution of the increase in labor absorption and capital accumulation to growth through integration with the Chinese economy will decrease and eventually come to an end. That is, economic integration with China may not help other East Asian economies to increase their TFP growth as much as their integration with advanced countries in the West. In the end, integration with China could frustrate their efforts at closing their income gap vis-à-vis advanced countries.

There is also a lingering doubt as to whether China will be able to find solutions to its entrenched structural problems that require deeper and extensive reform. The country suffers from widespread corruption and rent seeking. Reform of the financial sector, dominated by state-owned banks and ubiquitous state-owned enterprises that account for a large share of output of the inefficient capital-intensive manufacturing sector, has been slow. Inequality in income distribution may have reached a critical level. Unattended, these problems could easily drain China's growth potential and pull apart a society that has seen growing strife between regions and different income classes. Given these potential risk factors, East Asia's emerging economies will have second thoughts about going forward with deeper integration that entails harmonization of political, as well as economic institutions and policies with China.

However, ASEAN economies need to cultivate the huge market in China to drive their export-led development strategy, although they may not want to promote deeper integration with China. A compromise solution would be to form an FTA with China. This will at best bring about shallow integration, and secure their access to the Chinese market, but it will not necessarily force them to depart from their export-led development strategy as China itself will continue to adhere to it as well. For Japan and South Korea, China is also an equally important market for their exports, but the bulk of their exports to and imports from China belong to inter-industry trade. An FTA with China will precipitate therefore an extensive restructuring, of their labor-intensive industries and agriculture much more than a similar FTA would in ASEAN. Knowing the domestic opposition to such restructuring, an FTA with China is not an option Japan and South Korea can entertain at this stage of integration in the region.

China has in effect been leading Asia's trade and financial integration along with Japan, and will in the process increasingly wield greater influence in managing regional economic and political affairs. Japan is a democratic society and the second largest advanced economy in the world. However, it has suffered a decade-long recession, deflation, and an inefficient banking sector plagued with large amounts of nonperforming loans. Japan has not been able to project an image of a regional leader commensurate with its economic power that can lead liberal reform in East Asia. In a region where China and Japan are destined to vie for leadership roles, China will not provide peer pressure to other countries to speed up democratization and liberalization and neither will Japan.

As long as China and Japan lead economic integration in the region, there will be a limit to deeper integration through harmonizing institutions and policies among East Asian economies. If China is destined to serve as a large locomotive pulling the rest of East Asia, there is a high probability that it will determine the scope as well as the speed of economic liberalization in the region. Regional integration led by China and Japan may even interfere with introducing and enforcing global standards on banking, accounting, and corporate governance and establishing the rule of law in developing East Asia.

# 24

# New Paradigm for Development: A Mixed Economy Model

The political and economic reforms meant to develop an economic system closer to the Anglo-American model has stumbled over many roadblocks and met resistance in its implementation. Even if East Asia's emerging economies do not fully embrace Anglo-American capitalism, they will realize the necessity of introducing and fostering a large number of new economic and political institutions. To those export-oriented economies, the global realities leave little choice but to conform to international standards on and codes of practice in accounting, banking, corporate governance, and transparency of monetary and fiscal policy.[1] Developing a market-oriented open economy is also predicated on well-functioning legal and regulatory systems.

Most of the institutions that serve as the substructure of a democratic and open market-oriented economy are quintessentially Western and may not be easily transferable as they are inextricably interwoven with cultures, norms, history, and traditions of the West. The East Asian experience since the crisis is further proof that building institutions that constitute the Anglo-American system is much more difficult and may take longer periods of trial and error than is often assumed. These difficulties may stall or even turn back East Asia's convergence to the West.

Democratization has placed an increasingly heavy demand on governments to achieve growth, stability, and equitable distribution of income all at once. Liberal economic reforms have suffered from increasingly vocal opposition by those adversely affected by market deregulation and opening

---

[1] The setting of international standards, although heavily influenced by the US and UK, has been a matter that East Asia's emerging economies have to work out in dealing with the EU. Dominance of the Anglo-American model certainly reflects the political power of the two countries, but also to a lesser degree, the intellectual power of free markets and competition.

and as a consequence in some cases has run aground. Caught in between these divergent currents, some of the more advanced East Asian economies have been drawn to the corporatist or social democratic systems in Europe as evidenced by the election of a left-wing government in South Korea. Other less developed East Asian economies will muddle through or even drift to a populist policy regime. The gap between the political elites and the masses has, if anything, widened in much of East Asia. Failing to meet the pent-up demand for political freedom and distributive justice, policy-makers of those countries enduring political instability may indeed succumb to the populist approach of using macroeconomic policy to redistribute income by allowing large real wage increases. Since these countries have a comfortable reserve position and current account surpluses, temptation to do so is likely to be greater than before.

Whichever course East Asian emerging economies take in developing a new paradigm, one thing is clear: they will not regress into the pre-crisis regime. Nor will they blindly pursue competition, laissez-faire, and market opening policies. Given their limited reform capacity, East Asia's emerging economies will instead be searching for a new development paradigm that will help them catch up with advanced economies and at the same time facilitate gradual integration into the global economy. What types of a development model will satisfy these prerequisites? A development model is not a static concept, but rather path-dependent in the sense that its formation is greatly influenced by cultural, historic, and political factors. A new Asian economic system will therefore evolve over time with societal, political, and economic changes taking place in East Asia and throughout the global economy. What would then be the reforms needed to pave the way for such an evolution?

At the outset, it is proper to remember that East Asia covers a huge territory, is home to almost 2 billion people, and in 2002 accounted for 23 percent of total world GDP. It would indeed be presumptuous to talk about a new paradigm for all of East Asia, just as it would be to define the East Asian development model as if it applied to all East Asian economies. In what follows, this chapter summarizes those reforms that are presented in the preceding chapters critical to restructuring the old model and making it as effective in a new East Asian and global economic environment as it was before.

- *Governance*

A new governance system will be built around a set of democratic institutions, rules, and norms. The democratic polity should then be complemented by new institutions for conflict management, social insurance, and regulations that will make the market system function better. Many of these institutions are Western concepts and will have to be transplanted on an inhospitable East Asian cultural terrain. Unless this transplantation is carefully managed with due consideration of the capacity and constraints of the reforming economies, the reform may not succeed. Instead of introducing an ideal set of institutions and rules borrowed from the West in a haphazard manner, East Asia's emerging economies will have a better chance of enacting rules that they can enforce within the existing legal and judicial framework.

The following agenda includes East Asia's priorities for institutional reform for more effective governance:

 (i) Establishing and enforcing procedural and constitutional rules for the democratic system and market-supporting institutions;
 (ii) Improving the quality, effectiveness, and efficiency of the delivery of public service;
(iii) Enhancing the effectiveness of the judiciary and regulatory system; and
(iv) Reducing the incidence of corruption.

• *Role of Government*

The role of government has been undergoing a fundamental change from leading economic development to leading social development. This transformation, however, does not mean that there is no room for industrial policy. East Asia's emerging economies can and perhaps should develop a new framework of industrial policy designed to mitigate market failures and to help keep them abreast of technological advances in developed countries. East Asia's developing economies may have a better chance of making a smooth transition to a democratic and market-oriented regime if they first succeed in developing a strong but limited government. And within this framework of governance, they may be exempt from the rules of the World Trade Organization so that they can have a larger space for industrial policies to facilitate technology transfers and manage effective intervention in the market when market failures dictate stronger actions. To these countries the priorities of public sector reform are therefore establishing rules and norms that could provide government officials with incentives to act in the collective interest while controlling corruption and arbitrary actions.

- *Social Protection*

Most East Asian economies, except for China, may not be able to achieve the high growth of the pre-crisis period. This prospect for slow growth therefore undermines viability of the growth with equity strategy for social welfare of the pre-crisis period. However, the deceleration of growth does not necessarily mean that the European welfare system is an alternative mechanism for social protection. Nascent democracies will be under pressure to create a myriad of social welfare programs that will inevitably run huge deficits, imposing a large fiscal burden that will undermine their potential for growth. In order to militate against this possibility, East Asian economies should adhere to their fiscal conservatism. If targeting the poor is the objective of social welfare policy, one can make a strong case for East Asia's social contract, which places an emphasis on investment in people and communities.

Individual countries in East Asia will find it increasingly difficult to produce public goods for social welfare on their own as a result of economic regionalization and globalization. Resolving this difficulty may call for establishing a system of collective social security and harmonization of the tax system at a regional level.

- *Industrial Relations*

In managing industrial relations, East Asia's task would be to weigh the relative advantages of the Anglo-American system favoring labor market flexibility against the European 'corporatist' approach, which accommodates more extensive participation of labor in economic and social choices. After many years of suppressive labor policies, East Asian economies will benefit from making room for labor's participation in the political process to the extent that it does not compromise labor market flexibility. As far as labor participation is concerned, there cannot be a single approach acceptable to all East Asian economies. Each country is expected to fashion its own mechanism of labor participation compatible with its political system.

- *Financial Reform*

Theory and experience do not prove that a capital market-oriented financial system is more effective in mobilizing and allocating resources and safeguarding financial market stability in emerging economies. Many East Asian economies may have to depend on a bank-oriented financial system until they establish a well-functioning legal and regulatory system that can provide adequate protection of investor and creditor rights as a foundation for efficient securities markets. This means that in many East Asian economies, particularly those at earlier stages of development, the sequencing of financial reform would begin by improving efficiency and stability of the banking system before moving on to developing money and capital markets. Efficiency and stability of the banking system in turn require a medium-term strategy in which reforms accept and enforce international codes and standards on capital adequacy, loan classification, loan-loss provisioning, risk management and corporate governance.

The 1997–98 Asian financial crisis is proof that East Asian corporations will not be able to maintain robust growth with soundness in their balance sheets unless they reduce their leverage by going directly to equity markets rather than to banks for their financing. In fact, the backwardness of capital markets could serve as one of the major constraints on future growth in East Asia. Over time, East Asian economies are expected to develop a balanced financial system in which banks and financial markets are both complementary and competitive. Both the banking system and securities markets require a set of prudential regulations, supervision, and administrative rules, although the development of capital markets requires a more elaborate system of regulation and legal infrastructure. Introduction of a universal banking system deserves further consideration as it could under certain conditions serve as an intermediate step towards developing a balanced financial system in a bank-dominated East Asia.

### • *Reform of Industrial Organization*

Despite the problems of inefficiency, non-transparency, and inadequate governance of East Asian family-owned industrial groups, their physical breakup may cause more harm than good. The experiences of Western economies also suggest that the building of market institutions, better governance, transparency, and the protection of minority stockholders over time strengthen market discipline to which East Asian industrial groups will be subjected and which weeds out inefficient groups. Increased competition from domestic market liberalization and integration into global markets will further weaken the traditional advantages of a large, family-owned group. In particular, the growth of knowledge-based industries could accelerate the breakup of these groups.[2] It is also worth noting that

---

[2] World Bank (2000*b*).

East Asian industrial groups are not so much the products of Asian values as they are of a certain stage of economic development. Some of today's industrial giants, such as Ford, Thyssens, and Siemens, started out as family businesses. Over time, they have become modern, transparent, and shareholder friendly corporations. There is no reason to believe that East Asia's industrial icons will not follow a similar pattern of transformation as they become more multinational in their operations. What is needed at this stage of development is the strengthening of a bank-based corporate governance and other legal and judiciary reforms that will improve the transparency and accountability of these enterprises and the protection of minority stockholders.

- *Exchange Rate System and Capital Account Liberalization*

In the aftermath of the East Asian crisis, emerging market economies in East Asia have been given two alternatives: a free floating or fixed parity system for their exchange rate regimes. The experience of East Asian and other emerging market economies does not support the viability of either of the two corner solutions. East Asia's emerging economies will find a variety of managed floating systems more suitable and will be better off if they move to free floating as their financial systems mature and are integrated into the global financial system. As for capital market liberalization, this study agrees with the conclusion of a recent IMF study (Prasad et al. 2003) that until they develop good market supporting institutions and a macroeconomic framework, East Asian economies, particularly the developing ones, should exercise caution in deregulating the capital account as there is no optimal pace and sequencing for removing capital controls.

- *A New Paradigm*

What does the preceding discussion highlighting East Asia's reform priorities surmise in the way of constructing a new post-crisis paradigm of development for East Asia? East Asia's reform agenda suggests that an appropriate new model for a large number of East Asia's emerging economies will assign a larger role to the market than the old East Asian model described in Chapter 2. But it will have a larger role for government than the Anglo-Saxon model. In this sense the new model will be a mixed economy that combines the state and market (laissez-faire and intervention).

How is it then different from the old paradigm, which was also a mixed economy model? The new paradigm will be more democratic, market oriented, and a more open system than the old one, and will be built on foundations comprising a set of democratic political institutions. Depending on how market forces and still powerful governments fit together, different East Asian economies will develop different mixed economy models. Some of these models will be closer in their structure to the old East Asian model and others to the Anglo-Saxon model. In between, there will be models with different shades of the mixed economy. Many facets of the new Asian model that are envisaged in this study resemble the prototypical Anglo-Saxon model—democratic checks and balances, arm's-length relationships between banks and corporations, more spending on higher education, and government-sponsored R&D. The main way in which the new Asian model will differ from the Anglo-Saxon model is that it will value social goals, including equality, as well as growth. It may also have a more prominent role for industrial policy. The former is similar to the German social market economy, and the latter to French indicative planning.[3]

In developing the new system, there would be little disagreement that fundamentally sound development policies of the earlier periods will survive political as well as economic liberalization in East Asia. Indeed, East Asian economies will gain little if they deviate from the sound policies of the old model which include: (1) incentive schemes for promoting high rates of saving and investment; (2) ensuring large investments in education in general and research and development in particular; (3) sustaining macroeconomic stability; (4) maintaining market openness to acquire foreign technology and to be exposed to foreign competition; and (5) complementing social welfare policies with a growth and with equity strategy.

---

[3] Barry Eichengreen was helpful in conceptualizing a new East Asian development paradigm.

# 25

# Concluding Remarks

The 1997 financial crisis marked a watershed for economic liberalization and integration in East Asia. It exposed numerous structural problems and showed how unprepared East Asia's emerging economies were for preventing and, when they occurred, managing speculative attacks and other financial market turbulences. Not surprisingly, the crisis renewed the debate on the viability as well as replicability of the pre-crisis East Asian development paradigm in other developing economies. Although the crisis does not prove that the East Asian system was 'beaten' by the Anglo-American model, East Asia cannot afford to remain content with its vintage 1960s–1970s model, glibly laying the blame on foreign speculators for the 1997 crisis. In fact, except for the basic building blocks of economic fundamentals, all aspects of the model (and most notably), institutions governing the financial system, corporate sector, and labor market, will have to be reformed.

In the wake of the crisis, most East Asian economies voluntarily or otherwise chose to follow a structural and institutional reform that would lead to Anglo-Americanization of their economic systems. From the beginning, however, they realized that the liberal reforms of the Washington Consensus would neither be a safeguard from future financial crises nor help realize their growth potential. This realization has led them to fortify themselves with a large war chest of foreign exchange reserves and to explore the possibilities of creating a regional defense mechanism by strengthening cooperation for regional liquidity assistance. On regional financial cooperation, they have made considerable progress though they still have a long way to go to match the European collaboration. On filling up their war chest, they have been very successful, but at a high cost.

Most East Asian economies are not persuaded that liberal reforms will lead the way to catching up with advanced countries in terms of living standards and technological sophistication. They have therefore been searching for a new development paradigm that could, in addition to catching up, build crisis-resistant economic systems and integrate their economies into the global financial and trading system without breaking social harmony. They have yet to find such a system and perhaps they never will. Unprepared for pell-mell Anglo-Americanization and failing at finding an alternative paradigm, all East Asian economies have returned to their familiar and proven habit of export-led growth while some have even succumbed to the temptation of populist policies. These developments, though not inexplicable, have been unsettling in many respects. They have thrown into doubt the further liberalization of capital account transactions and whether to remain with a flexible exchange rate system. They have in part given rise to the proliferation of bilateral FTAs, which may or may not promote region-wide trade liberalization. Most of all, they have been responsible for exacerbating the transpacific imbalance for which both East Asia and the US have been unable to find a solution.

East Asian emerging economies may be able to mount a more effective defense against financial crises if they coordinate their policies and form more efficient regional economic cooperative arrangements. With a better framework of policy cooperation and coordination in force, they may also be able to determine the scope and the speed of economic reforms that will facilitate their gradual and smooth integration into the global economy. Small East Asian economies have found it increasingly difficult to provide many of the important public goods needed for social protection, combating corruption, securing financial stability, and resolving the conflicts between domestic politics and economic globalization. Some of these countries may not be able to develop efficient domestic capital markets and may have to rely on regional capital markets. These public goods may be more efficiently produced at a regional level. East Asia's efforts for regional economic integration have culminated in a number of regional initiatives, such as the Chiang Mai Initiative in 2000 and the Asian bond market development initiative in 2003.

Recent developments such as the low probability of another crisis, Japan's recession, the China–Japan rivalry on political and economic leadership in East Asia, and other disputes on trade, territorial, and historical issues have dampened initial enthusiasm for regional cooperation and integration. Nevertheless, the collective interest in creating a larger market and preventing financial turbulence will be strong enough to overcome and reconcile the different interests of different economies to move the integration process forward. In fact, deepening economic ties among ASEAN+3 appears to have mitigated growing tensions on the political and security fronts in the region. However, growing economic ties and mutual economic interdependence will not be enough. In order to push the integrationist movement forward, the East Asian economies will have to find ways in which the rivalry on political and economic leadership in East Asia and other regional disputes between China and Japan can be resolved. One approach to unraveling the political entanglements in the region is to espouse open regionalism which has its ultimate goal in achieving global integration and which will bring in other major powers as mediators on regional disputes. Given the region's extensive trade and financial ties with North America and Europe, East Asia cannot afford an integrationist movement that discriminates against other partners from different regions.

What implications do these developments have for East Asia's growth and stability in the future? One of the main messages of this study is that a new development paradigm for post-crisis East Asia will not be an Anglo-American system of free capitalism, but a mixed economy model as was the pre-crisis system. The new model, distinct from the old system, will be a more deregulated and open regime with a government oriented to social rather than economic development. To be effective in meeting the challenges posed by the new global economy, the new model will have to incorporate a new governance system that embraces a set of democratic institutions, rules, and norms and to be complemented by a host of new institutions for conflict management, social insurance, and regulations, thus allowing the market system to function better. In particular, regulatory and judicial mechanisms for enforcing investor and creditor rights need to be improved by reforming securities, commercial, and bankruptcy laws. Many of these institutions are Western concepts and will have to be assimilated into an inhospitable East Asian cultural terrain. The reform may not succeed unless this transplantation is carefully managed with due consideration of the capacity and constraints of the reforming economies.

Another message is that East Asian regionalism is at risk of developing into a more insulated region integrated in a shallow form with China as the center or a hub economy. This pattern of shallow integration centered on China may not be desirable for both East Asia and the rest of the world. It may not help bridge East Asia's technological gap vis-à-vis advanced countries. It may also not develop a region capable of working out the growing transpacific trade imbalance, thereby aggravating trade and other frictions in the region's relations with North America and the EU. Although the transpacific imbalance is at risk of escalating into serious frictions, neither has been able to provide a realistic solution except that the US, EU, and major international financial institutions have been repeating the same mantra that East Asian economies should revalue their currencies and open their trade and financial regimes, fully knowing they are not able to do so. How then could this impasse be broken?

This study urges that the G-7 countries develop institutions that will facilitate economic globalization and make it easier for East Asia to integrate into the global trading and financial system. They should in this regard resurrect the initiative for building a new international financial architecture that will among other things help prevent future financial crises and rescue East Asia's emerging market economies in the event that they occur. They should also lead and revitalize the Doha Development round to its successful conclusion to hold at bay the proliferation of FTAs in East Asia.

A third message concerns the apprehension that would result if regionalization were to be dominated by China. It would therefore be in the interest of the US and EU to encourage and support regional economic integration in East Asia. Expansion and consolidation of the CMI network will reduce the need for East Asia to hold so much in reserves as the network can serve as a regional liquidity support system. The ABMI, if carried out successfully, will contribute to capital account liberalization and deepen financial integration. Bilateral FTA negotiations underway in East Asia could be managed in a way that could advance region-wide trade liberalization and integration that will loosen East Asia's fixation on its export-led development strategy. As far as the US and EU are concerned, their choice is either an economically integrated or warring East Asia. There is little doubt that they will gain from an economically integrated East Asia. And to assist the region's efforts in this regard, they could as a first step balance the roles of both China and Japan so that they can cooperate rather than compete for regional supremacy.

The United States has an important role to play in East Asia's regional integration. Using its market as leverage, it has the ability as well as interest in steering East Asia to an open region. To this end, the US may revive the APEC movement to bring regional economic arrangements under its auspices, such as the CMI, ABMI, and bilateral FTAs. Alternatively the US could articulate its interest in participating in and supporting the regional integration movement in East Asia, which will lead to cooperation rather than confrontation between the two sides across the Pacific.

# References

ADB (Asian Development Bank) (1997), *Emerging Asia: Change and Challenges*, Manila.

AKAMATSU, KANAME (1961), 'A Theory of Unbalanced Growth in the World Economy,' *Weltwirtschaftliches Archiv*, Vol. 86, No. 2.

AOKI, MASAHIKO (2001), 'A Note on the Role of Banking in Developing Economies in the Aftermath of the East Asian Crisis,' in Boris Plekovic and Joseph E. Stiglitz (eds.), *Governance, Equity and Global Markets*, The World Bank.

AOKI, MASAHIKO, and HUGH PATRICK (1994), *The Japanese Main Bank System: Its Relevance for Developing and Transforming Economies*, Oxford University Press, New York.

AOKI, M., K. MURDOCK, and M. OKUNO-FUJIWARA (1997), 'Beyond The East Asian Miracle: Introducing the Market Enhancing View', in M. Aoki, H. K. Kim, and M. Okuno-Fujiwara (eds.), *The Role of Government in East Asian Development*, Clarendon Press, Oxford.

ARTETA, C., B. EICHENGREEN, and C. WYPLOSZ (2001), 'When Does Capital Account Liberalization Help More Than It Hurts?', *NBER Working Paper* No. 8414, August.

ASEAN (2005), The Joint Ministerial Statement of the 8th ASEAN+3 Finance Ministers' Meeting, Istanbul, May 4.

BAEK, S. G., and C. Y. SONG (2002), 'Is Currency Union a Feasible Option in East Asia?,' in Han Kwang Joo and Yunjong Wang (eds.), *Currency Union in East Asia*, Korea Institute for International Economic Policy, July.

BALDWIN, RICHARD E. (2004), 'The Spoke Trap: Hub and Spoke Bilateralism in East Asia,' *CNAEC Research Series* No. 04–02, Korea Institute for International Economic Policy.

BALIÑO, TOMÁS J. T., CHARLES ENOCH, ANNE-MARIE GULDE, CARL-JOHAN LINDGREN, MARC QUINTYN, and LESLIE TEO (1999), 'Financial Sector Crisis and Restructuring: Lessons From Asia,' *IMF Occasional Paper* No. 188, September.

BANK FOR INTERNATIONAL SETTLEMENTS (2004), 'Foreign Direct Investment in the Financial Sector of Emerging Market Economies,' Committee on the Global Financial System, March.

BARDHAN, PRANAB (1996), 'Efficiency, Equity and Poverty Alleviation, Policy Issues in Less Developed Countries,' *Economic Journal*, September.

BARDHAN, PRANAB (1997), 'Corruption and Development: A Review of Issues,' *Journal of Economic Literature*,' September.

BARTH, JAMES, STEVEN B. CAUDILL, THOMAS HALL, and GLENN YAGO (2000), 'Cross-country Evidence on Banking Crises: Do Financial Structure and Banking Regulation

Matter?', in George G. Kaufman (ed.), *Banking Fragility and Regulation: Evidence from Different Countries*, JAI press, Amsterdam.

BAUMS, THEODOR (1994), 'The German Banking System and its Impact on Corporate Finance and Governance,' in M. Aoki and H. Patrick (eds.), *The Japanese Main Bank System: Its Relevance for Developing and Transforming Economies*, Clarendon Press, Oxford.

BAYOUMI, TAMIM (1996), 'Exchange Rate Movements and Their Impact on Trade and Investment in the APEC Region,' *IMF Occasional Paper* No. 145, December.

BEKAERT, GEERT, CAMPELL R. HARVEY, and CHRISTIAN LUNDBLAD (2001), 'Does Financial Liberalization Spur Growth?' *NBER Working Paper* No.8245, October.

BERG, ANDREW, and ANNE KRUEGER (2003), 'Trade, Growth, and Poverty: A Selective Survey,' *IMF Working Paper* No. 03/30, April.

BERGSTEN, C. FRED (2005), 'Lesson for China from Japan is: Revalue your currency soon and far enough to avoid bubble,' *Financial Times*, March 24.

BERGSTEN, C. FRED, and YUNG CHUL PARK (2002), 'Toward Creating a Regional Monetary Arrangement in East Asia,' *ADBI Research Paper* No. 50, December.

BERNANKE, BEN S. (2005), 'The Global Saving Glut and the U.S. Current Account Deficit,' the Federal Reserve Board Speech at the Sandridge Lecture, Virginia Association of Economics, Richmond, April.

BHAGWATI, T. (1998), 'Why Free Capital Mobility May Be Hazardous to Your Health?: Lessons from the Latest Financial Crisis,' *NBER Conference on Capital Controls*, November 7.

BHANUPONG, NIDHIPRABKA (2003), 'Thailand's Macroeconomic Policy after July 1997,' *Asian Economic Papers*, Vol. 2, No. 1, MIT Press, January.

BLINDER, A. S. (1999), 'Eight Steps to a New Financial Order,' *Foreign Affairs*, September/ October.

BLUSTEIN, PAUL (2001), *The Chastening: Inside the Crisis that Rocked the Global Financial System and Humbled the IMF*, Public Affairs Books, New York.

BRANSON, W., and HANNA NAGY (2000), 'Ownership and Conditionality,' *World Bank OED Working Paper* Series No. 8, Summer.

CALVO, A., and C. REINHART (2001), 'Fixing for Your Life,' Brookings Trade Forum 2000, The Brookings Institution, Washington, DC.

CALVO, A., and C. REINHART (2002), 'Fear of Floating,' *Quarterly Journal of Economics*, Vol. CXVII No. 2, May.

CAMPBELL, DUNCAN (2000), 'Globalization and Change: Social Dialogue and Labor Market Adjustment in the Crisis-Affected Countries of East Asia,' ILO/EASMAT, November.

CAMPOS, J. E., and ROOT, H. L. (1996), *The Key to the Asian Miracle: Making Shared Growth Credible*, The Brookings Institution, Washington, DC.

CARDOSO, JAIME, and BERNARD LAURENS (1998), 'Managing Capital Flows—Lessons from the Experience of Chile,' *IMF Working Paper* No. 98/168, October.

CHANG, ROBERTO, and ANDRES VELASCO (1998), 'Financial Crises in Emerging Markets: A Canonical Model,' *NBER Working Paper* No. 6606, June.

CHARI, ANUSHA, and PETER BLAIR HENRY (2002), 'Capital Account liberalization: Allocative Efficiency or Animal Spirits?', *NBER Working Paper* No. 8908, April.

CHEONG, INKYO (2002), 'East Asian Economic Integration: Recent Development of FTAs and Policy Implications,' *Policy Analysis* No. 02-02, Korea Institute for International Economic Policy.

CLAESSENS, STIJN, SIMION DJANKOV, and DANIELA KLINGEBIEL (1999), 'Financial Restructuring in East Asia: Halfway There?' *World Bank Financial Sector Discussion Paper* No. 3, September.

CLAESSENS, STIJN, SIMION DJANKOV, and LARRY LANG (2000), 'East Asian Corporations: Growth, Financing, and Risks,' *Emerging Markets Quarterly*, Spring.

CLINE, WILLIAM R. (2005), *The United States as a Debtor Nation: Risks and Policy Reform*, Institute for International Economics, Washington, DC.

CORSETTI, G., P. PESENTI, and N. ROUBINI (1998), 'What Caused the Asian Currency and Financial Crisis,' *NBER Working Paper* No. 6833, December.

CRYSTAL, J. S., B. GERARD DAGES, and LINDA S. GOLDBERG (2001), 'Does Foreign Ownership Contribute to Sounder Banks in Emerging Markets? The Latin American Experience,' *Staff Reports* No. 137, Federal Reserve Bank of New York, September.

CRYSTAL, J. S., B. GERARD DAGES, and LINDA S GOLDBERG (2002), 'Has Foreign Banks Entry Led to Sounder Banks in Latin America?', *Current Issues in Economics and Finance*, Federal Reserve Bank of New York, January.

DEMIRGUC-KUNT, ASLI, and ROSS LEVINE (1999), 'Bank-Based and Market-Based Financial Systems: Cross-Country Comparisons,' *World Bank Country Economics Department Papers* No. 2143, July.

DEMIRGUC-KUNT, ASLI, and ROSS LEVINE (2001), *Financial Structure and Economic Growth: A Cross-Country Comparison of Banks, Markets, and Development*, MIT Press, Cambridge.

DOLLAR, DAVID, and AART KRAAY (2002), 'Growth is Good for the Poor,' *Journal of Economic Growth*, September.

DOOLEY, MICHAEL, DAVID FOLKERTS-LANDAU, and PETER GARBER (2003), 'An Essay on Revived Bretton Woods System,' *NBER Working Paper* No. 9971, September.

DOOLEY, M., R. DORNBUSCH, and YUNG CHUL PARK (2002), 'A Framework for Exchange Rate Policy in Korea,' *Korean Crisis and Recovery*, IMF and Korea Institute for International Economic Policy.

DORNBUSCH, R. (2001), 'Malaysia: Was it Different?', *NBER Working Paper* No. 8325, June.

EASTERLY, WILLIAMS, and ROSS LEVINE (2000), 'It's not Factor Accumulation: Stylized Facts and Growth Models,' *Development Research Group*, World Bank, December.

EAVG (2001), 'Towards an East Asian Community: Region of Peace, Prosperity and Progress,' *East Asia Vision Group*, July.

EDWARDS, S. (2000), 'Interest Rates, Contagion and Capital Controls,' *NBER Working Paper* No. 7801, July.

EDWARDS, S. (2001), 'Capital Mobility and Economic Performance: Are Emerging Economies Different?', *NBER Working Paper* No. 8076, January.

## References

EICHENGREEN, BARRY (1998), 'International Economic Policy in the Wake of the Asian Crisis,' University of California, Berkeley Center for International and Development Economics Research (CIDER) *Working Paper Series* C98-102, August.

EICHENGREEN, BARRY (1999*a*), 'Strengthening the International Financial Architecture: Where Do We Stand?,' paper presented for the East-West Center Workshop on International Monetary and Financial Reform, October.

EICHENGREEN, BARRY (1999*b*), *Toward a New International Financial Architecture*, Institute for International Economics, Washington, DC, February.

EICHENGREEN, BARRY, and RICARDO BAYOUMI (1999), 'Is Asia an Optimum Currency Area? Can It Become One? Regional, Global and Historical Perspectives on Asian Monetary Relations,' in Stefan Collignon, Jean Pisani-Ferry, and Yung Chul Park (eds.), *Exchange Rate Policies in Emerging Asian Countries*, Routledge, London.

EICHENGREEN, BARRY, and RICARDO HAUSMANN (1999), 'Exchange Rates and Financial Fragility,' *NBER Working Paper* No. 7418, November.

EICHENGREEN, BARRY, and YUNG CHUL PARK (2004), 'Financial Liberalization and Capital Market Integration in East Asia,' in Takatoshi Ito, Yung Chul Park, and Yun Jong Wang (eds.), *A New Financial Market Structure for East Asia*, to be published by Edward Elgar.

FELDSTEIN, MARTIN (1998), 'Refocusing the IMF,' *Foreign Affairs*, March-April.

FISCHER, STANLEY (2001), 'Exchange Rate Regime: Is the Bipolar View Correct?' *Journal of Economic Perspectives*, No. 15, Spring.

FRANKEL, JEFFREY (1999), 'No Single Currency Regime is Right for All Countries or At All Times,' *Essays in International Finance* No. 215, Princeton University Press, Princeton.

FUKUYAMA, FRANCIS (1998), 'Asian Values and Civilization,' the ICAS Lectures in ICAS Fall Symposium, No. 98-929-FRF, September 29.

FUKUYAMA, FRANCIS (2004), *State Building: Governance and World Order in the 21*st *Century*, Cornell University Press, Ithaca.

FURMAN, JASON, and JOSEPH STIGLITZ (1998), 'Economic Crises: Evidence and Insights from East Asia,' *Brookings Papers on Economic Activity* II.

GALINDO, ARTURO, ALEJANDRO MICCO, and GUILLERMO ORDONEZ (2002), 'Financial Liberalization and Growth,' World Bank and George Washington University conference, Financial Globalization: A Blessing or a Curse?, Washington DC, May.

GENBERG, HANS, ROBERT MCCAULEY, YUNG CHUL PARK and AVINASH PERSAUD (2005), *Official Reserves and Currency Management in Asia: Myth, Reality and the Future*, Geneva Reports on the World Economy 7, International Centre for Monetary and Banking Studies and Centre for Economic Policy Research, September.

GOLDFAJN, I., and G. OLIVARES (2001), 'Can Flexible Exchange Rates still Work in Financially Open Economies?' *UNCTAD G-24 Discussion Paper series* No. 8, January.

GOLDFAJN, I., and S. R. C. WERLANG (2000), 'The Pass-through from Depreciation to Inflation: A panel study, ' *Working Paper Series* No. 5, Banco Central do Brazil.

GOLDSTEIN, MORRIS (2002), 'Managed Floating Plus,' *Policy Analyses in International Economics*, No. 66, Institute for International Economics, Washington, DC, March.

GOLDSTEIN, MORRIS (2003), 'IMF Structural Programs,' in Martin Feldstein (ed.), *Economic and Financial Crises in Emerging Market Economies*, National Bureau of Economic Research, University of Chicago Press, Chicago.

HAGGARD, STEPHAN (2000), *The Political Economy of the Asian Financial Crisis*, Institute for International Economics, Washington, DC.

HAHN, CHIN HEE (2004), 'Exporting and Performance of Plants: Evidence from Korean Manufacturing' *NBER Working Paper* No. 10208, January.

HAUSMANN, R., M. GAVIN, C. PAGES-SERRA, and E. STEIN (1999), 'Financial Turmoil and the Choice of Exchange Rate Regime,' *IADB Working Paper* No. 400, March.

HELLMANN, F. THOMAS, KEVIN C. MURDOCK, and JOSEPH E. STIGLITZ (2000), 'Liberalization, Moral Hazard in Banking, and Prudential Regulation: Are Capital Requirements Enough?' *American Economic Review*, March.

HERNANDEZ, L., and P. MONTIEL (2001), 'Post-Crisis Exchange Rate Policy in Five Asian Countries: Filling in the Hollow Middle? paper presented at the IMF Institute high-level seminar, *Exchange Rate Regimes: Hard Peg or Free Floating?* IMF, Washington, DC, March 19–20.

HOOD, R. (2001), 'Malaysian Capital Controls,' *World Bank Working Paper* No. 2536.

HSIEH, CHANG-TAI (2002), 'What Explains the Industrial Revolution in East Asia? Evidence from the Factor Markets,' *American Economic Review* Vol. 92, No. 3, June.

HWANG, S. I., I. KIM, and I. SHIN, (2001), 'The Liberalization of Banking Sector and the Effect of Foreign Entry in Korea,' *Policy Analysis* No. 01–03, Korea Institute for International Economic Policy.

IMF (2003), *The IMF and Recent Capital Account Crises: Indonesia, Korea, Brazil, Evaluation Report*, Independent Evaluation Office, IMF.

IMF (2004), *China's Growth and Integration in the World Economy: Prospects and Challenges*, Eswar Prasad (ed.) *IMF Occasional Paper* No. 232, June.

ITO, TAKATOSHI (2000), 'Perspectives on Asian Economic Growth: Neoclassical Growth vs. Flying Geese Growth,' *The Economic Analysis*, Economic Research Institute, Economic Planning Agency, Tokyo, No. 160, December.

JEANNE, OLIVIER, and ANDREW K. ROSE (1999), 'Noise Trading and Exchange Rate Regimes,' *Quarterly Journal of Economics* Vol. 117, No. 2, May.

JEON, JONGKYOU, YONGHYUP OH, and DOO YOUNG YANG (2005), 'Financial Market Integration in East Asia: Regional or Global?' *Working Paper* No. 05–02, Korea Institute for International Economic Policy.

JOHNSON, CHALMER (1983), *MITI and the Japanese Miracle: The Growth of Industrial Policy, 1925–1975*, Stanford University Press, Stanford.

JOHNSON, CHALMER (2001), 'Japanese Capitalism Revisited,' *JPRI Occasional Paper* No. 22, August.

JOHNSTON, B., M. SWINBURNE, A. KYEI, B. LAURENS, D. MITCHEM, I. OTKER, S. SOSA, and N. TAMIRISA (1999), Exchange Rate Arrangements and Currency Convertibility: Developments and Issues, *World Economic and Financial Surveys*, IMF.

JOMO, K. (2001), 'Capital Controls,' in K. Jomo (ed.), *Malaysian Eclipse: Economic Crisis and Recovery*, Select Books Pte. Ltd., Singapore.

## References

KAMINSKY, GRACIELA LAURA, and SERGIO L. SCHMUKLER (2002), 'Short-Run Pain, Long-Run Gain: The Effect of Financial Liberalization,' *World Bank Working Paper* No. 2912, October.

KANG, JUN-KOO, and RENÉ M. STULZ (2000), 'Do Banking Shocks Affect Borrowing Firm Performance? An Analysis of the Japanese Experience,' *Journal of Business* Vol. 73, Issue 1, January.

KAPLAN, E., and D. RODRIK (2001), 'Did the Malaysian Capital Controls Work?' *NBER Working Paper* No. 8142, February.

KAUFMANN, DANIEL, AART KRAAY, and PABLO ZOIDO-LOBATON (1999), 'Governance Matters,' *World Bank Working Paper* No. 2196, October.

KAUFMANN, DANIEL, AART KRAAY, and PABLO ZOIDO-LOBATON (2002), 'Governance Matters II: Updated Indicators for 2000/01,' *World Bank Working Paper* No. 2196, January.

KAUFMANN, DANIEL, AART KRAAY, and MASSIMO MASTRUZZI (2002), 'Governance Matters III: Governance Indicators for 1996–2002,' *World Bank Working Paper* No. 3106, June.

KHAN, A. HAIDER (1999), 'Corporate Governance of Family-Based Businesses in Asia: Which Road to Take?' paper presented to the 2nd anniversary symposium of ADBI, Tokyo, December.

KHANNA, TARUN, and KRISHNA PALEPU (1999), 'The Right Way to Restructure Conglomerates in Emerging Markets,' *Harvard Business Review* Vol. 77, July–August.

KLEIN, M., and G. OLIVEI (1999), 'Capital Account Liberalization, Financial Depth, and Economic Growth', *Federal Reserve Bank of Boston Working Paper* No. 99–6, August.

KLINGEBIEL, DANIELA (2000), 'The Use of Asset Management Companies in the Resolution of Banking Crises Cross-Country Experiences,' *World Bank Working Paper* No. 2284.

KNACK, S., and P. KEEFER (1995), 'Institutions and Economic Performance: Cross-Country Tests Using Alternative Institutional Measures,' *Economics and Politics* 7(3), November.

KOCK, UDO (2000), 'Institutions, Incentives and Social Policy in the "Dutch Model",' *Serie Research Memoranda 0003*, Free University of Amsterdam, Faculty of Economics, Business Administration and Econometrics.

KRAAY, A. (1998), 'In Search of the Macroeconomic Effects of Capital Account Liberalization,' mimeo, The World Bank, October.

KRUEGER, ANNE O. (1995), 'East Asian Experience and Endogenous Growth Theory,' in Takatoshi Ito and Anne O. Krueger (eds.), *Growth Theories in Light of the East Asian Experience*, NBER-East Asia Seminar on Economics Vol. 4., University of Chicago Press, Chicago.

KRUGMAN, PAUL (1994), 'The Myth of Asia's Miracle,' *Foreign Affairs*, November.

KRUGMAN, PAUL (1997), *The Age of Diminished Expectations*, MIT Press, Cambridge.

KUHNLE, STEIN, AKSEL HATLAND, and SVEN HORT (2003), 'A Work-Friendly Welfare State: Lessons from Europe,' in K. Marshall and O. Butzbach (eds.), *New Social Policy Agendas for Europe and Asia*, The World Bank.

LALL, SANJAYA (2003), 'Reinventing Industrial Strategy: The Role of Government Policy in Building Industrial Competitiveness,' The Intergovernmental Group on Monetary Affairs and Development (G-24), October.

LANE, PHILLIP, and GIAN MARIA MILESI-FERRETTI, (2001), 'Long-Term Capital Movements,' *IMF Working Papers* 01/107, August.

LANE, TIMOTHY, ATISH GHOSH, JAVIER HAMANN, STEVEN PHILLIPS, MARIANNE SCHULZE-GHATTAS, and TSIDI TSIKATA (1999), 'IMF-Supported Programs in Indonesia, Korea, and Thailand: A Preliminary Assessment,' *IMF Occasional Paper*, No. 178, June.

LA PORTA, R., F. LOPEZ-DE-SILANES, A. SHLEIFER, and R. VISHNY (1998), 'Law and Finance,' *Journal of Political Economy*, December.

LA PORTA, RAFAEL, FLORENCIO LOPEZ-DE-SILANES, ANDREI SHLEIFER, and ROBERT VISHNY (1999), 'Investor Protection: Origins, Consequences, Reform,' *Financial Sector Discussion Paper* No. 1, The World Bank, September.

LARDY, NICHOLAS (2001), 'Foreign Financial Firms in Asia,' a paper presented to a conference on Open Doors: Foreign Participation in Financial Systems in Developing Countries organized by The Brookings Institution, World Bank, and IMF, April.

LAYARD, RICHARD (2001), 'The "Third Way" and Its Relation to the Labour Market,' in Boris Plekovic and Joseph E. Stiglitz (eds.), *Governance, Equity and Global Markets*, The World Bank.

LEE, JONG WHA, and CHANGYONG RHEE (2000), 'Macroeconomic Impacts of the Korean Financial Crisis: Comparison with the Cross-country Patterns,' University of Rochester—Center for Economic Research (RCER) Working Paper No. 471.

LEE, JONG WHA, WARWICK J. MCKIBBIN, and YUNG CHUL PARK (2004), 'The Transpacific Imbalance,' *Brookings Discussion papers* in International Economics, No. 162, August.

LEE, JONG-WHA, YUNG CHUL PARK, and KWAN HO SHIN (2004), 'A Currency Union in East Asia,' in *Monetary and Financial Integration in East Asia* Vol. ii, edited by the Asian Development Bank, Palgrave Macmillan, London.

LEVINE, ROSS (2002), 'Bank-Based or Market-Based Financial Systems: Which is Better?' *NBER Working Paper* No. 9138, September.

LEVINE, ROSS (2003), 'More on finance and growth: more finance, more growth?', *Review*, Federal Reserve Bank of St Louis.

LEVY-YEYATI, E., and F. STURZENEGGER (2005), 'Classifying Exchange Rate Regimes: Deeds vs. Words,' *European Economic Review*, Vol. 49, Issue 6, August.

LIN, JUSTIN YIFU, FANG CAI, and ZHOU LI (2003), *The China Miracle: Development Strategy and Economic Reform* (revised), Chinese University Press, Hong Kong.

MCCALLUM, N. (1996), 'Inflation Targeting in Canada, New Zealand, Sweden, the United Kingdom, and in General,' *NBER Working Papers* No. 5579, May.

MCCAULEY, ROBERT N., SAN-SAU FUNG, and BLAISE GADANECZ (2002), 'Integrating the Finances of East Asia,' *BIS Quarterly Review*, December.

MCINTYRE, ANDREW (1994), 'Power, Prosperity and Patrimonialism: Business and Government in Indonesia,' in A. McIntyre (ed.), *Business and Government in Industrializing Asia*, Cornell University Press, Ithaca.

# References

McKibbin W. J., and A. Stoeckel (2004), 'What if China Revalues Its Currency?' **www.EconomicScenarios.com**, Issue 7, February.

McKinnon, Ronald (1973), *Money and Capital in Economic Development*, The Brookings Institution, Washington, DC.

McKinnon, Ronald (1993), *The Order of Economic Liberalization: Financial Control in the Transition to a Market Economy*, Johns Hopkins Press, Baltimore.

McKinnon, Ronald (2003), 'The World Dollar Standard and Globalization, New Rules for the Game?' in Leo Michelis and Mark Lovewell (eds.), *Exchange Rates, Economic Integration and the International Economy*, APF Press, Toronto.

McKinnon, Ronald (2005), 'The East Asian Exchange Rate Dilemma,' *Exchange Rates under the East Asian Dollar Standard*, MIT Press, Cambridge.

Manzano, George (2001), 'Is There Any Value-added in the ASEAN Surveillance Process?' *ASEAN Economic Bulletin*, Vol. 18, No. 2, August.

Mauro, Paolo (1995), 'Corruption, Country Risk, and Growth,' *Quarterly Journal of Economics*, No. 110, October.

Miniane, J. (2000), 'A New Set of Measures on Capital Account Restrictions,' *IMF Staff Papers*, Vol. 51, No. 2, February.

Moon, Hyungpyo (2001), 'The Korean Pension System: Present and the Future,' *Korea Development Institute Working Paper* 2001–01, March.

Moon, Hyungpyo (2005), 'Korea's Pension Reform Agenda,' prepared for the KDI International Conference on Population Aging in Korea: Economic Impacts and Policy Issues, March 17–18.

Mussa, M., P. Masson, A. Swoboda, E. Jadresic, P. Mauro, and A. Berg (2000), 'Exchange Rate Regime in Increasing Integrated World Economy,' IMF *Occasional Paper* No. 193, April.

Obstfeld, Maurice, and Kenneth Rogoff (2004), 'The Unsustainable US Current Account Position Revised,' *NBER Working Paper* No. 10869, October.

Pack, Howard (2000), 'Industrial Policy: Growth and Elixir or Poison?', *The World Bank Research Observer*, Vol. 15, No. 1, February.

Pakorn, Vichyanond (1999), 'Financial Reforms in Thailand,' Thailand Development Research Institute, February.

Park, Yung Chul (1993), 'Capital Movement, Real Asset Speculation, and Macroeconomic Adjustment in South Korea,' in Helmut Reisen and Bernard Fischer (eds.), *Financial Opening: Policy Lessons and Experiences in Developing Countries*, OECD Development Center.

Park, Yung Chul (1994), 'Concepts and Issues,' in Hugh T. Patrick and Yung Chul Park (eds.), *The Financial Development of Japan, Korea and Taiwan: Growth, Repression, and Liberalization*, Oxford University Press, New York.

Park, Yung Chul (1996), 'East Asian Liberalization, Bubbles, and the Challenge from China,' *Brooking's papers on Economic Activity*, II.

Park, Yung Chul (2001), 'East Asian Dilemma: Restructuring Out or Growing Out?' *Essay in International Economics*, No. 233, Princeton University, August.

Park, Yung Chul (2002), 'Does East Asia Need a New Paradigm of Development?' in Dani Rodrik and Susan M. Collins (eds.), *Brookings Trade Forum 2002*. The Brookings Institution, Washington, DC.

Park, Yung Chul, and C. Y. Song (2001), 'East Asia's Experiences with the Free Floating Exchange Rate System,' in *New Challenges of Crisis Prevention*, Forum on Debt and Development (FONDAD), The Hague.

Park, Yung Chul, and Jong Wha Lee (2003), 'Recovery and Sustainability in East Asia,' in Michael P. Dooley and Jeffrey A. Frankel (eds.), *Managing Currency Crises in Emerging Market*, University of Chicago Press, Chicago.

Park, Yung Chul, and Charles Wyplosz (2004), 'Exchange Arrangement in Asia: Do They Matter?' paper presented to the KIEP conference on Monetary and Exchange Rate Arrangement in East Asia, August.

Park, Yung Chul, and Yun Jong Wang (2004), 'Toward a Regional Financial Architecture for East Asia: Korean Proposal,' paper presented to the ASEAN+3 Research Group Meeting, Manila, March 16–17.

Park, Yung Chul, Wonho Song, and Yunjong Wang (2004), 'Finance and Economic Development in East Asia,' in Takatoshi Ito, Yung Chul Park, and Yun Jong Wang (eds.), *A New Financial Market Structure for East Asia*, to be published by Edward Elgar.

Park, Yung Chul, Jae Ha Park, Julia Leung, and Kanit Sangsubhan (2004), 'Asian Bond Market Development: Rationale and Strategy,' paper presented to a Conference on Regional Financial Arrangements, United Nations, New York, July 14–15.

Park, Yung Chul, Shujiro Urata, and Inkyo Cheong (2005), 'The Political Economy of the Proliferation of FTAs,' paper presented to the PAFTAD 30 meeting in Honolulu, Hawaii, February 19–21.

Pistor, Katharina (2000), 'The Standardization of Law and Its Effect on Developing Economies,' *G-24 Discussion Paper Series*, No. 4, United Nations Conference on Trade and Development, June.

Political and Economic Risk Consultancy, Ltd. (2001), 'The Trend of Corruption in Asia in 2001,' *Excerpt from Asian Intelligence Issue* No. 579, March.

Prasad, Eswar S., Kenneth Rogoff, Shang-Jin Wei, and M. Ayhan Kose (2003), 'Effects of Financial Globalization on Developing Countires: Some Empirical Evidence,' *IMF Occasional Paper 220*, March.

Quibria, M. G. (2002), 'Growth and Poverty: Lessons from the East Asian Miracle Revisited,' *ADB Institute Research Paper*, February.

Radelet, S., and J. Sachs (1998), 'The Onset of the East Asian Financial Crisis,' *Development Discussion Paper*, Harvard Institute for International Development, August 7.

Radelet, S., J. Sachs, and Jong-Wha Lee (1997), 'Economic Growth in Asia,' *Development Discussion Paper* No. 609, Harvard Institute for International Development, November.

Rajan, R. G., and L. Zingales (1998), 'Which Capitalism? Lessons from the East Asian Crisis,' *Journal of Applied Corporate Finance*, Vol. 11, No. 3, Fall.

# References

RAVENHILL. J. (2004) 'The Political Economy of the New Asia-Pacific Bilateralism,' paper presented to Beijing Forum, August 24.

REINHART, CARMEN M., and IOANNIS TOKATLIDIS (2002), 'Before and after Financial Liberalization,' paper presented to the 14th World Bank ABCDE Conference, Washington, DC, April.

REINHART, CARMEN M., and K. ROGOFF (2004), 'The Modern History of Exchange Rate Arrangements: A Reinterpretation,' *Quarterly Journal of Economics*, February.

RODRIK, DANI (1995), 'Getting Interventions Right: How South Korea and Taiwan Grew Rich,' *Economic Policy*, No. 20, April.

RODRIK, DANI (1996), 'Coordination Failures and Government Policy: A Model with Applications to East Asia and Eastern Europe,' *Journal of International Economics*, 40(1–2), February.

RODRIK, DANI (1997), *Has Globalisation Gone Too Far?* Institute for International Economics, Washington, DC.

RODRIK, DANI (1998), 'Who Needs Capital-Account Convertibility?', in Peter Kenen (ed.), *Should the IMF Pursue Capital Account Convertibility?*, Essays in International Finance, No. 207, Princeton University.

RODRIK, DANI (1999), 'Governing the Global Economy: Does One Architectural Style Fit All?' Susan Collins and Robert Lawrence (eds.), *Brookings Trade Forum: 1999*, The Brookings Institution, Washington, DC.

RODRIK, DANI (2000a), 'Development Strategies for the Next Century,' Annual World Bank Conference on Development Economics, Fall.

RODRIK, DANI (2000b), 'Institutions For High-Quality Growth: What They Are and How to Acquire Them,' *Studies in Comparative International Development*, Vol. 35, No. 3, Fall.

RODRIK, DANI (2000c), 'Participatory Politics, Social Cooperation, and Economic Stability,' *American Economic Review*, May.

RODRIK, DANI (2001), 'Four Simple Principles for Democratic Governance of Globalization,' paper prepared for the Friedrich Ebert Foundation, May.

RODRIK, DANI (2004), 'Industrial Policy for the Twenty-First Century,' paper prepared for UNIDO, September.

ROGOFF, KENNETH, ASIM M. HUSAIN, ASHOKA MODY, ROBIN BROOKS, and NIENKE OOMES (2003), 'Evolution and Performance of Exchange Rate Regimes,' *IMF Working Paper* 03/243, December.

ROLAND-HOLST (2002), 'An Overview of PRC's Emergence and East Asian Trade Patterns to 2020,' *ADBI Research Paper* No. 44, Tokyo, August.

ROUBINI, NOURIEL, and BRAD SETSER (2005), 'Will the Bretton Woods 2 Regime Unravel Soon? The Risk of a Hard Landing in 2005–2006,' paper prepared for the Symposium on the 'Revived Bretton Woods System: A New Paradigm for Asian Development?' February.

RUBIN, ROBERT E. (2004), *In an Uncertain World: Tough Choices from Wall Street to Washington*, Random House Inc., New York.

SACHS, JEFFREY (2000), 'A New Map of the World,' *The Economist*, June 24–30.

SACHS, JEFFREY D., and ANDREW M. WARNER (1995), 'Economic Reform and the Process of Global Integration,' in *Brookings Papers on Economic Activity: 1*, The Brookings Institution, Washington, DC.

SCHMITZ, H., and KHALID NANDVI (1999), 'Clustering and Industrialization; Introduction,' *World Development*, Vol. 27, No. 9, September.

SENHADJI, ABDELHAK S., and CLAUDIO E. MONTENEGRO (1999), 'Time Series Analysis of Export Demand Equations: A Cross-Country Analysis,' *IMF Staff Papers*, Vol. 46, No. 3 (September/December).

SIMONE, F., and P. SORSA (1999), 'A Review of Capital account Restrictions in Chile in the 1990's,' *IMF Working Paper* 99/52, April.

STIGLITZ, JOSEPH (1996), 'Some Lessons from the East Asian Miracle,' *World Bank Research Observer*, August.

STIGLITZ, JOSEPH (1998a), 'Towards a New Paradigm for Development: Strategies, Policies and Process,' *Prebisch Lecture*, UNCTAD, Geneva, October.

STIGLITZ, JOSEPH (1998b), 'More Instruments and Broader Goals: Moving toward the Post-Washington Consensus,' *WIDER Annual Lectures 2*, UNU/WIDER.

STIGLITZ, JOSEPH (2002), *Globalization and Its Discontents*, W.W. Norton & Company, New York.

STIGLITZ, JOSEPH, and MARILOU UY (1996), 'Financial Markets, Public Policy, and the East Asian Miracle,' *World Bank Research Observer*, 11(2), August.

STIGLITZ, JOSEPH, and SHAHID YUSUF (2001), *Rethinking the East Asian Miracle*, Oxford University Press, New York.

SVENSSON, LARS (1991), 'Assessing Target Zone Credibility: Mean Reversion and Devaluation Expectations in the ERM 1979–1992,' *NBER Working Paper* 3795.

SVENSSON, LARS (1997), 'Inflation Forecast Targeting: Implementing and Monitoring Inflation Targets,' *European Economic Review*, Vol. 41, November.

SVENSSON, LARS (2000), 'Open-Economy Inflation Targeting,' *Journal of International Economics*, Vol. 50, February.

SWANK, D. (1998), 'Funding the Welfare State: Globalization and the Taxation of Business in Advanced Market Economies,' *Political Studies 66*, Political Studies Association.

TEMPLE, JONATHAN, and PAUL JOHNSON (1997), 'Social Capability and Economic Growth,' *Quarterly Journal of Economics*, 113, March.

THE ECONOMIST (2000), 'The End of Tycoons,' April 22–28.

THE ECONOMIST (2003), 'Stop Worrying and Love the Deficit,' November 22–28.

THE ECONOMIST (2004), 'Asia's Other Miracle', April 24–30.

THE ECONOMIST (2005), 'In Europe's Midst,' July 16–22.

THE ECONOMIST (2005), 'Lessons from the ten-year-old darling of e-commerce,' June 11–17.

TRANSPARENCY INTERNATIONAL (2002), *Corruption Perceptions Index,* **www.transparency. org/cpi**

TYBOUT, J. R. (2001), 'Plant- and Firm-Level Evidence on "New" Trade Theories,' *NBER Working Paper* No. 8418, August.

# References

VALDES-PRIETO, SALVADOR, and MARCELO SOTO, (1996), 'New Selective Controls in Chile: Are they Effective,' *Working Paper*, Catholic University of Chile.

VELASCO, ANDRES, and FELIPE LARRAIN (2001), 'Exchange-Rate Policy in Emerging-Market Economies: The Case for Floating,' *Essays in International Economics*, No. 224, Princeton University, December.

VENEROSO, FRANK, and ROBERT WADE (1998), 'The Case for an Asian Monetary Fund: Asia Should Look to its Own Resources,' *The Economist*, November 7–13.

VERNON, RAYMOND (1966), 'International Investment and International Trade in the Product Cycle,' *Quarterly Journal of Economics*, May.

VISSER, J., and ANTON HEMERICK (1997), *A Dutch Miracle*, Amsterdam University Press, Amsterdam.

WADE, ROBERT (1990), *Governing the Market: Theory and the Role of Government in East Asian Industrialization*, Princeton University Press, Princeton.

WALL, DAVID (2002), 'Koizumi Trade Pitch Misses,' *Japan Times*, April 21.

WANG, YUNJONG, and WING THYE WOO (2004), 'A Timely Information Exchange Mechanism, an Effective Surveillance System, and an Improved Financial Architecture for East Asia,' in *Monetary and Financial Integration in East Asia: The Way Ahead*, Vol. II, Asian Development Bank, Palgrave Macmillan, London.

WILLIAMSON, JOHN (1997), 'The Washington Consensus Revisited,' in Louis Emmerij (ed.), *Economic and Social Development into the XXI Century*, Part II, Inter-American Development Bank, Washington, DC.

WILLIAMSON, JOHN (2000), 'Exchange-Rate Regimes for East Asia: Reviving the Intermediate Option,' *Policy Analyses in International Economics*, 60, Institute for International Economics, Washington, DC.

WORLD BANK (1993), *The East Asian Miracle: Economic Growth and Public Policy: Policy Research Report*, October.

WORLD BANK (1998), *East Asia: The Road to Recovery*, Richard Newfarmer (principle author), October.

WORLD BANK (2000a), 'Pension Systems in East Asia and the Pacific: Challenges and Opportunities,' *Social Protection Discussion Paper* No. 0014, June.

WORLD BANK (2000b), *East Asia: Recovery and Beyond*, East Asia and Pacific Region, May.

WORLD BANK (2000c), *World Development Report 1999/2000: Entering the 21st Century*, September.

WORLD BANK (2000d), *East Asia's Recovery: Gathering Force: An Update*, East Asia and Pacific Region, September.

WORLD BANK (2001a), *Special Focus: Financial and Corporate Restructuring in East Asia Update*. East Asia and Pacific Region, March.

WORLD BANK (2001b), *East Asia Update*, East Asia and Pacific Region, October.

WORLD BANK (2002), 'East Asia Regional Update: Making Progress in Uncertain Times,' November.

WORLD BANK (2004a), *East Asia Update*, East Asia and Pacific Region, April.

WORLD BANK (2004b), *East Asia Update*, East Asia and Pacific Region, November.

YANELLE, M. O. (1989), 'The Strategic Analysis of Intermediation,' *European Economic Review*, 33, March.

YOO, KYUNG JUN and HYUN KYUNG KIM (2001), *Changes in Economic and Societal Environment and the Role of Public Finance*, Korea Development Institute (KDI), KDI Press, Seoul.

YOSHITOMI, MASARU, and ADBI STAFF (2003), *Post-Crisis Development Paradigms in Asia*, Asian Development Bank Institute, Tokyo.

YOUNG, ALWYN (1995), 'The Tyranny of Numbers: Confronting the Statistical Realities of East Asian Growth Experience,' *Quarterly Journal of Economics*, 110, August.

YUSUF, SHAID (2001), 'The East Asian Miracle at the Millennium,' in Joseph Stiglitz and Shahid Yusef (eds.), *Rethinking the East Asian Miracle*, Oxford University Press, New York.

ZAKARIA, FAREED (1994), 'Culture is Destiny,' a conversation with Lee Kuan Yew, *Foreign Affairs*, Vol. 73, No. 2, March/April.

# Index

Figures and tables are indexed in bold as **t**. If more than one appears on a page, they are indexed in bold using lower case letters.